All My Love, Mary

Letters from War-Time Swansea

෧෬

DEBORAH STATHES

Fulton Books, Inc.
Meadville, PA

Published by Fulton Books 2021

ISBN 978-1-63860-425-9 (paperback)
ISBN 978-1-63860-426-6 (digital)

Printed in the United States of America

This compilation is dedicated to my mother,
Hilary Mary Thomas Deems, and her
family, whom she loved dearly.

An Introduction to Swansea in Wartime and to Mary and Her Soldier

Swansea, South Wales, had been at the heart of early industrialization. Coal and copper came from the valleys. Much of the coal and copper stayed in Swansea, where factories produced copper, steel, and tin. The town became known as Copperopolis. Fortunes were made. Grand buildings went up. Workers came to Swansea to become part of this new way of life. Between the wars, markets fell, jobs were lost, poverty ruled, and hope for a promising future seemed a distant dream. On June 20, 1940, the Nazis dropped the first bombs on Swansea, an initiation to war. The next February, Nazi bombs fell on the town for three consecutive nights, destroying the docks and the inner city. There were no more blitzes for Swansea, but Nazi bombers dropped leftover bombs from other raids on other towns on Swansea as they returned to the continent. This random bombing continued until February of 1943.

In the fall of 1943, Swansea was filled with rubble and young people in the middle of a war.

Mary Thomas left her school, the Swansea Intermediate and Technical School for Girls, damaged in the bombing of June 27, 1940, and became an office worker at Glamtax, a car company kept busy because of government limits placed on petrol and private cars. The alternative to office work was work as a land girl, and she knew life on a farm wouldn't suit her. Mud, animals, rough clothes, boots? She knew she was suited to the city and dances and nice clothing and films and wonderful city busyness. She also knew she wouldn't want to leave her home with its comings and goings with her mother at the center. Her mother had kept the family together in their home on Manselton Road after the sudden death of Mary's father in 1937. Two brothers, Ken and Harry, were away in the service. Harry was in the army and married to Kit. Ken was a navigator in the RAF. Two brothers remained in Swansea, Con and Walter. Con was married to Mair, and Walter was the bachelor living away from home. Her sister, Dorothy, two years younger, was at home, interested in riding bikes and running around with packs of kids—a world away from Mary. In the course of Mary's letters, Dot's boyfriend, Sid, enters the picture. Mary's younger brother, John, was…her younger brother.

"Mam, it's me, Mary!" she whispered loudly through the letter slot in the front door of 117 Manselton Road. Mary knew her mother had heard her, knew she'd be up waiting. And she knew her mother would refuse to answer her because she knew Mary had stayed out late dancing with soldiers, maybe even Americans, and she didn't approve. American troops had come over and set up camps in South Wales in the fall of 1943 in preparation for the European invasion. And yes, she had been dancing and had met a lovely American. Her new soldier was stationed at Penclawdd. Lucky for her, the Yanks had petrol to fill up their tanks, so the soldiers could drive into Swansea. There was no petrol for civilians, but that just meant more trade for Glamtax. They met November 6, 1943.

Soldiers marched and trained, went on maneuvers, and prepared to invade the continent. Mary and her American soldier continued to meet and dance and become a couple, one person steeped in innocence and one more experienced, possessing guarded secrets. They were together in Swansea until the summer of 1944, when Irwin, Mary's soldier, became part of the Allied invasion. Thanks to a fairly efficient postal system, complete with wartime censors, letters were able to cross the Channel and get delivered. Most of Mary's letters survived, as did her spirit, which was filled with hope and doubt, faith and fear.

When they met she was seventeen and he was thirty-one.

Irwin left Swansea for further invasion preparation in England and then landed in France in July of 1944. He was part of the 28th Artillery Division from Pennsylvania, which became part of the 1st Army. He marched in the victory parade in Paris with the 28th Division on August 29, 1944, and then engaged in battle the next day.

Mary's correspondence begins with a letter dated October 8, 1944. She's eighteen years old. Through these letters, we get to know her family, including her cousin Nancy and Nancy's mother, who tells fortunes. We learn about her friends Gwenda, Hazel, Elaine, Eva, and Althea and the people in her office, especially Mr. Clement. We learn of Mr. and Mrs. Humphreys. We also learn about Irwin's family, those in Pennsylvania and those fighting in Europe. Mary shares with Irwin the songs she's listening to, the movies she sees, the books she reads, and lets him know when his American magazines arrive at her house. Mary can be thoughtful, wistful, and sometimes critical and questioning. She clearly loves her family. She turns twenty in March of 1946.

In her letters, Mary creates a vivid picture of Swansea at war and its aftermath as she expresses the hopes and fears of a young woman in love with her soldier. These letters are unedited. A clear narrative emerges amid declarations of love and doubt and hope.

He is her first and only love.

These letters have been divided into ten parts, each part determined by Irwin's visits or Mary's periods of silence.

Part One

OCTOBER 8, 1944–
FEBRUARY 28, 1945

The ladder is still outside my window.

October 8, 1944

My Darling,

Still taking care of yourself for me? You'd better. This morning when I was walking down the road on my way to work, I met the postman. He must have seen the questioning look on my face because he fished down in his bag and handed me three letters from you. Was I happy? I couldn't read them in the bus because I had to stand but took time out when I went to work. They were nice ones too.

Things must be in a bad way if you can't even remember what day it is. How do you know when Saturday night comes round so you can celebrate? Am I kidding? So glad my calendar has moved with you, though. Remember the Sunday morning I gave you that? I thought I wouldn't see you again, that morning. You fooled me though. I'd like to be fooled like that all the time. You'd make a good boss, Darling. I wouldn't work at all, but I'd love being at work.

Will I be excited when I'll be seeing you again? That's a silly question to ask. What I'm worrying about is whether or not I'll be able to stand the excitement. I'm sure I'd be a nervous wreck by the time that train came in. I'd like to be, love to be, in your arms right now, having the longest kiss of my life. It's too wonderful to even think about, but it will happen one day, I'm sure.

Sometimes I wonder about you loving me, Darling. All right, don't get mad. I know I should be convinced by this time, but once you told me you wouldn't want me if I was married, and in this letter you wouldn't want me if I wanted you to take me back to the States. The way I feel about you is quite different from that. I wish I wasn't alone so much as I am now, then I wouldn't have time to think these things out. Forgive me, Darling. Guess I do need a bit of convincing.

Your brother wasn't in England very long, was he? I'm glad I didn't run into him. I felt bad enough when I met your brother-in-law in Sennybridge. I could feel myself shrinking down. I felt so small, but I've never been in a position like that before. Hope I can meet all your family with a clear conscience one day.

Wish I could have helped you boys out with the gin. Sound as though I drink a lot, don't I? You know better. I probably would have ended up on your shoulder anyway. Wouldn't that be nice, though?

The ladder is still outside my window. Every night I wake up and wonder if someone has used it and am disappointed to find no "invader." That's what Gwenda says about the balcony around her window. Don't go around with her these days. Found something out that I didn't like, and if she cares to give an explanation for it all, I might like her again. Girls can be awfully catty about other girls. Couldn't do what she did though. I'm not sorry about not going out with her as she wasn't very reliable.

Went to a show on my own tonight, *Lady in the Dark*. It was rather ridiculous but good entertainment. Want a nice cold? I have a super one. That's through being a bridesmaid. Don't tell. I know. Use Vicks.

Keep loving me, Darling.

All my love,
Mary

Mary's younger sister and brother, Dot and John, had been evacuated to the countryside in Carmarthen after the three-day blitz in February of 1941. They were placed with people who spoke only Welsh. Their mother grew up speaking Welsh but encouraged her children to speak only English. They, especially Dot, were traumatized by this experience, stayed on the farms only a few months before being brought home by an older brother. For Mary, Carmarthen was a world away from the Swansea. For safety, the family had an Anderson shelter in their back garden in Manselton.

October 11, 1944

My Darling,

Just returned from my stay on the farm. I had quite a nice time. That's surprising, isn't it? I got to Carmarthen about three on Monday, waited at the station for Gwenda to come collect me, wishing all the time it was you who would come. I felt like a package waiting to be claimed. Eventually Gwenda comes strolling down the road and warned me of the journey ahead. You'd have laughed if you had seen the bus we traveled in. It started to rain, and the roof of the bus was leaking. People put their umbrellas up. I was soaking after the hour's ride then, to my disgust, found we had three miles to walk. I had to change my shoes on the roadside, and believe me, I felt like something the cat had dragged in after walking through the country lanes. Gwenda's aunt has a beautiful house there, and she had a super dinner in readiness for me. I took writing paper with me, imagining having hours to spare in which I could write to you, but that was out. I hope you forgive me, Darling. But after dinner, the neighbors who live four hours away started their visit. This was about nine o'clock. They don't keep very good hours there. Gwenda met a farmer there last week, and he came later. He apologized for being so late, but he had to milk the cows first. This amused me. I was thinking of you saying a thing like that. He took Gwenda for a car ride, while I helped to entertain the guests. Gwenda had told her aunt about you, so she kept asking me questions. She wants me to take you down there, if I get the chance. It would be lovely for us. She's a tactful old dear and full of fun. Gwenda and her boyfriend came back to supper about midnight, after which the neighbors went home, and Aunty went to bed. Gwenda went to say good night to her friend in his car. Only the maids and myself were left downstairs. We talked quite a bit then, after about an hour, went to get Gwenda to bed. I was feeling quite tired after all this, and it was about 2:00 a.m., so I was glad to get some sleep. I woke in the morning to hear the cows making an awful noise. I was sleeping with Gwenda, and she was saying some funny things in her sleep, so I woke her up. The maid brought us a cup of tea and asked when we wanted breakfast. We both said twelve o'clock. That was when we got up and had lunch instead. I cycled into the village, which consists of one small store and a few houses, bought a long cigarette holder to shock the yokels with, then back to the house for tea. An old woman came there and told my fortune. She told me I'd be married very shortly and have a very happy life. I hope she's right. I love you, Darling. Aunty arranged a surprise for me. She had the village pianist and invited a couple of farmers and their wives there for the evening. The maids brought their boyfriends too, some handsome specimens, and we had a very entertaining evening. Got to bed about one thirty. You should have seen their faces when I used the cigarette holder. I thought they'd never get over the shock. This morning I got up around seven, as Gwenda wanted to say goodbye to some of the people she had met. We used Aunty's car and must have traveled a number of miles around the different farms. Then back for lunch and then into the town to get the train home. It's hard to settle down here even after those few days of plenty of food and not having any work to do. I wouldn't like it always though. I'd hate to get fat like Gwenda's aunt. All she does is sit and order the maids around. I wish you could have been with me though. We'd have had fun. You'd have caused a sensation, as a new face around those parts is something for them to talk about for weeks. Somebody asked if I was an evacuee. Gwenda started giggling at that.

The best part of it was coming home and finding three wonderful letters from you, also a *Look*, a *Yank*, and a *Reader's Digest*. Thank you, Darling.

I'm glad payday is over for this month. I hate that time. Doc gets some brilliant ideas, doesn't he? His tent is certainly well fixed up. Glad he remembers me, and thanks for all of your love too. You know where mine is.

You should have been on the farm with me. I also made some doughnuts for them. I'm clever, only nobody knows it or won't appreciate it. There's something wrong. That place where you had the beer reminds me of one of the farms that we visited. I was just about leaving there, glad to get some air, when a cow put its head through the doorway. I gave one yell and then dived back into the house. I was scared, honest. There were two evacuees there, lovely little boys, but I felt sorry for them.

Everyone likes my new suit. Darling, I hope you will too. It's a lot nicer than the one I used to wear to work. If you must know everything, it's navy and white. Want me to send you some fluff from it? It seems such a waste of time looking nice for Gwenda or some other girls. I'm going to start complaining as you did in the letter. I want to be near you, taste your tobacco, have my hair messed up, and my face looking a wreck. Listen to you talk about yourself, which you did on times, laugh with you, dance to a slow number, even to see you looking miserable as you did on times. As a matter of fact, I'd do anything just to be able to see you again.

Did you get wedding cake from Nancy? I gave her your address when she asked for it.

Well, Darling, I'm being terribly good. Your account is untouched, and I'll always love you and miss you.

All my love,
Mary

PS: What are you playing at, moving back to the place you were a few days ago? I don't want to say what place I'm talking about, in case the censor might pounce on this letter, so I hope you understand what I'm talking about. I'm a little confused myself. You know though, one day you're in one place, and next day you're in the place you were the day before that. I'm not crazy, just about you. Just be careful.

Be good,
Mary

October 13, 1944

My Darling,

Hurry up and get the war finished so that I can see you again.

Remember the American who came to the garage the same time as you did that morning? He came to see me today. He's back from France, wounded, and now having treatment at a hospital in England. Nothing serious, I don't think. He's spending a forty-eight-hour pass in Swansea. Thought he was doing me a big favour. Wanted me to spend a few days with him in England. I didn't think he was serious about it, but apparently he was. I'm sure if I couldn't manage to see you before you left here, when I love you so much, I wouldn't even want to go with him. I think they take advantage of their battle scars. I know we should show our appreciation to them, but that's taking advantage of our good will. He knows where I live, so he says, and when I wouldn't go out with him tonight, he said he'd come to the house. I've warned my mother, so if he should come, I won't be at home. She says I should have asked him to supper since there's nothing else to do in this place. If he was a different type, I might have, but he'd get ideas if I did a thing like that.

Can't get envelopes for you, Darling. Sorry. It seems a little thing to do for you, but they are very scarce at the moment. I hope you'll understand.

My picture, the main topic of every letter I get from you. The ones I have aren't so good. I know I'm not as bad as that. People who have seen them say they don't even look like me. Naturally, I don't want you to have one of those. The photographer who took our picture in Nancy's wedding made a good job of them, so tomorrow I'm paying him a visit. I called Nancy this morning. Asked her if it was Mrs. Howells speaking. That's her name now. She hesitated a few minutes before saying yes. I suppose it's hard to get used to.

Don't remember if I told you about Connie's husband, the Canadian flyer. Not very long ago, I was at their wedding. He's missing, believed killed. She heard that once before, and he turned up, so she's still hanging on to her hopes. I hope everything's all right, as he's all she talks about and loves him as much as I love you. She phoned me today. Asked if I'd go out with her tomorrow. She's alone in the house all day and gets too much time to think. I don't know what to talk to her about, as I know she couldn't forget about him, not even for a minute, but I'll do my best. Go to a show where we won't have to talk and that's all I can think of.

All my love,
Mary

October 21, 1944

My Darling Irwin,

Nancy phoned me this morning. She has the snaps they took at her wedding. I had forgotten about those. She said they are very good too, so naturally I'm very curious to see them. Nancy is going to stay with her husband's people for a few days. His brother has just returned from Canada. He's a flyer, and Nancy hadn't met him. She was all excited about seeing her brother-in-law when she gets there today.

Believe me, I won't keep you waiting two minutes when our day comes. Might even get there before you. Wouldn't that be terrible? I'd love to come home and just say I'm married. That's what I've always wanted. Weddings usually end up in a family quarrel because one of the relations wasn't invited. There used to be a place in Scotland called Gretna Green, where you could get married at a minute's notice. Have you ever heard of it? It was banned when war broke out for some reason. Supposed to be very romantic. The ceremony took place over an anvil. I'm not scared of you, so don't pat yourself on the back, but I just have to wear my nightdress, it's transparent anyway, so don't start worrying. Even Gwenda thinks it's disgusting. She made me try it on the other night. But she thought it would be nice for one of those lovely weekends. She's full of brilliant suggestions like that.

Are you listening to the radio now? I am. It's Saturday night. One of the girls from the Food Office phoned me this afternoon. Wanted me to make up a foursome tonight. She had two Norwegian fliers on her hands. Told her I had another date, which as you know wasn't true, but she's a very determined girl. and I couldn't say I had nothing to do tonight. I hate dancing with anyone these days, and especially at Langland. I only want to dance with you. I can't be with you tonight, so I'll just have to dream about you and remember how everything was when I had you near me. I would kick myself too for those times I was so nasty to you. I was, wasn't I?

Glad you enjoyed the USO show. In the show I saw the other night, *Destination Tokyo*, that American girl broadcasting from Germany came on the radio. A bunch of sailors were listening to her, and you should have heard what they called her. Didn't think they'd allow that sort of thing to reach the troops. We had to listen to an Englishman and his propaganda every so often, broadcasting from Germany. Everyone has a good laugh at his expense. Haven't heard our song for a long time and never heard "I'm Thinking of You Tonight." Just heard "I'll Walk Alone," though it's nice too. The one I like best at the moment is "I'll Be Seeing You."

Soon fix you so you can walk up hills without being exhausted, don't worry. This morning, when I was at the bottom of the slope leading to our garage, a few Canadians came along, wanting to race me to the top. I'm not a sissy, so I took their challenge. I was at the top before they were halfway up. They couldn't get over it.

Had a nice afternoon. Mother in a generous mood. Bought me a new suit on the spur of the moment. We were looking at it. I told her how nice it was, never thinking I'd get it. She's a wonderful mother. It's nice, Irwin. Keep loving me.

All my love,
Mary

November 4, 1944

My Darling,

This is the first day of another year that I'll be loving you. I wonder what this year holds in store for us. If it could only be as wonderful as the first six months of the last year, having you near to me, my only fears being that you'd be moved a few miles away, not as it is now, wondering if you're all right and if I'll ever see you again.

Should like to have seen you with a two-day beard. It's not a bit of wonder that I wake up in the middle of the night sometimes and feel my face burning. Don't you dare turn up without shaving again.

You certainly think of some wonderful methods of transportation to this country, but keep thinking hard and maybe you'll discover a practical means. A flying bomb, indeed. What if they thought you were a secret weapon and capture you? I'd have to fight to get you back, because I'd have a hard time convincing them just why you came that way. You're crazy, but I love you so much.

What happens when you hit the ditch, Darling? I'm longing to see the poem. Do you think that if I wrote to Hitler and explained that I didn't like the idea of you hitting ditches that he wouldn't do it again? No, neither do I, but I can't have anything hurting you, ever. So see that the ditch is deep, and take good care of yourself, or else— I'll never speak to you again, honest. The war will be over one day, then you can forget about the ditches and all the other things that go with war, except me, of course, as I'm a part of your wartime life too.

Don't blame you for not liking Germany, besides the reasons that we all hate the place, but it's good training experience for a married man. All men should try it sometime, then they'd appreciate their wives more. I'd like to send my brother there, not that I'd wish him any harm, but it would teach him a thing or two.

Your loving me could never be too consistent, and I'll always love you the same way, and you won't have to scrub floors, sew, or cook. You might have to help with the dishes sometimes if I'm in a hurry, but loving me will be a full-time job for you, so be prepared, Darling.

Today has been my day off. I spent the afternoon reading in the room where I've arranged the flowers. I had some beautiful roses and carnations as well as chrysanthemums, which were the best I've seen for a long time, and a bunch of violets, which I wore tonight when I visited my brother.

All my love,
Mary

November 6, 1944

My Darling,

Our anniversary and how can I put into words how I feel about the flowers you sent. This afternoon, Mother phoned me to tell me about the beautiful flowers that had come for me. I almost screamed at her with excitement. She said it didn't say who they were from, but there was an envelope inside. I knew my Irwin had sent them and told her so. She told me I was crazy as you were so far away. It had me wondering too, but I knew no one else would send me flowers, especially on November 6. I wish it was our wedding anniversary too, but today's date will always be as important to me as our wedding day. A lot has happened in a year, Darling. I met you, which has turned out to be the happiest thing that has happened in my life. I was glad when I fell in love with you and have never regretted it. I'll never forget the first time you told me you loved me. It was in a taxi, remember? I thought you were handing me a line as it seemed too good to be true, and as you know, I'm not easily convinced. My dreams were shattered a couple of times after that, but I never stopped loving you. I tried to be unselfish a few times too, telling you I wanted to end everything, but that didn't work either. Then you moved further away, but nearer to my heart, and never realized that I could miss a person the way I miss you. That was when you were in England. It seems so long since that day in Sennybridge, when I tried to break my own heart by trying to finish things once more. I'm glad you realized that it wasn't what I wanted to do at all.

Thank you, Irwin, for the best year of my life.

All my love,
Mary

December 2, 1944

My Darling,

Your operation, you crazy person, two teeth filled. I told you your teeth needed filling, didn't I? You won't listen to a thing I tell you, though. Now you'll be able to bite me with full strength.

Can't understand why you are moving around the way you are, but I'm not supposed to. That must be some hill you have to climb. You'll be too good for me if you stay there much longer. That would be awful.

It isn't Vera Lind, Darling. It's Vera Lynn. She was discovered when war broke out, as she has a way of putting sentimental songs over and is now the sweetheart of the forces. I saw her in person once, here. She had her audience crying, all except me. I was hardhearted then. I like her very much, though, and the songs she sings too. Nothing compared to my voice though. Ask any of the men that I work with. I drive them crazy. When I start, they take a walk. These last few days, I've had "It Could Happen to You" on my mind all the time. The men hate that song now. Guess I murdered it. You have yet to hear me in top form. I'm warning you, I'm wicked.

Thanks for the Belgian money. I have quite a collection now. You certainly have a lot of work with all this money.

The boy I was writing to when I met you has his picture on the local paper tonight. He's had a promotion, and my brother does nothing but tease me about it. I often see this boy's mother in town. She always wants me to visit her. I'd much rather have nothing to do with his family. I don't like them. They're a scheming bunch of people. He was a queer person too. Someone I could never love.

All my love,
Mary

December 3, 1944

My Darling,

This is one of those days when people, whatever they say or do, annoy me. It's still raining here, and everything looks miserable. I'm sure I'll go crazy if things don't change soon. I was ready to go home from work this afternoon, when two girls came wanting to go to Penclawdd. The driver said he'd take me home the same time. So I had a trip to Penclawdd first. I didn't know it took so long to get there. It didn't seem so long, anyway, when you and I used to make the trip. Time always used to fly when I was with you though, and I never wanted to leave you. These girls were going to the American camp; two soldiers were waiting for them. I'd never been to that place in daylight before. It looks awfully dreary but holds some wonderful memories for me, and how I wish you were there now. The driver asked if it brought back any memories to me, the same driver who came for us the night of the party, remember? Doc and Eva came too. He shouldn't ask such silly questions.

I want to be with you all the time. Dream about me, and keep loving me, Darling, and take extra good care of yourself.

All my love,
Mary

December 4, 1944

My Darling,

They must have heard our pleas for speeding up the mail, as I had two wonderful letters today, written on the twenty-fourth and the twenty-ninth. Also some magazines. I love you, Darling.

You seem to have quite a comfortable time in your new abode. It's no wonder Doc envies you. Are you sure the women who look after the place aren't too nice? If they are, please don't tell me, or I'll get so jealous and start suspecting things. I'd much rather think of them as the usual type who do that sort of work. Doc will tell me though, but I won't worry about them then, as you'll be around too, and I'll be able to guard you from other females. First I read about your housekeepers, then that paper you sent me concerning the march through Paris and how you were greeted by the grateful French girls. Are you sure my account is untouched?

The boy I sit next to in the bus asked me to go to his home tonight and listen to some of his wonderful records. But when I asked him what the records were, it finished things, strictly symphony and opera. Can you imagine me going through agony listening to those? I told him it wasn't my type. He said he'd buy "Slaughter on 10th Avenue" tomorrow so I wouldn't have any excuse. I told him not to waste his money. He'd be a nice boy if he wasn't so dumb.

All my love,
Mary

December 5, 1944

My Darling,

You don't mind me calling you honey? I know you don't as you made me say it quite a few times. So, Honey, I love you. You love me too? Oh, you're a real honey. Lots of honey, no bees, though.

Heard on the radio today that all British troops that have been in France for six months will get seven days' home leave shortly. I thought they might say something about the Americans, but no. I just have to keep wishing and hoping. This is a terrible war. Quite a lot of our Johnnies came marching home yesterday. Four weeks home from the Middle East. We are hoping my brother may come home soon.

Mary's brother Ken was in the RAF and away from home for six years. According to Mary's brother Con, Ken was in the air dropping bombs on his brother Harry, who was with British forces on the ground during the Battle of Monte Cassino between January and May of 1944. Mary goes on to speak of Harry's wife, Kitty. Interesting to note that Mary knew Irwin was a married man. It's not clear if she knew he had children at this point in their relationship.

My sister-in-law, Kit, paid us a visit this morning. She's sorry for what she's done and wanted to know when we heard from her husband and how he was, etc. She should have thought about those things before. My mother understands how she feels now though, and to show her how much she'd like things to be right between them, she asked her to come and live with us until my brother comes home. I hope she doesn't. Things wouldn't be the same, and I, for one, could never accept her as one of the family, not because of how she hurt my brother, but I don't like her herself.

This afternoon I went to see *White Cliffs of Dover* on my own again. It was sad, but I couldn't cry as you feel so conspicuous when you're alone. The whole show took a bit of believing, but I didn't notice it until I got home and thought about it.

All my love,
Mary

December 6, 1944

My Darling,

Tonight is one of those nights when I miss you more than usual. All night on the radio they've played nothing but sentimental numbers until I couldn't listen to them any longer. I'm so glad I love you, though.

We had a visitor tonight, a boy who's been stationed with my brother in Italy, home on leave. My brother asked him to call and see us and let us know just where he was. He's staying at Lady Hamilton's place (she was Nelson's woman) in Naples. He particularly wanted this boy to see Mary. I didn't know I had such a loving brother, but apparently, he's always talking about me. I'll have to write him more often if that's true. This is the brother whose wife you met. He's always been a great brother to me. Anything I wanted very badly, I'd always go to him for it and usually got it. It seems such a long time since I saw him really, almost four years. I suppose he still thinks of me as I was then, always taking the rise out of someone and thinking the whole world was mine. I wish this war would end soon so that we could all get back to normal again. I'd like a lot of things to be different. I'd have everything if I had you, and I wish so much that it could be that way.

All my love,
Mary

December 8

My Darling,

Got to work at ten this morning, and between that time and eleven, I had six people call me, all females. My two sisters-in-law, rushing me with invitations to supper, etc. Nancy wants me to go to the Garrison Ball with her on December 20. It's all right; her husband is going too. I haven't decided whether or not I'll go yet. I wish you were here, then I'd love to go. It's the ball of the year, dancing until 1:00 a.m. Imagine how nice it would be if I could tell you I love you all night while you were holding me close to you. It's too wonderful to even think about. When Nancy asked me about it, I said I'd be there for certain if my Irwin could come too. She knew that, of course. Her husband has fourteen days leave for Christmas. Isn't she lucky? And he is too.

They've started having Christmas parties at work. I want to keep way from there as much as I can. I had a bottle of gin given to me today, but I had to give it towards the need of these parties. It's no fun drinking on your own or with people you don't like, is it?

How are the ladies who clean house for you? I wish I was one of them. I could take care of you properly and love my work. I'd make you tea all day like we did at Bryn. I like tea when it's made like that, don't you?

I've never wished so hard in my life as I have since you left here. Nobody takes any notice of my wishes, though.

Can't write in bed like this much longer. My hands get too cold. I'll have to find some other place where I can write in peace.

All my love,
Mary

December 9, 1944

My Darling,

Had quite a nice time this evening. Went to tea with my sister-in-law then afterwards to a show at the place where we saw the opera. My favorite singer was there in person. You've probably never heard of him, Issy Bonn, he has a wonderful voice and sang all nice numbers tonight, "I'll Be Seeing You," "All of My Life," "Kiss Me Again," and "Deep Purple." What more could I want? Yes, I know. You more than some hair. The whole thing would be a lot more romantic if you couldn't see him, but you can't have everything. Saturday night doesn't seem so bad if you can go somewhere like that, as generally I hate to see this night come around.

Today has been quite nice all around. I had two super letters from you this morning, written on November 29 and December 1. Oh, you're wonderfully honest, you are, and I know you're not kidding me. It's funny you should mention Mr. Humphries. I didn't know until today that he's one of our regular customers. I've heard the name at work dozens of times but never thought it was the same person. This afternoon, one of the drivers mentioned that he wanted a car. Me, being inquisitive, asked where he lived. It was quite a shock when he said 13 Bryn Road. I didn't think he liked us too much, did he? Who cares anyway? We liked his place very much. I wish we could be there for Christmas. Darling, I could go without sleep for a couple of weeks after the time I've spent in bed lately. You'll never hear me complain one little bit, and all in favor to be loved, well, not quite to death. I want it to be a happy ending, you know, me love you to death, sleep, I mean.

All my love,
Mary

The next letter from Mary is hard to read. In it, she uses the word n——in a derogatory and familiar way. In order to frame Mary as positive and engaging, I considered eliminating this passage but then reconsidered in order to convey the truth of the times. Mary had been brought up in a town where everyone pretty much looked the same. Irish and Italians lived in Swansea and were considered exotic. Gypsies roamed and had their place among the people of Swansea. She also speaks in stereotypical terms about Jews. Her world view was limited. With experience, she evolved and became interested in and accepting of all the people she later encountered. To omit portions of her letters which we would find offensive today would do disservice to this record of the time.

December 10, 1944

My Darling,

Missing me lots? I know you are as I miss you so much that you must feel me haunting you, wherever you go and whatever you do. I wish I could haunt you personally, you know, just appear from nowhere when you least expect me. Wouldn't that surprise you. I have you on my mind so much that I expect to see you there in front of me sometimes. Crazy, ain't I? Should have said 'honey' to finish that question. I heard a n——call a girl honey this morning. It sounded terrible, the way he said it, maybe because he was black. When I saw him with that girl, I thought about you asking me if I'd been out with one of them. The very thought of it makes me shudder. We no longer have soldiers here. The town is almost back to normal again, not to mention the fact that business at our place isn't so good. Surprising really the difference those boys made to the town. Glamtax has to start advertising its service once more, and we have enough calendars printed to supply the whole of Swansea.

Heard on the radio tonight about the new advance the 1st Army is making. Wish my Irwin was making a new advance towards Swansea. Before I met you, I was never interested, well, not very interested, in the news. All I thought was we just had to win this war one day. Now I scan the newspapers for any details of the 1st Army's activities, and everyone at home has to keep quiet when they mention it on the radio. How I wish it was all over, then at least I wouldn't have to worry about you being safe and when I'd see you again. If things could be as I wish, I'd always see you; otherwise it would be never, as though hundreds of miles that separate us nor wouldn't be very much in comparison to the thousands that will when you return home. I hate to even think of it, as life would be very empty if that should happen, Darling. You're all my life and always will be.

Been reading since I finished work today, a book called *Blanche Fury*. Have you read it? It's very interesting, nice parts in it too. I think you'd like it. This fast life I'm leading is killing me. Those thirty days. I wish I was in America waiting for you to come home. What's the good of wishing, anyway? I'm curious to know who the neighbors find to talk about these days. I used to be their pet subject. They must be wondering what happened to me. I could tell them, "You know why I don't come home late, don't you? Irwin is far away, and I love him lots, so why would I want to stay out late?" Have to keep my date with you now, so can't write anymore. Keep loving me, Darling. Be good and take extra good care of yourself. Good night, Honey.

All my love,
Mary

December 11, 1944

My Darling,

Heard some big news today. Americans from Germany are being flown to the USA for thirty days' leave. I was wondering if you were one of the fortunate ones. It's a big break for you boys, I know, but I'm selfish. I don't want you to go there. You should know why. The only good thing I can find about it is you'd be out of danger those thirty days. I wish I was in America waiting for you to come home. What's the good of wishing anyway? I'm still here just loving you more and more every day, and nothing I can do about it. But I do consider myself very fortunate to spend as much time as I did with you, and I'm glad I love you the way I do, Irwin. I'll never regret meeting you. I don't think I ever lived until then.

Went to a show with Nancy tonight. I was bored stiff with it, an English production. Richard Greene was quite nice though. I managed to get a bus home for a change, otherwise that long walk wouldn't have been so good tonight. It's colder than I ever remember it. Too cold to write in bed tonight. I've sent the family to bed and have a nice big fire all to myself. If you were only here, then I wouldn't need a big fire to keep me nice and warm, and I wouldn't be writing. I think that's become a part of my life now, and I look forward to writing you every night. It's terribly important actually as that's all we have to keep us together.

Tomorrow means a morning in bed for me. Don't you envy me? You'll have an awful time getting me out of bed on Tuesday morning, Irwin. It's a habit I have, not only on one particular day, but on every day. I guess I must have sleeping sickness or something. But I always start thinking of you when I wake up in the mornings and hate to get up, leaving my thoughts in bed. When I got to work this morning around ten, this girl in the office went to get us tea, etc., so I started my work while I was waiting for it. Mr. Clement came in the meantime, so I forgot about the tea, when this girl, not knowing Mr. Clement had arrived, yelled into the office, "Mary, come and get it." He just looked at me and remarked what a noisy little so-and-so she was. Anyway, I did get my tea, and that's all that mattered.

It's getting late, Darling, twelve thirty. I had a terrible time getting my brother to bed. He likes being difficult, otherwise I should have started writing earlier than I did. I know I'll dream about you tonight. I feel so tired. Keep loving me, Honey, and be good.

All my love,
Mary

December 12, 1944

My Darling,

Only today, I realized that I hadn't mentioned our year-and-one-month anniversary. You know I didn't forget about it though, so I hope you'll forgive me. That's a date I'll never forget, Darling, because I loved you the day I met you and love you thirteen months more now. That's an awful lot, Irwin. This time last year I was missing you the nights in between the times I didn't see you, so you can guess how much more I miss you now, so much that life seems terribly mean to me. I've been thinking so long that I'll see you soon, but nothing ever seems to happen. I just go on, knowing that one day

I'll see you again and be able to revive all those wonderful memories I have.

Haven't done anything today except shopping with Mother. I must be good because we haven't had any rain today. It was quite nice to be able to walk around without any fear of getting soaked. Bought all my Christmas presents this afternoon. There's not very much you can buy here now, but after all, there's a war on. (See, I said it before you had a chance to.)

It's funny at home when they mention the 1st Army on the radio, there's an automatic silence. Until they've heard how they're advancing. Everyone looks at me, and I don't know what they expect me to do, but I feel silly. You see, they know your name, where you're from, what army you're in, and I think they know I like you more than I've liked anyone else. I can't tell them how much I love you, naturally, but they're certainly very inquisitive as to why I don't go out like I used to and why do I write to you so often. I often wonder myself why I believe everything you say, even though I love you the way I do. I know you're not kidding me though. You're too wonderful to do a thing like that, and what use would it be?

Tonight I really felt like dancing. We wouldn't have stayed in tonight, Darling. I'd have requested all slow numbers. You weren't here though. So I'll just have to dream about it instead. Be good and dream nice dreams all about me. Love me lots like I love you.

All my love,
Mary

December 14, 1944

My Darling,

Didn't write last night, did you notice, Irwin? Went to one of the Glamtax parties. I had to go to one of them and thought the one last night would be best. It was awful, though. Not only was I disgusted with it, but everyone there. They were so bored with themselves that they didn't even feel like drinking. It was raining heavily all night. We couldn't walk home. Just had to wait until the cars came for us. Well, we waited until two this morning. I'm walking around in a dream today and can hardly wait until it's time to go to bed. I had to walk on my toes up the road, when the car left me this morning. It was funny after all this time. Darling, it's a big relief to get to bed without anyone hearing when you're late getting home. While I was waiting for the car last night, I was mad to think I couldn't write to you because I was wasting my time there. I've never felt as tired as I do today. These late-night parties take some getting used to.

Was very pleased to receive a letter from you today, written on the fifth, the first since last Saturday. Were you drunk when you wrote it, Darling? I know you weren't. I'm only kidding. You tell me not to stay in on your account, to go and have a good time if I want to, then you say you don't like to think of me going out. You know as well as I do, Irwin, that if I want to go out, I will, but I don't, Darling. I'm much happier at home, reading and thinking these days because, as I told you, you have my heart, and I don't see any point in going out. You don't believe me, do you? About all these nights I spend at home, I mean. Well, Darling, I can't prove it to you, but I wish I could, and I do stay in, really I do, because I want to. I've read it about six times, and when I do that, I imagine things that you didn't say but want to all the same. When I said you haunt me, I didn't mean it the way you thought I did. What I meant was, wherever I go, I think so hard about you that I lose interest in everyone and everything around me. You have no reason to cross your fingers on my account. You have all my love wherever you are. There's not one little bit to spare for anyone else.

Started this letter before supper. Now I'm in that bed I was talking about. You know that letter I had today is going to start me thinking quite a bit before I go to sleep. I've read it about six times, and when I do that, I imagine things that you didn't say but want to just the same. You do want my love, don't you, Irwin? I wish we didn't have to rely on letters so much. If you were here, I'd know just how you felt about me. Maybe I'm crazy for loving you the way I do, but I don't think I am. You're a wonderful person and deserve more than my love.

My aunt, Nancy's mother, was here tonight. They had a letter from Walter today. He's looking forward to visiting all his friends in Swansea in January. He said all the other officers with him would spend their leave here too. My aunt is quite excited. She likes Walter very much and wants to have a big party for all of them. She's just the person to do it too. She asked about my Irwin. I liked her for that.

I'm always missing you. Be good.

All my love,
Mary

Mary and Irwin's relationship is complicated. He is married and has four boys back in Pennsylvania, the youngest born in 1943. He has asked Mary to marry him. Mary knows of his marriage, but it is not clear who else in Swansea knows. Whether or not she knows of his children at this point is unclear. Rumors do abound.

December 15, 1944

My Darling,

It is really a long time, no see, and I miss you so much. Give anything if I could see you soon. Been helping Mother to make Christmas cake tonight. It's not like the cake we used to have, no nuts to put on it, and lots of other things that we can't get. I suppose we're fortunate to have the rest of the things though. It looks all right anyway, even though I did have a hand in things.

Received a very lovely letter from you today written on the second after you had visited Doc. I wasn't too disappointed about the lawyer's advice, Irwin. You see, I've never really set my mind on all those lovely plans we made. They seemed too good to be true. Maybe it is better for you to return home before starting things. Then you'll know for certain how you feel about me and everything else. I won't start thinking things, Darling. I know you've done all you can to make my dreams possible, and those things that stand in our way don't make the slightest difference to the way I love you. I want very much to be your wife, so I'll wait for you, Irwin, until you don't want me to. You knew that, didn't you? I have complete faith in you, Darling, and nobody will ever shake that faith, no matter what they say. There's no one but you for me. I'm quite sure about that, especially after not seeing you for all this time. I've never wanted to go out with anyone else even though at times I feel lonely and miserable. Nobody could ever take your place. I don't want anyone to, though. Waiting for you and being as good as I am is no effort really, as you loving me is worth lots more than that. Thanks for offering to write my brother, but it isn't necessary. That, by the way, is a great relief to me (my fears being unfounded, I mean). In any case, Irwin, I don't think it would have helped any. He doesn't know what it is to want anything very much, and it's impossible to make him understand these things. If a thing looks wrong on the surface to him, he'd never change his mind about it. I think he's one of the most selfish persons I know even though he's my brother, but he seems to get all the luck. I'd hate to be as self-satisfied as he is. If anything should leak out about us, I'll take everything that's coming to me, but I can't see anything wrong in what I've done, and nobody can break things up now. I love you too much. I'm all yours for as much as you want me. I hope that's always.

Keep loving me, Darling. Miss me too. Going to dream about you now.

All my love,
Mary

The Battle of the Bulge begins on December 16, 1944, and ends officially on January 22, 1945. Mary becomes aware of this military action after it has begun and then realizes the danger Irwin was in only after the action. He had been reported Missing in Action but turned up with frostbite in one leg and in his feet. The 28th Artillery Division is involved in some of the heaviest fighting during this period.

December 16, 1944

My Darling,

All I need now to complete my loneliness is someone to start singing "This Is a Lovely Way to Spend an Evening." Saturday night always seems to drag. All the family find somewhere to go. And tonight, again, I have only myself to talk to. I've read your wonderful letters over and over again, the two I had this morning, I mean. You're a real honey. You don't mind me calling you that, do you?

I must be ignorant. I didn't know that they celebrated Christmas on December 6 in Belgium until you told me. Did you do any celebrating, Darling?

Thanks for the five francs you sent. Who's that gorgeous-looking thing that has her face imprinted on that note? Their money is certainly very colourful. I wouldn't want to spend it if I lived there.

It's wonderful to know that you love me, Darling. You know that I love you too, don't you? Keep loving me, Darling, and miss me lots.

All my love,
Mary

December 17, 1944

My Darling,

What do you do when you miss someone very much? I don't know what to do with myself, especially when I'm as cold as this and no Irwin to keep me warm. Never mind, I can wait, and how I'm waiting. It's a good thing you don't know what I'm thinking right now, the only part I can tell you is that I love you, and I love you until it's impossible for me to love you anymore. Here's me in bed and you're there in bed when I could be reading to you or something. I like the sound of that something, biting your ears, I mean, Darling.

One of your sucker-bites would be more than welcome right now, anything, as long as I could be with you.

Had a very exciting day. (I'm even trying to fool myself these days.) Went to see my dear sister-in-law Kitty. Her nephew was there, and you should have seen the way he messed me up. He's only two, but he's almost as good at the job as you are. He kept me going the whole afternoon. I was sorry to see him go to bed.

When I got home tonight, my brother and his wife, Con and Mair, were there. All my fears about my brother hearing about you were unfounded. They are both getting lonely, together in their house all the time. I can't imagine me feeling lonely or bored for one little minute if you were around. Anyway, they wanted to know if you were coming here on leave. If so, they'd like to have you stay there and a friend as well. The suggestion was very nice of them I thought. They really want to entertain somebody. Asked me if I knew of some Americans who'd like to spend Christmas there. A good many boys would want to, I suppose, but as I don't know any Americans here. I can't do anything for them, as I explained to my brother. Something's come over him. He told me to find somebody. I don't know if I should go out carousing, but I'm not.

Have to go to sleep now.

All my love,
Mary

December 19, 1944

My Darling,

I'm so worried about you having heard the bad news that I don't know how to write to you. I could never explain how I feel about you being in the centre of things. I'm not very clever, Irwin, but I hope you'll understand just how much I'm thinking of you because of the way I love you. It's strange what a difference a year can make to our lives. This time last year, I had you near, no fear of what may happen, just being happier than I had ever been in my life before, but this is war, I guess. At times like these, you fully realize how much a person means to you. Makes me realize how very much I love you, Darling.

Went shopping with Mother this afternoon. Couldn't get a thing we wanted, so we went to a show. It was very good too, *2000 Women*. I thought there might be a letter from you when we got home. That's what I was hoping, I mean. No letter, though, but a *Yank*. You must have sent it some time ago. It was a November 5 issue but very welcome. Thanks, Darling.

On our way into town today, we met a lady Mother knew. I'd never seen her before, but she knew all about me. She works in the same office as a girl I know. The first thing she asked me was if she could see my bracelet. I didn't know what she was talking about for a minute, then she explained that this had told her about a bracelet she saw on me one day. She thought it was an identity disc. It was your bracelet she wanted to see, and when I showed it to her, she thought it was absolutely wonderful, like I do. Naturally, she had to examine it thoroughly and wanted to know who Irwin was. Mother explained quite nicely that he was the boy I stay in every night for. She might just as well have said that I'm crazy about you. This woman rambled on then about how nice it would be if my father could see me now and lots of other tactless remarks. After she left us, Mother told me she was engaged to my father at one time. It's funny meeting people like that. I was wondering why she was so interested in me.

We had a letter from my brother Ken today. He said that if he should tell us to expect him home in five years' time, he'd be saying and expecting too much ten. He doesn't think the war will end for years and years. It was not what we needed to cheer us up for Christmas. He must have been in a wonderful mood when he wrote that because he was fed up with everything and everybody, including Churchill. I was saying to my brother Walter today about how different things would be if the war was over. We've got so used to living under wartime conditions that any other sort of life seems another world. My bothers Harry and Ken have been away so long too it seems crazy to think of them being home again. My brother then asked if I had gotten used to this idea and you being away and never expecting to see you again. I said yes but didn't mean it as I'm always expecting to see you, Darling.

Wherever you are, Irwin, I'm always near you. I love you and miss you every minute of the day.

Keep loving me. I'm thinking about you.

All my love,
Mary

December 22, 1944

My Darling,

You have every reason to think I'm a meanie for not writing for two days. During which time I was, and still am, more worried about you than I've ever been about anyone else in my life before. I've heard the news and read the newspapers, until everything is getting on my nerves, and to make things worse, I haven't had a letter from this week at all. Wednesday night I went to the Garrison Ball, a wonderful hen party. I shared Nancy's husband with her and kept thinking about you the whole time I was there. Somebody else must be worrying about you, just the way I am, if it is possible for any other person to be so worried. Last night we had a party at home. All the relations were present in full strength. I was wondering when they'd go home so I could write you, but nobody went home until 1:00 a.m. Then I had a bedmate, one of my many cousins, which made it impossible to even think about writing. I wish Christmas was over. I don't feel in the celebrating mood at all with things as they are.

Irwin, do you think you made too big a promise to me? I think you do and won't love you any less if you tell me about it. We can't have everything we want, I guess. I want you more than anything in the world, as you know, but other people probably think the same thing. I'd have to be absolutely perfect to make up for what you'd do for me, and I'm afraid I couldn't make it, but I'd always be thinking about all you gave up, etc. You can tell by this letter how miserable I feel. I am. I can't help it though. If only I knew you were all right, I'd feel lots better. I don't think I'd like to be married in wartime. It's bad enough just loving you as much as I do.

Well, Darling, I'm awfully tired after two late nights. I wouldn't be surprised if I did snore tonight. Take extra good care of yourself.

All my love,
Mary

January 2, 1945

My Darling,

Did you think I had forgotten about you? Believe me, Irwin, I can never do that. I haven't any excuse for not writing. Well, not that you'd understand. It was just that somehow I couldn't write a letter. I know what you're thinking, that I was having too good a time over Christmas to find time to write, but that isn't true. I spent most of my time last week at home alone just thinking about you and wondering if things were all right. Christmas Day I worked until one, then when I got home, there was a really wonderful letter from you, which rated an immediate reply. Then I started feeling sorry for myself, and I had a super cold as well, so I thought I'd better wait until I was in a better mood before attempting to write. In the evening, Mother and the rest of the family went to Nancy's place. Her husband is home on leave, and we had a nice evening. The men played cards, while my aunt told our fortunes. Eating took up most of the time, but we were home at twelve. Tuesday, my sister Dot had a party. Some party. I don't know where she found all the people she invited. Mother went to a neighbor's house because they didn't want her around, and I had to play all those games with them. You can imagine what a kick I had out of it. The rest of the week I just stayed home every night thinking how different things were a year ago. I was awfully optimistic, Darling. I thought maybe you'd be here for Christmas. Wasn't I silly to even suppose it? Do you know what I did because of my dreaming? I kept that something I had for you until I could see you. Now I know how crazy I was. But even so, as long as you didn't mind not getting it in time for Christmas, I think it was a good idea. You have a better chance of receiving it now that the mail rush is over. I have to make some excuse for being crazy.

New Year's Eve was a very sad affair. Just my mother and I at home. My brother was working, and the others were at a party. We listened to the greetings on the radio until the New Year came in. We both felt so lonely. The quietest way we ever spent an occasion like that. My sister brought a dark boy into the house. Supposed to be lucky. He insisted on kissing me. It's all right, he's only sixteen, but he has ideas. Remember last year? You were the first and last person to kiss me. I wish it could be that way this year. I won't give up hope though.

Last night my brother Walter was invited to a party. My other brother and his wife, Con and Mair, visited us, looking for a party actually. We all went and gate-crashed this party my brother had. We were very welcome though. At least that's what they told us. I didn't enjoy myself very much. One of the girls there and I sat on the stairs all night, as we didn't want to join in the necking games with the males who were there. We drank about twelve cups of tea while we froze on the stairs, but we both agreed it was better than the rest of the party. I couldn't get my brother Walter to come home with me. He was having a hectic time. In the end I put his coat on him and dragged him away. He made me laugh. He had his eyes on some blonde there, and he wanted to take her home until she said she only lived next door. He lost interest and heart then. We finally got home around one. I nagged him for staying there so long. He told me that if my Irwin had been there, he'd never have got home. He's right too.

Well, Darling, I'll answer your letter tomorrow. It's getting late now. I wish I could have a letter from you tomorrow. The last one I received was on December 25, written on the tenth. I love you with all my heart, Irwin, and miss you more every day. Keep loving me, Honey, remember I'm thinking about you all the time and you're in my prayers every night. Happy New Year to us, Darling. Take extra good care of yourself.

All my love for always and always,
Mary

January 3, 1945

My Darling,

How I wish that you were here or I was there. As long as I could see you and know that you were all right, everything would be perfect. No letter came today, but I have your other wonderful letter to answer yet. I'm awfully disappointed with our postman. He used to be so good to me. Now he just looks at me and says, "No letters for you," as those he's to blame. I persuade myself that the mail is held up the other side, as you said you'd write me on the eleventh, and I haven't had that letter yet.

The letter I'm answering now is the one in which you convinced me that you still loved me after me telling you that I thought your letters had changed. I should have understood that often you wrote when conditions were pretty bad and made allowances for that, but you must know how it is just relying on letters to keep us together. You know, you read things that aren't there. I don't know, but I just love you such an awful lot that I'm afraid of all sorts of things. When I read about the bad news you had from home, I was wishing I could be with you because, Irwin, you don't deserve these tough breaks you get. I'm sorry for complaining about that letter. Just when you needed extra love, I went and nagged you. Why do you love me when I do things like that? You know how much I love you, though, don't you? I want so much to be with you always, and when I said I wouldn't be too disappointed if things didn't turn out as planned, I was kidding myself. Being honest with myself, I'd be the most disappointed person in the world. I realize that bad news you had about your home will set things back, but when I know, as I do, that there's no one else I could ever want or love, I'll wait for you, forever. I hope I won't have to wait that long, though. If the war lasts as long as people think it will, we will have an awful long wait. I hope it doesn't. The end of it means more than ever to me now.

There are quite a number of Americans here on leave at the moment. Nancy called me this morning to tell me who she had seen, etc., making me green with envy. They aren't on leave from hospital either, so I don't know what they are doing here.

Mrs. Bent's husband has returned to this country seriously wounded. The first time I've ever seen her looking really miserable was this afternoon. She isn't allowed to visit him yet. All she had was the telegram telling her the bad news on New Year's morning. I felt sorry for her, but you don't know what to say to people when things like that happen.

Mother went to a show tonight. She came home all excited. I thought the *Seventh Cross* must have been good the way she acted. It wasn't that at all. She saw pictures of the 1st Army Artillery men. She said that if she had known any of them, they would have been easily recognized. I must go and see this tomorrow, but it will just be my luck if they change the programme.

Have to dream about you now. It's a habit, a wonderful habit I have. You don't mind me bothering you the way I do, do you? Wish we could dream together. Then I wouldn't have to dream, would I? Keep loving me, Darling. I love you so very much.

All my love,
Mary

January 5, 1945

My Darling,

Didn't write last night but you still love me, don't you? We had unexpected guests who will be with us for an indefinite period, unfortunately. My aunt and her dear little ten-year-old daughter. After hearing their sad tales, we could do nothing but let them stay. My aunt married a widower who has a daughter my age and lived about three hundred miles from here. It didn't work though. The daughter didn't want her there, and my aunt wasn't getting on too well with her new husband, so she left the place. Now we have them. I have this little girl as my bedmate. I'm wondering when I'll sleep on my own again for any length of time. I'd rather have somebody nice to keep me warm though. Guess who?

Haven't told you of my good fortune today yet. Two super letters from you. You're wonderful. They were written on the twelfth and the fourteenth, and you said you loved me lots. Oh, I'm happy. You say in your letters the things I want to tell you. I think we think alike, even though you're American and I'm English Welsh.

I'd love to be able to keep your new stove warm for you. When you shake it, does it look just like a fire? I remember too well the way you roasted on times when I couldn't feel any heat from the thing. Weren't those wonderful days? I'd give anything to live them over again. Irwin, you shouldn't talk about that kiss when I see you again. It makes me go out of this world. It's a wonderful thought, though. Doc's nice to remember me too. Does he get letters from Eva now? Our telephonist at work saw her at the garage a few nights ago. It's funny how she never comes to see me.

I'd love to have seen you having your picture taken. Can I have one, please? Why don't you smile when a thing like that happens to you? After all, it's just like visiting the dentist. Even though you say you look like a sourpuss, I saw you're the best-looking man I ever saw. It isn't all because I love you either. I thought that a few minutes after I met you the first time, and I felt so good about being with you at those parties at Penclawdd and all those other places we went. I told you that before, didn't I? It's wonderful knowing that you love me too.

Guess what happened here yesterday? It snowed. No buses or cars could travel the roads were so bad. I had to walk to work, and as I had a cold, Mother made me wear my stockings. They were nice too. I was almost in work safely, then a couple of crazy Americans threw snowballs at me. Naturally, I had to fall right then, and so ended another beautiful pair of silk stockings. Those grinning Americans thought it was a huge joke. I was in a terrible mood when I did get to work. I ignored everybody, sat down in my office, and started to take those fatal stockings off. I was so mad I didn't notice Mr. Clement coming on until he coughed. Was his face red. Mine too. He didn't look at me all day yesterday after that.

Where do you want me to meet you in Paris, Darling? Just say. I'll be there. Well, close your eyes and I'll be there. I know, I'll wait for you at Bryn instead of the station. Wish I could do all these things I dream about. We'll do them all one day, though, won't we? I miss you lots and lots. There can never be any intruder into my heart, as you have it. I love you so much. Your turn to say "me too" now. No sucker bites, please. Let me give you one instead. It's twelve thirty, Darling. I had to wait for everyone else to go to bed before starting to write. Mother said, "Aren't you going to write tonight? You'd better wait until we're all out of the way." I've got them all used to the idea that you're the only person that I'm interested in. Nobody could guess how much I love you though, only you. Take care of yourself and keep loving me, Darling.

All my love always and always,
Mary

PS: Forget to tell you, I went to the show after work today, just to see the pictures of the 1st Army Artillery. Yes, they changed the news around. All I saw was Churchill. I was disgusted.

I love you.

Mary

January 6, 1945

My Darling,

It's our anniversary today. I thought of it as soon as I woke this morning, and I had the letter I'd been hoping for during these last two weeks. It was the one you wrote on the twenty-sixth, telling me you were safe. You'll never know how worried I was, Darling. I just didn't care what happened as long as you were all right. I love you so much, Irwin, and realize it more and more as each day passes. I also received your Christmas card and two wonderful letters written on the thirteenth and fourteenth. I think, excepting the times we were together, this has been the best anniversary day for me yet. I will wait for you always, just as I'm waiting for you now, loving you with all my heart and always remembering what a wonderful person you are.

Imagine the Jerries having the nerve to take my letters, especially after you took the trouble of filing them. Did I really write to you 145 letters, Irwin? That's good going, even though I skipped a few days now and then. I'll beat that record this year, and I hope nothing will happen to them. You needn't worry yourself about the financial side of them. That's little enough that I can do for you, and remember, if I wasn't in love with you, and being as good as I am, I'd get rid of a lot more money. I'm quite proud of myself and my savings. See how good you are for me in all respects? You love me too, don't you? I suppose I'm just about the luckiest person in the world, having your love and being able to love you.

Thought of calling Eva to tell her that Doc was all right, but I don't know if that would be the right thing to do. I'm awfully glad he came through that lot safe, and I know you must have felt good about it too. I always think of Doc as someone much older than you and me and not a person you'd think of in a romantic way, but I like him.

It's only nine o'clock, but I'm in bed. I have that wonderful cold still. All right, you can finish it with Vicks, Doctor. I wish you were here so you could share my cold and pitch lots and lots of woo. The thought of getting your breakfast and kissing you, even though it has to be six o'clock in the morning, is wonderful. I'm sure I wouldn't let you leave me at that hour even though we went to bed at six o'clock the night before. It would be too long before you came home again. Can I go back to bed after you leave in the morning? Only for an hour, I promise. Don't be a meanie. Say I can. If you don't, I'll keep you in bed. Yes, I can or can I? Just remembered the way you used to get out of being tickled. You're too strong for me, but I love you the way you are.

Going to sleep this cold away now. See you in ten minutes' time after I say my prayers. We'll stay in tonight. It's our turn for the drawing room. Keep loving me and miss me. I know you're taking good care of yourself. I want to make a withdrawal from this account of mine. It's much too much. What can you do about it? I miss you and love you more every minute, and you're always in my thoughts.

All my love,
Mary

January 8, 1945

My Darling,

Today was lucky for me again. I got the letter you wrote at eight fifteen on December 15. You must love me to take the trouble of writing at that time in the morning. Though, if you're going to get me out of bed to make you breakfast at six o'clock in the morning, I'll be writing letters at eight fifteen too. You told me once that you wanted to see me properly dressed for breakfast, so I wouldn't feel like undressing again just to go back to bed. Will you love me early in the morning too, Darling? I know I'll be loving you all the time, even though you'll rag me now and then. You know what I keep imagining? How happy we'll be together all the time. Whenever I'm alone for a few minutes, I've decided it's going to be wonderful to have you to mess up and make me happier, if it's possible, than when I used to see you as often as I did. You'll be all mine then, and I'll do all I can to prove to you how much that means to me.

You'll be an expert at fixing fires, Darling. I give in. Maybe I did finish a fire one night. But you forget about the wonderful fire we had at Mrs. Blewell's, all my own work too. I'll make you suffer for all those cracks you are giving me. Remember, I know where to hug you so it hurts, then you'll be sorry. Wish I could give you an extra big hug now along with two or three or one hundred kisses, so I could sloe on your shoulder but not have to say good night and walk home. I'd like to wake and still find your arms around me. I want an awful lot, don't I, Darling? But I love you an awful lot.

Missed writing last night, sorry, Honey. My brother and his wife wanted my brother and I to go to some party with them. We decided it was a good idea as it was Sunday night, and things were pretty dull. It was a bad night for me from the start. My brother found a shortcut to get to this place. The result was I found myself in mud up to my ankles, and I already had a cold. There weren't many people at this party but plenty to drink. I couldn't stop my brother and kept thinking of the long walk home. I was ready to go home at ten thirty, tired and bored to tears. They played a few crazy games, one in which I had my head pushed in a bag of flour. I was quite a mess by the time they had finished with me. I couldn't get either of my brothers to come home until two thirty. My sister-in-law nagged my brother all the way home, and I was too tired to talk. I don't remember anything after putting my head on the pillow after getting to bed.

My cold wasn't improved any after that. Went to see the doctor tonight. I was waiting for him to recommend Vicks, but he gave me some horrible medicine instead and told me to take a few days off. Tomorrow is my day off officially, so I came to bed at eight o'clock tonight, and I'll stay here until Wednesday morning. Wish you were here too. I'm lonely.

Dream about me. I'm always with you and always missing and loving you all I can. Keep loving me, Darling.

All my love,
Mary

January 9, 1945

My Darling,

My cold is much better. Are you interested? I only stayed in bed until two o'clock. By that time I had read the letter I received today, the super one, written on the twenty-sixth, about a dozen times. Then, after feeling lonely in bed, I got up and sat by a nice big fire for the rest of the day. Our visitors have gone to stay with some friends, so we're all happy at home again.

Darling, I was near you when you were in trouble, and I prayed harder than I ever have in my life before, those nights I didn't write. I just didn't know what to say but felt sure you must have felt me right there with you. I knew something was wrong, though, but kept thinking that nothing could happen to take you away from me. One night I read on the paper how the Germans were shooting their prisoners. All the dreadful details were given, and that night I cried myself to sleep. I don't care how skinny you may be, that or anything else that might change your appearance could never change the fact that I love you with all my heart, and as long as you love me and want me, Darling, I'll always be yours. The thing that's much more important is that you're safe. I'm glad you got your Christmas dinner even though it was a little late. I can imagine how you ate after five days' starvation. Wish I could see you, Darling, to give my thanks for all you've been through.

That little bed of yours sounds very comfortable. Is it big enough for both of us? I'd love to try to get the other side of you right now, and a small bed would be a very good excuse. I miss those bruises I had where your tags dug into me. Oh, Irwin, I just miss everything about you. And after all this time without your wonderful kisses, I do feel love-starved. You asked me how I intended to protect your account. Since you left here, only one person has kissed me, and that's a sixteen-year-old on New Year's Eve. You don't mind that, do you? The only person who'll kiss me this year is you, Irwin. We had mistletoe in work over Christmas, but I steered clear of it. The very thought of one of those men, or any other man, kissing me makes me shudder. You've done something to me, and I like being this way. I love that thought of belonging to you and knowing that you want me. Yes, Darling, our love is true love, and for my part, I'm sure it will stay that way.

Love me lots, Irwin, then I'll know you'll be missing me like I miss you. Don't snore in my dreams tonight. You woke me last night.

All my love,
Mary

47

January 10, 1945

My Darling,

Missing me? You must be because I'm missing you so much. It's ten thirty, and I hope you're thinking about me. I'm in bed and imagining all sorts of things about us, of course. Nice though, having an imagination like mine. I know you're wonderful and that I love you with all my heart. Also we had lots and lots of fun together, and you made me very happy, so it doesn't take a lot of imagination to think of how perfect everything could be if we could be together for always. Somehow I don't think all our love will be wasted, do you?

It just can't be.

Went to see *Marriage Is a Private Affair* tonight. Lana Turner is beautiful, isn't she? It wasn't a very good show, though. It was all about marriages and how they go wrong and how people who seem happily married aren't happy at all. The whole thing seems like a warning—never get married. I wish I had the chance to marry you. I know just how happy I'd be. Sometimes, when I'm really miserable, I think what an absurd idea I have, that I'll ever marry you. Other times, it seems quite a natural thought. It's all so complicated, I get mixed up on times. Don't you ever wonder how things will turn out? I have a selfish dread, Irwin, when I think of you going home for thirty days' leave. You can guess what that dread is, but I could never blame you if that's what happened.

Didn't get to work until ten this morning. Mr. Clement was there. I didn't know what explanation to give him for being two hours late, thought the best plan was not to say anything until he asked me for one. He just stood there looking mad. I went to sit down, and as I did, the chair collapsed, and I landed on the floor. Luckily, he saw the funny side of things and laughed. Whoever the person was who put that chair ready for me didn't know at the time, but he did me a great favor as Mr. Clement seemed to forget about me being late after that.

Do you still sleep in that little bed? Think how warm I could keep you if I were there too. I'm cold, all alone in my little bed. Can't you do something about it? I dream about it, but it isn't the same.

I don't have sore lips when I wake in the morning, and I never get headaches, do you? Good night, Honey. I love you all I can. Keep loving me. I'm yours.

All my love,
Mary

January 12, 1945

My Darling,

My New Year's resolution to be in work on time isn't a bit successful. Ten thirty again this morning, but I was awfully tired. Last night I went to a party at that place you nearly went to last year, remember, Irwin? We waked to the top of a small mountain. It was raining quite a bit, and we took shelter in a doorway. Then it was time for you to catch your train. I was thinking about that night as I climbed the same hill last night, but this time on my own. All our drivers and their wives were there. I don't know why I went except that I wanted to be in a crowd instead of boring myself with my own company. Wish I had stayed home, though. I would have written you a nice long letter instead of sitting amongst these people, having the wives watch every move I made. I went into the other room to help cut sandwiches, and when I got back to the rest of the party, I was accused of taking somebody's husband away. I had a lovely time, as you can imagine. I wouldn't ever want one of their husbands. I've got my Irwin, haven't I? The whole bunch of them aren't worth your little finger. I love you, Darling, you have my heart, so how could I even spare a thought for anyone else? It's cold in bed on my own like this. I'd give anything to be in your arms right now, getting rid of some kisses I have waiting for you. How much longer do we have to wait, Darling? Make it soon. I happen to love you, remember?

This morning I got that lovely letter you wrote on the thirtieth, also quite a number of magazines. Thanks, you're a honey. You're so wonderful to me. Can you tell me just why I'm so lucky? Your description of the mayor's wife made me grin all morning. You're a crazy darling. I'm glad your Johnny Monson is with you. I've heard so much about him that I just have to meet him one day. He seems a likeable person. You must be staying in a quaint old place, wild boars and shouting news out in the streets. I can't think how I'll ever get you to settle down when it'd all over. Will you be very much trouble?

You asked me how your plan for our future sounded to me. Darling, you know I'm waiting for that day, don't you? The day I'm talking about is when I'll be Mrs. Deems. It's so wonderful that I'm in another world when I think about it. Don't ever change your mind, Irwin. Aren't I selfish? I can't help it though. All I know is that I want you for always and always. I won't have any cold, then you'll be there with Vicks. No good night. It's all so wonderful to me. Please keep loving me, Darling, and miss me lots.

All my love,
Mary

January 13, 1945

My Darling,

It's Saturday night again, and I'm missing you extra. It's disgusting. Not even having a quickie from my Irwin. I had a lovely letter today, though. Don't know how I'd be able to exist without you being able to tell me that you love me even though it's by letter. Been sitting by a nice big fire all night, reading your magazines. It's nice to think that you've been reading the same things, brings you closer to me. Wish I could make myself invisible and surprise you by just appearing in front of you. I could stay with you for a long time, and when there was anyone important around, I could make myself invisible. Aren't I crazy? This is what love does to me. It's all your fault. If you were still in England, even a few hundred miles from me, I wouldn't hesitate. I'd get there as soon as I could without asking anyone. I know I had that opportunity once and turned it down, but I'm always regretting it.

The letter I received today was written on New Year's Eve, and your New Year's ambition is also mine. I wonder where we'll be this time next year. You know where I want to be, don't you? Wherever you are. You had quite a time in that jeep on your way to collect liquor. You seem to get quite a lot of that stuff now. I don't want a drunken husband, Darling. You know I'm kidding, because you deserve something after what you've been through. My brother Con, the miserable one, rarely drinks, and in one party we went to after Christmas, he had a few beers and started singing and told everyone what a nice sister he had, when all he does when he sees me is criticize me. His wife was there, and she got mad. He was having quite a time with the girls. She nagged him all the way home, and I couldn't stop laughing at him.

That bed of yours sounds nice and comfortable. Wish I could try it sometime. I'd rather put my feet on your back than on a hot brick. I can do that anytime. When you wrote "we crawl into bed," I didn't think anything until you explained you were talking about yourself and Johnny. Who else could it be? I'm being dumb now. I'll haunt you if anyone steals you from me. I've always had set ideas about the person I'd fall in love with, and except for the fact, a very important fact, that you're married, you are my ideal. Good-looking, good manners, able to mix with all kinds of people, and well-educated. I never thought I'd meet anyone as perfect as that, but I did, and I'm so glad I fell in love with you. Don't ever let anyone make you forget me, Darling.

Have to go. Byes now. Keep loving me. I'm always loving you.

All my love,
Mary

January 15, 1945

My Darling,

Tonight I feel more impatient than I ever have before. I'm all alone, and it's only seven thirty now. I've been thinking of all those times I saw you and how wonderful everything would be if I could see you tonight. We wouldn't go out, would we, Darling? It's going to take an awful lot of time to deliver all the loves and kisses I have waiting for you.

Had a letter from my brother Harry today. I don't know what the army has done to him, but it's certainly changed him a lot. He was suffering from a hangover when he wrote to me. I think he must have been drunk. He'd spent Christmas seeing the sights of Rome. He thinks it's a wonderful place. Also added that the women were wonderful, but it costs $30 just to look at them. Mother said, "Can I read the letter?" I thought it was better that she didn't as I'm sure she thinks he's a missionary out there. All I'm hoping is that his wife doesn't visit us, as she always wants to read letters she gets from him, though I think it's all her fault that he has changed like this. Of course, his explanation is that Continental life is a lot different to ours. Shocked him at first, but he rather likes it now. Do you like it, Darling?

Read on the paper today about the first troops from France to arrive in America for leave. It said the first things they wanted were a glass of milk and honey. When do you get your leave, Darling? Don't look for honey when you get home.

Gwenda is leaving Swansea this week. Her people are going to keep a hotel in another town. I'm wondering if she'll come to see me before she goes because I haven't done anything to hurt her, unless I disgusted her, but I don't think so. Mother wants to know why I don't go and see her. That's the awkward part. I can't explain. As long as I've got my Irwin, everyone else can go. You mean more to me than the rest of the people in the world put together. I love you, Irwin.

Had a wonderful dream all about you last night. You loved me so much, and we were together. I wish we could be together soon, just like that dream, but I suppose I have to do a lot of dreaming before that happens. Keep loving me, Darling, and take good care of yourself. I'm loving you all the time.

All my love, Darling,
Mary

January 16, 1945

My Darling,

Done nothing today, not even work. It's been raining, and it's so cold here, colder than last winter when my nose got so red. I promised to see Nancy tonight, but instead, I stayed home and thought about you. That's the next best thing to being with you that I can do. If you had let me go when I asked you, I don't know what I'd do now, because I know I'd still be loving you. Nobody can take your place. Time goes so slowly these days, or maybe it seems that way because I'm waiting to see you. Sometimes it makes me wonder if I ever will. Then I'm ashamed of myself for being so impatient as I know if you should get a chance to come and see me, you'd come. Do you find it difficult being true to a person, Darling? I don't. When anyone asks me to go out, I don't hesitate about my answer as I know I'd be thinking about you all the time, and it would be a waste of time, boring the other person.

Have to get to work early in the morning. Auditors are there again for three days. They're two very conscientious girls, and we had to find a hotel for them to stay. They wanted separate beds as they both hated sleeping with anyone else. That's what they wanted but won't get. You can imagine what they look like. One of the men suggested having a party while they're here and inviting them. I don't think they'd come to Swansea again if we did a thing like that. I wouldn't mind a job like theirs though. They travel around the country quite a bit. I wish I could change my job. It's getting very monotonous, but if I try to, they'll put me in the army or in a factory. At least I'm home now, even though I'm bored to tears on times.

Mother tells me I'm the most dissatisfied person she knows. Just like my father was, always wanting to be somewhere else. What I really want is to be with you for always. This afternoon, I heard Dinah Shore sing "Always." I like it. Did you hear it? They played it in that programme *Hello G.I.s*. Also heard Bing singing "I'll be Seeing You" today. Frank Sinatra is improving too. I like his version of "Dancing in the Dark" and "Kiss Me Again." My brother expects me to swoon every time I hear him, but he isn't that good. I only swoon for my Irwin when he tries to give me a sucker bite. I frightened Mother when I went home with a sucker bite one night. She couldn't make out what it was, and I couldn't tell her. I was crazy to let you do that. It was nice though. Why can't you be here, to stop me from getting so much sleep. I get tired so early now. You'll have an awful job with me, or will you? I'm loving you and missing you more and more each minute. Dream about me and love me lots.

All my love,
Mary

January 1945

My Darling,

If I don't dream about Chinese tonight, there's something wrong with me, as I went to see *Dragonseed* after work today. It was a wicked show. I had the horrors after looking at Katherine Hepburn and all the other people with slant eyes for two hours. I was home at seven o'clock, then I played cards with my young brother. I'm awfully unlucky, but I don't mind because I know I am lucky in love. It seems such a waste of time all these evenings that I stay home when I could be with you if there wasn't a war to be won. I was reading today about the people who are able to go to Paris from England. I wish I had business to see to there. Then I could see you and wouldn't have to worry about getting home early as there wouldn't be anyone to say anything to me. Not that I was worried too much when you were here. You got less sleep than I did those days after the walk you had when you left me. Remember the place we used to say good night? I do. I see it every day of my life, and I always think of the wonderful memories attached to it. I wonder if anyone else makes use of it now that we are unable to? We'll be back though, won't we, Darling?

The news seems quite good to us people at home now. It was only last week we were told how serious things were right before Christmas, and it made me mad to hear silly old men in the bus criticising all the boys who are fighting for them. My brother gets a kick out of teasing me about the Americans. He told me that they were all out with girls instead of keeping their minds on the fighting, but his real opinion was that nobody could have done any better than they did. He's a Home Guard too, and they usually think that they can do better than the soldiers.

It's about ten o'clock now. I'll finish this letter before ten thirty, then I can think really hard about you. I like to think of you in a nice, warm bed safe from harm. But the way you're advancing right now, I get other thoughts. I haven't had a letter this week yet, so I guess you must be busy. As long as you're safe, Darling, and let me know once in a while, that's all that matters. It's funny the way I trust you, but I do. I know you'd have no difficulty in finding yourself a date, but I never think about it. Maybe it's because I'm being so good. I love you, Irwin. That calls for a super kiss. I can't wait, but I'll have to. Keep loving me, Darling, and miss me a lot.

All my love,
Mary

January 19, 1945

My Darling,

My lucky day today. Three lovely letters from you. I love you lots. You're so wonderful. Can't you hear me telling you that right now? You're so near to me when I read your letters that I expect to be kissed now and then, but I'll have to wait for something as wonderful as that to happen to me. It's snowing here, but I don't mind a bit. It just makes me feel more comfortable sitting near the fire as I've been doing tonight. I'd feel much more comfortable in your arms, though. It's cold, and I'd have a good excuse to get closer to you. I imagine that all day long. I miss you so much, Darling. I guess you know that though even if you have the nerve to ask me if I remember you once in a while.

It looks as though they've mixed the mail up. The letters I got today were written on the third, fifth, and sixth of January. You seemed to have changed houses. Do you like being on a farm, Darling? Your description of shaking a bottle of milk to make butter was funny. Let's try it sometime if and when we don't have anything to do. Can you imagine us wasting precious time together like that? I can't. I have much nicer plans, same as you, Irwin. I wish I could start putting my plans into action right now. It's cold in bed alone like this.

Do you think I'd be any use helping you with all that extra work you have? Don't work late again tomorrow night, Honey, I have to see you. I'm lonely, remember? Bring your work home. After all, I know what some of those letters stand for. You told me once, s2 and all the others I mean. I'm sorry about your clerks, Irwin. When you think of all those nice people you met not so very long ago, it seems terribly unfair the way they have to sacrifice their lives, and I feel so selfish moaning about little things that don't really matter. I'm praying for you just as hard now as when you were in trouble, Darling. Don't let anything happen to you. You're my all.

Can you imagine how Doc feels about his Purple Heart Medal? It's a good thing that he didn't have to pay too dearly for it. I'd like to see him again too. You don't have to tell me to kiss you on the platform when you arrive here. I know I won't have any control over my feelings when that longed-for day arrives. I'll be in your arms before you have a chance to look for me, so prepare yourself for a super kiss. Don't think of Germans when you're alone in bed, Darling. Think of me and lots of other things, like I do. It's much nicer, and you go to sleep quicker too, feeling nice and warm. I kiss my pillow every night, making believe it's you. I know I'm crazy, but I like to imagine things.

Are you keeping something from me? What's wrong with your leg that I didn't know about before you mentioned it in this letter? Doc had better see it's all right as I'll have something to say to him. I know he'll look after you though. I don't suppose we people at home will ever realise just how much you boys are doing for us, but I can imagine what you've been through, Darling, and I hope I'll get a chance to prove with my love just how I feel about it all.

Do you think we'll ever get to Hawaii, Irwin? I want to wear a grass skirt and a necklace of flowers, that's all. Maybe they'll think I'm a native girl if I get a good tan as well. See how easy it will be for you to get rid of me, but once you're mine, I won't let you out of my sight. I love you for always, remember?

Wish you could keep me awake tonight. There's no fun in sleeping, especially when I don't dream about you. Keep loving me. I love you lots and lots.

All my love,
Mary

January 20, 1945

My Darling,

Here I am all ready to do that town, or village of yours, even though you say there's not much to see. What would I want to see anyway? If I could only be near you, I'd have my whole world in sight—you're all of it. I'd even take my turn shaking milk to make butter as long as I could just talk to you; then we'd let the rest of the family go to bed, and I could have you all to myself. I'll have to polish up my French before I see you. I can't have you showing off. I know some good phrases, but I suppose you know them too, standard phrases for all the soldiers. You're looking after my account, though, aren't you, Darling. Yours has to be as big as mine, and mine is in perfect condition. I hope it won't be that way for much longer. I want you to make a big withdrawal soon. It's all yours. You won't have a big balance either. I don't think you'll have one at all after I finish with it. It says on posters everywhere that you can never save enough for the fighting me, but I'm only saving for one fighting man. I wish I had bonds or something to prove to that one man just how enormous my account is. If he knows just how much I love him, he'll have a rough idea. You know I love you with all my heart, don't you, Irwin?

Went to see *Pin-Up Girl* tonight. I've seen it once before, but there was nowhere else to go. It's good, though. I like to hear the remarks made by men around me. When Grable makes a wonderful appearance, some just give a big sigh; others find something wrong with her. They can either see her dark parting or some other little fault. She is nice, though, but I prefer Lana Turner, don't you? You're my pin-up boy. I don't have any etchings like you have. I told Tyrone I didn't want to see him again. He's too big for me anyway. My Irwin is too much for me to handle as it is. He can bite my ears and give me sucker bites without me being able to stop him. I'd love it though. You just wait until I'm big. I'll have my revenge, when I can kick you out of bed. No, I wouldn't want to do a thing like that. It's much nicer to fit in your arms and say "me too," not forgetting hearing you snore. I'm glad you can't say I snore because I don't.

Have to dream about all the lovely things now. I love you, Irwin. Keep loving me.

All my love,
Mary

January 21, 1945

My Darling,

Oh! I'm frightened! I'm in bed, and there's a spider right over my head. I can hear you saying I'm a sissy, but it's a big one, honest. Wish you were here so you could make me forget about it. If it crawls down the wall, I'm going to hide my head. Wouldn't I make a wonderful jungle-mate? Spiders are supposed to be lucky. I hope this one is. The only luck I hope for is to see you soon, and I'm actually hoping and praying for that.

Supposed to have gone to my brother Con's place for tea this afternoon. I was late getting home from work, and by the time I dressed, it was too late to expect tea by the time I walked two miles to get there, so I had it home instead, deciding to go and see how Nancy was this evening, but fate was against me. As I was leaving the house, it started to snow quite heavily, so I resigned myself to another night at home. My sister's boyfriend, Sid, came. She was busy doing something, so I had to stay and be polite to him for almost an hour, then they left. Mother came home from church and brought a few of our delightful neighbors with her, and it was funny to listen to all the local scandal. They seem to know every move I make, but I have a clear conscience, so I don't worry. There's one woman, I see her almost every day, and she says the same thing to me, how dark my hair is going. I was a redhead once, Darling, but I'm not now, am I? I'm glad you don't remember me like that. You'd never let me forget about it.

Had the most wonderful dream about us last night. When I woke this morning, I thought sure you'd be there, but no Irwin. How much longer do I have to go on dreaming, Darling? I feel as though I can't wait until the time comes when I'll be able to open my eyes and see you there. I'm not tired of waiting, but these dreams I have make me that way, and I'm always expecting you to turn up suddenly, a big surprise. That's not considering the fact that over where my Darling is, there's a big fight going on. I hate to think of you in the middle of things, though. Perhaps if I stay as good as I am now, as I know I shall, they'll let me see you before too long. Well, it's a heavenly thought anyway. Just imagine, I'll be able to kiss you without having to dream and see me in your eyes just like I used to. I love you more than ever, Irwin, and can't miss you any more than I do. Love me lots, dream about me.

All my love,
Mary

January 22, 1945

My Darling,

Haven't been able to get warm today yet. It's still snowing here, and I think just to look at that stuff makes you feel colder. I know of a good remedy though, but he happens to be a few hundred miles away. So what can I do? Think I'll have to write to Dorothy Dix again and see if she can help me. I seem to be getting quite a name since I don't go out anymore. People don't see me, so they're inventing stories. I think I told you about Brookman going around with our telephonist. He still is, but last night he took his wife to a party at this girl's house, making everything look decent. He was afraid in case her people had heard something about them. He had a shock though as this girl's mother asked him if he was still taking me out. That's what Hazel's been telling her people just to clear herself. Brookman has one or two good points. Believe it or not, he never talks about other people's affairs. He rags me about you but never tells anyone else about it. He told this woman that I wouldn't go out with him because he was married. She didn't believe that as she knew I went around with an American who was married for quite a while. So now Brookman has taken over. If that should ever get to Mother's ears, she'd know different, as she knows how often I've been out since you left here and just where I go and who I go with. I asked Brookman if he told this girl you were married, but he swore on his oath that he didn't, so I'm worrying now where she heard it. He was quite annoyed about it himself, and his latest romance has ended. I'm not worried about this supposed affair with him, as I can deny it all with a clear conscience, but I'm waiting to see the person who started the story. I wish I could change my work as from what I've heard, whenever the drivers and their wives get together in a party or some place, I'm the sole topic of conversation. When I go home from work in a car, the driver tells me to sit at the back, in case his wife should see me. I don't want any part of them, and they know it too, but obviously other people don't. I've been miserable about it all day today, thinking about it all, except tonight when I came home and just thought about you, Darling. They can talk as much as they like about me and only make me love you more.

Heard Dinah Shore sing "I'll Walk Alone" on Command Performance tonight. It made me miss you more. But it's nice. The rest of the programme wasn't so good though, or maybe I'm getting critical by listening to the radio so much. My young brother wanted me to go see *The Fleet's In* tonight, but I've seen it twice before, and I don't like the Navy. I'm only interested in the Army, one person in the Army. I think he loves me too. What more could I want? That reminds me. The cashier in the bank said to me today, "Have you got everything you want?" I thought he meant money bags and forms, so I said yes and got a good answer. "You're lucky." He's a nice man, though, gives me a piece of chocolate every day and a nice smile.

You are taking extra good care of yourself and looking after your part of our account, aren't you? Dream about me and love me all you can. I love you, Irwin.

All my love,
Mary

January 25, 1945

My Darling,

The snow is about five inches deep here today. I've never seen so much in my life before. There's no transport running, including our cars, but being conscientious, I walked to work. I only fell about six times before I got there. It was funny at work. The drivers had nothing to do, and they didn't bother to answer the phone. Naturally, I had work to do though. The other girl in the office couldn't get home to lunch, so we both decided to find something to eat in town, but everybody else had the same idea, and we didn't get any lunch. We went back to work, and the men challenged us to a snowball fight on the roof, so that's what we did. I'm sorry now though. They rubbed my face in the snow. I was soaking. Then some Americans in the street below decided to play. They thought better of it after a few minutes and left. All the time I was handling this snow, I thought dye was coming off my gloves, but it looked just like blood. I had cut myself somehow. I was scared and couldn't find anyone to help me, then a wounded American came looking for a car. He asked if he could warm his hand "by the fire." You should have seen him, Irwin, I thought he was going to die. His four fingers had been shot off, and the frost had affected them. He sat in the chair, and then he asked for water. All this time, my hand was still bleeding. I thought I'd need water too. I didn't know what to do for him. He wanted to get ten miles from here to see his wife, and the roads are so bad that every driver I asked wouldn't take the risk. Mr. Clement took him at last, and I had my hand seen to. It's quite a nasty cut but not as bad as I thought it was. I'd make a hopeless nurse, Darling. I won't play tomorrow. I had enough, between cutting my hand and one man I hit who told me he'd break my so-and-so neck for me if he caught me. It's all in a day's work, I suppose. One of the drivers said it was all right to take me home, so I took the risk, what a risk. We had people pushing the car most of the way, but I did get home, and it was a lot better than walking.

Haven't had a letter from you this week, Darling. As long as you're all right, that's the main thing. I do pray for you every night, and I'm being so good that I'm sure my prayers will be answered. Our hopes are raised again by the good news. When this is all over, I hope I can take care of you instead of you doing it on your own. I wish I could be with you now, wherever you are. If I go on missing you more and more each day, I think I'll go crazy if I don't see you soon. It's been a long time now. It seems longer though. This time last year, everything was so wonderful, and now all I can do is imagine that I'm with you. All the time, I'm scared in case you should forget about me. You won't though, will you, Irwin? If I could only be asking you that in person and have reassurance the way I used to. Well, if I could only be near you, that's all I want. I love you so much that it hurts, Darling.

Keep loving me and remember that I'm thinking of you and loving you every minute. Please take extra good care of yourself. If you don't, I'll never speak to you again. You can haunt me as much as you wish, in person though. I've lots and lots of kisses waiting for you. See what you're missing? I love you, Darling, with all my heart.

All my love,
Mary

January 30, 1945

My Darling,

Did you think I'd forgotten about you? You're wrong again. See, you can't get rid of me. I've been in bed and still am, since last Thursday. When I've stayed in bed for so long, I can't remember. It's awful. But things could be a lot worse. I slipped with a kettle of boiling water in my hand and scalded my hands. I was scared more than anything, though, as I imagined the water came all over me. I'm fated to have something wrong with my hands this time every year.

Thanks, Darling, for the two wonderful letters I received yesterday. I wish I could have answered them right away, but the doctor bandaged my fingers up as well. I had to tell him about that this morning so I could write to my Irwin today.

That letter Mr. Humphreys sent you was nice, wasn't it? I wish we could impose on his good nature soon so I could read to you and have you pester me all the time, just like you do in my dreams. You were annoyed last night, though, because I kissed you when you wanted to go to sleep. You were a sissy, but I still loved you.

Hope your feet aren't bothering you too much, Darling. I know you'll take care of them. I hate to think of anything hurting you at all. You're so wonderful, and I love you so much.

Missed all the fun since I've been in bed. We've had quite a heavy fall of snow here, and there's been moonlight skiing. I could kick myself for being so careless, but I'd want you with me in the moonlight, before I'd appreciate it. I want to be with you all the time.

Old Mr. Harris died last Friday. He was a millionaire, but he wasn't very happy with all his money. He was going to take me for a trip around the world when the war ended. I guess I've had that. I didn't believe him anyway.

Wrote you a letter last Thursday before my accident and remembered today that I hadn't sent it. So don't blame the mail when you do get it. It's all my fault.

Wish I could find my way into your arms right now, and tomorrow was Sunday morning, so we could both sleep late. I love you more and more each day and longing so much to see you again.

My hand is tired or something. It's burning. I'll write again tomorrow. Keep loving me, please.

All my love,
Mary

February 1, 1945

My Darling,

Feeling fit once more except that I still have my hand dressed twice a day. You're so wonderful that I can't explain how I love. Today I had two *Esquires*, nice one too; a *Red Book* and *Cosmopolitan*; and a very special letter written on the 22nd. You make me so happy, Irwin. I hope I can repay you one day soon. If I could only be with you right now, I'd try and prove it to you, how grateful I am for you loving me.

You asked me what I was doing when you were writing to me. You know, and I don't have to think very hard to remember, just thinking of you, that's what I like doing most, since I can't see you. I'd give anything to prove if you did have a good shave, and whenever I think of you, I'm always in the mood for love, and that's not worrying about your beard, either.

It must have been a horrible experience you had. One day, Darling, we'll be so happy that those days when you thought our hopes were crushed will seem like a bad dream. Irwin, you didn't say before that you were reported missing. If anything happened to you, I wouldn't want to live either. I'm so sure about loving you, more than

I've ever been about anything in my life before, though sometimes when I'm feeling sorry for myself, I wonder why I couldn't have you all to myself, all mine. But I know how fortunate I am to have your love. Whoever it was that kept you safe for me, when you couldn't see a way out, must have designs for our dreams to come true. I can never think of giving you up, as I should, as something has to come of our love. It just can't be wasted. You'd say I was crazy if you knew some of the things I imagine. But it is so wonderful to think of getting your breakfast, even though it's very early in the morning and only being without you for a few hours. I suppose that would be too long, but I won't complain, honest. Life would be terrible without an imagination. I don't know what I'd do without mine. You don't mind my building my dreams around you, do you? I don't care what you imagine about us. I'm all in favour with any of your plans.

It would be nice if you could get your brother transferred. I worry enough about you now. I don't know what I'd do if you were in the infantry. You haven't met your brother over there, have you? It must be maddening to be so near and yet so far. Only a mountain parts my brothers in Italy, but they've tried all ways to get to one another and failed.

Time for bed. All this sleep is killing me. Come home and keep me awake all the time. I don't ever want to sleep when you're around. I love you with all my big heart, Darling, and I'm getting impatient to see you. Love me all you can. Take good care of yourself and be good.

All my love,
Mary

February 3, 1945

My Darling,

Saturday night and I'm lonely, sitting here, pitying myself, just thinking what we'd be doing. If only someone would grant my wishes. It's about eight o'clock now, but not going to work makes the day seem so much longer. I don't know what I'd do without your letters to read over and over again. This morning I had two lovely letters written on the eighteenth and the twentieth. Don't you envy me being able to take all the time I want reading them? I like writing you when it's almost time to go to sleep, and that's what I intended doing last night, but my brother and his wife came and kept me talking until twelve o'clock, and I wondered if Irwin would think I was a meanie if I wrote a long letter tonight instead. I don't mean to be such a meanie, Darling, because I love you all I can, and writing isn't any effort at all. I like to tell you what I'm thinking and what I do, knowing that you are interested. You're so wonderful to find time to write me. You're so busy with all the extra work you have now. I'm looking forward to having a new bar with a long stripe. I'll be promoted too. And I know how pleased you'll feel about it. That's one of your ambitions, isn't it? So it's mine too. It does make me impatient waiting, Darling. But when I have you to wait for, it would be a very, very long time before I'd get too impatient. And I have something wonderful to look forward to, as I know you love me almost as much as I love you.

Would like to have seen you doing your washing. I bet that sweater wasn't any use after you had finished with it. Though you looked nice washing dishes one night, with that correct domestic air. Maybe you will make a useful husband after all.

Of course I remember Sherry. I'm sorry that I was nasty to him that night at Penclawdd now. It's not a bit of wonder those boys drink the way they do, as they must wonder themselves how many more months or days they have to live. I remember him at the garage one night, asking me to get him a taxi. We already had one, but he grinned when I said he could share ours, as though he knew I didn't want him to. Doesn't a year make a big difference, Darling? I don't remember Corporal Webb, only saw him once, I think, but I feel as though I knew him very well, hearing you speak about him. I wonder how his wife feels about it now. One of the girls who works at the bus offices in the same building as ours lives at Penclawdd and knows Mrs. Webb very well. She didn't think that her marriage meant very much to her, but you can never tell. Does Doc still hear from Eva? I saw her one night, did I tell you? She ignored me, so I didn't bother to make her see me.

It would be wonderful, Darling, if I could be waiting there, where you are, when you return from work. We'd forget about the war for a few hours, wouldn't we? We are allowed to dream, and that helps a lot. I wouldn't like to tell you what I dream either, but you're wonderful. You haven't any idea just how wonderful you are.

Oh, I forgot to thank you for the snaps you sent. Why couldn't I see more of you, though. I didn't send that picture, Darling, but I believe it was in the letter I wrote on the twenty-fourth of December. I mean, I sent you two snaps my brother took indoors one night. They'll catch up with you, I suppose, I hope. Next Tuesday afternoon, I promise to go through the ordeal once more, and then my Irwin won't be disappointed with me. I hope you got pictures for Christmas, though, so you could be like the rest of the boys. That long, low building doesn't look too comfortable to me. I can see the aerial. It doesn't look very safe, but it did work, didn't it? Wish I could have shared that place with you. Any place as long as I could be with you, even that tent. Seems as though I'm always wishing, doesn't it? Well, I am.

Nancy's mother visited us this afternoon. Nancy is staying in England with her husband now. She's lucky. My aunt gave me a shock when she brought her knitting out. I asked her who she was knitting those little things for. She laughed and then broke the news, for Nancy. It seems funny to think of things just a year ago. Nancy was having a good time with Walter, hadn't even met her husband, and now this. My aunt's still waiting for Walter to come here. She thinks a lot of him even though she knows he's married. He was quite nice though but not good-looking, like you said.

One of our drivers is getting married Monday. They're having some sort of celebration tonight. I'm glad I had a good excuse to stay away from that. I intend starting work tomorrow morning. I'm tired of staying home like this with so much time to waste. I think about you until I end up envying myself being with you when you were here. If you ever dare to insinuate that I don't love you after this, I'll get mad with you. Irwin, do you realize I dread the thought of going out with anyone else? I do. You can be quite certain of the fact that I'm all yours, even though you keep saying you want to be sure, and I'm serious about your account, so you take good care of mine too. If I hear any sentimental number on the radio or read a sentimental story, I always think of you and us. I'm glad my thoughts are secret to me, or people around would think I was crazy. I do love you with all my heart, Darling, that's what I'd give anything to whisper in your ear right now.

The fire needs coal again, and I won't put it out either. Suppose I need sleep after that, so do you. Mind if I say good night now. Love me all you can and think about me all the time.

All my love,
Mary

February 4, 1945

My Darling,

Haven't got any lipstick on, my hair is down, and now, well, what I'm trying to tell you is, I'm all ready to be messed up more while pitching lots of woo with you. So have a nice shave and come right over. On second thought, don't bother to shave, I can't wait. It's Sunday, seven o'clock, time to make tea, Irwin, but don't let's bother. I have so many kisses to catch up on that we can't waste a minute for anything else. I'm tired of dreaming. I want you near to me, very near, in person, and not opening my eyes to find you've left me. All I ever want to dream about is you though. They're such super dreams. It's a good thing I sleep on my own; otherwise things might get complicated.

Started work again this morning. I walked and was in the office at eight thirty. It was a lovely morning. No rain or wind, and the sun was actually shining. I worked until two o'clock and walked home again. I'm missing our walks, Darling. I miss everything that has anything to do with you. This afternoon while the rest of the family were out, my brother at his club and the others at church, I did some cooking and surprised them when they returned. They're still living, anyway, so no sarcastic remarks from you, Honey. Been reading your magazines until now, looking at those pin-up girls and wondering why you love me.

Every day we're expecting the Russians to reach Berlin. They're doing all right, not to mention the 1st Army. That's my main interest. How I wish this would end so I could see my Darling again. I have a funny feeling, just to think about it, but I want it to be soon.

They told me at work today that I missed a wonderful night out last night. All the staff invaded the New Moon Club. I believe you went there once. It's near Penclawdd. They looked stupid this morning, so I can imagine what last night was like and am more than glad I was out of it. I wouldn't like to get drunk with any of those men around. I only want to get drunk when my Irwin is around to take care of me.

My hands are almost cured now, except for a red patch on one which doesn't look so good, but the doctor assured me it would wear off. My left hand wasn't so bad. It's just dry now, so maybe I'll get right one day altogether. I forgot to tell you, I also have a sore knee where I fell. You can imagine I was in a bad way. They wanted to know at work had I been helping the Russians in their new advance.

My young brother wants me to help him with his algebra now. Would you like to help too? Help me instead. I need some lessons in love. Be good, Darling, and think about me all the time, then I know you'll be missing and loving me. I'll always love you, Darling.

All my love,
Mary

February 5, 1945

My Darling,

Are you nice and cosy in bed now? I am. I could be much cosier if I had you to keep me warm. I can't wait, but I have to, I guess. They're nice thoughts right now, though. When I write these things, I close my eyes for a few seconds and think just how heavenly it would be. I love you and love you more than you'll ever know.

On the local paper tonight, there's a wedding anniversary greeting for Corporal Webb from his wife, so I imagine he's safe. That's good news anyway. It's the first greeting of that kind to anyone in the US Army that I've seen in our paper. This time last year you were on leave, Darling. Someone tried to steal you from me at that wedding, didn't they? I'm so glad that you never took any of those opportunities you had. You've always been wonderful to me, Darling, even though I've been mean to you on times. You've always known I love you, though, haven't you?

Did you hear Command Performance tonight? Dinah Shore sang "Long Ago and Far Away." She was good. All the important people took some part in it. Bing and Bob Hope were quite good, but I don't think much of Judy Garland lately. My strong, silent man Gary Cooper was silent, but I like him lots. English programmes are bad after those.

We have the auditors again tomorrow, but I'm still taking my day off. I've made an appointment for your picture, and that's more important, isn't it? Will you love me more when you get it? I know you're saying yes so I'll hurry it to you. I want you to love me as much as it's possible for you to love anyone. I'm selfish about your love, Darling. Suppose that's natural when you have all my love. I missed you in my dreams last night. You didn't show up, but I'll be waiting again tonight. I'm always waiting, though. Have to get lots of sleep tonight for a good picture tomorrow. Love me all you can. Dream about me, and miss me all the time.

All my love,
Mary

February 6, 1945

My Darling,

Happy anniversary. Fifteen months now. I hope I can remind you of this date every month of my life. Had three lovely letters waiting for me when I returned from the photographers this afternoon.

That's for being nice to you. I'm worried about you not receiving any of my mail, in case you think I've forgotten about you. You must know I haven't though. I never will, Darling. I can't imagine me doing that when I know I'll always love you so very much. I do, honest. I know too that you are doing all you can to make my life perfect even though Doc's lawyer made a suggestion contrary to our plans. But I'll always be waiting for you whatever stands in our way right now.

You don't know how I felt when I read that article that you sent about leaves being granted to England. It's wonderful. I too can hardly believe it. Seven whole days with you, and then you ask me if I want you to come to Swansea. It's something to look forward to. Before I've been wondering how long this war could last so I could see you again. You'll get plenty of food this time too. I'll cook for you. It will be more than a pleasure, and Mr. Humphreys did say to consider him as a relative, Darling, so I'm sure he'll fix you up. I'm going to be around all the time too, so don't get ideas about sleeping until 2:00 p.m. If they change their minds about this leave now, I don't know what I'll do I'm planning so much. Hope they've found some people to help with your work too, but you certainly deserve a rest after what you've been through. I'll forget while you're here that you have to leave me again and just think how wonderful it is to have you back again. I wish I could sleep until the time came for me to see you again, when I can have Irwin's super kisses.

Your description of the show was funny. I bet you were all mad after heating the place and then smoke obliterating the screen. You put up with some terrible things, but we'll all laugh at them someday, won't we?

You're a honey not to go to that club looking for nurses like the rest of the boys. It would be so easy for you to have a good time, but I know you feel the same way as I do about things. I have no interest in going anywhere since you left. They're having quite a number of big dances at the Brangwyn Hall lately. My brother and his wife don't like going just the two alone and keep asking me to go with them, but I don't like the thought of trying to be nice to anyone when all the time I'd be wishing you were there, like I was at the Garrison Ball, when I spent most of my time talking to girls I knew and hadn't seen for a long time. Shall we go to one of those dances while you're here, Darling? It would be nice, and it's a lovely place. Are your feet in good shape now? I'm longing to dance with you again. As long as I can be with you, I don't care where we go, but I'd rather have you all to myself instead of being surrounded with people. You have such an enormous account waiting for you. It's going to take all your time to withdraw it all. How's mine doing?

Tonight I'm going to dream about your trip. I'll be doing that every night until I'm actually waiting for you at that station. Keep loving me, dream what you like about me. I'm all yours. I hope that very soon I'll be able to whisper in your ear just how much I love you and tell you how much I'm missing you all day and every day. Take good care of yourself, Darling. You're wonderful.

All my love,
Mary

February 7, 1945

My Darling,

Every day seems just like a year now, waiting until I can see you. But it's so good knowing that I don't have to wait very long before that wonderful day rolls around. You've made me more excited than I've been about anything in my life before, but you're the most wonderful thing that's ever happened to me. I love you lots, Irwin, much more than when you left here, so maybe you'll have an idea of how I've missed you. I believe I've told you about the girl who cleans our offices. She's married to an American. This morning she told me about the leaves, but she heard that only men with wives were getting them. That isn't right, is it? Say it isn't or It'll break my heart. I just have to see you soon so that my dreams can be realized. I've done lots of dreaming.

When the blackout was on here, all the windows in our garage were painted black. Now the men have to scrape the paint off again. I thought I'd help this afternoon so we'd get some light in the office.

I had to leave this particular window I was doing for a few minutes, and when I got back to it, someone had the shape of a heart there, with "Irwin" alongside it. There were a few men standing around, and I was asking which one took all the trouble for my benefit, couldn't make out why they were all so quiet. Then I heard Mr. Clement say, "Jolly good." He'd been standing behind me all the time. I had to work an hour extra to get the heart off the window. I have to put up with all sorts of things when they start teasing me about you. That stone heart they presented me with is still in the office with your name written on it, and Mr. Clement gets a big kick out of it. Shows it to all his visitors. They must be able to tell that I love you an awful lot. I don't want to hide the fact anyway, because I do.

Hope you're thinking hard about me now. It's ten thirty, and I'm ready for loving. Are you, Honey? What I mean is, I'm in bed, ready for sleep so I can dream about you. I had a lovely dream last night, but don't you ever tell me I'm scandalous in your dreams, or I'll start telling you how you behave. Oh, but you're wonderful, and I love you so much. Have to go now, Darling, but I'll be back. Start saving all the kisses and love you can for me. I want all I can have. Love me lots and miss me.

All my love,
Mary

February 8, 1945

My Darling,

How am I ever going to cure myself of this habit of going to bed so early every night? You'll have me sleeping on your shoulder at ten o'clock. Now I am kidding. Sleep is the last thing on my mind when you're around, even though you snore when you're with me. Don't get mad. Remember, I'm not there for you to bite my ears as a reprisal, and please don't remember me saying that when my ears are available. I was alone sitting near the fire tonight, thinking the loveliest things about us, then my brother returned home. I could have kicked him for disturbing my thoughts, and he doesn't stay quiet like all brothers should. He teases me, and I don't bother to answer him until I have a few bruises to say something about. Mother gets mad with him, the way he pushes me around. He doesn't mean to hurt me, but he doesn't realize his strength. He thinks it's good for me to have this experience in case I get a tough husband. You won't be cruel, will you, Irwin? I know I wouldn't be able to do anything about it if you were unless I talked myself out of things, like I did to avoid sucker bites. I love you, Darling, and I'll never let you forget it. That rates a kiss. When can I have it please? Maybe I'm not able to collect it right away, but put it to my account.

Forgot to thank you for three lovely magazines I received today, all *Collier's*. They have good article in them too. What amuses me is the whole family reads them before I'm allowed to look at them, but I do get lots of time these days to appreciate magazines when it comes my turn to see them. So thanks a lot, Darling, you're wonderful to me.

Don't have very much to tell you tonight. I wish I could put my thoughts into words. Though all I can say is, you are all my thoughts, because you're always on my mind. Missing you and loving you more and more all the time. So keep loving me, Darling, and remember I'm all yours. I'll be there tonight in your dreams. May be a little late if your train doesn't come to time. But you know I'll be waiting. Take care of yourself, Honey.

All my love,
Mary

February 9, 1945

Irwin Darling,

We're having unusual weather for Swansea. It's raining again. It's a lovely place if you want to recuperate after pneumonia. People are still walking around looking miserable. I'm glad I don't have to go out to feel happy. Now that you're not here, all the good times I have are spent at home thinking of you and being able to write you letters. That's the next best thing to walking in the rain with you. Didn't get a letter today. I know you love me, but I'm worrying in case you think I've forgotten about you, as you don't seem to be having my letters. I think so hard about you that you should sense my love. I hope you do, Darling, as you loving me is the only thing that matters in my life. So please don't stop.

Finished my work very early today, and I don't know why, but I can't stay in that place a minute longer than it's necessary, so I got home at four thirty and spent the rest of the evening reading your nice magazines until it was time to come to bed and dream about my Darling. Wish we could dream together though. Do you talk in your sleep. They tell me I do. I wonder what I say. Mother tells me I'm talking when she wakes me in the morning, so it's no wonder I don't say very much when I'm awake if I'm talking all night. I wouldn't mind you hearing what I say as I'm sure it's all about you. Nice things too. Was listening to a man on the radio today, speaking about dreams. He said that before we say something when we're awake, there's a part of the brain that censors it. But when we're sleeping, the censor isn't at work. Maybe that's a good thing or the censor would be very shocked at the things I dream. I'm terrible lately, but you're bad too. But do we have fun. I'll tell about it one day. You don't mind me dreaming these things about you, do you? It's just too bad if you do as I can't do anything about it, and I don't care what you dream about me as long as you love me.

Have to go now, but I'll be back. Remember how much I love you. I hope to tell you about it in person soon. You're wonderful, and I miss you lots. Dream about me.

All my love,
Mary

February 10, 1945

My Darling,

While I'm writing this, Harry James is playing "You Made Me Love You" on the radio. You did too though it didn't take the slightest effort on my part. Do you love me on Saturdays too? I love you more as I miss you extra. There's an American Red Cross Ball at the Brangwyn Hall tonight. If you were only here, then I'd want to go. It's strictly evening dress tonight too. It should be good. Let's go. You can hold me as close as you want and even bite my ears while we're dancing, anything, as long as I'm with you. I love you, Darling, and can't help imagining all these wonderful things. I'm not really crazy, honest. It's just that it's Saturday, and I want to be so near you instead of thinking what I would be doing. It's all your fault for being so wonderful, or is it mine for loving you so much? I don't know, but I want to feel this way until I can see you again.

When I was leaving home this morning, the postman called after me. No letters, but two *Yank* magazines. That's what I've been reading this evening. Those articles on the German towns you've occupied are awfully interesting. And those letters written to the editor bring up some funny subjects, don't they? My brother didn't like the pin-up girls, though. That's the first page he looks at. I think they had too much on to suit him. He's almost as bad as you with your etchings. Do you still have them, Darling?

Remember Mr. Dent's daughter? I saw her today. She certainly surprised me, as the first thing she said to me was "I'm engaged." I thought she was kidding even though she showed me her ring. She insisted it was right though. He's an American. Surely he has eyes, though. Maybe she helped him get mistakes in French sentences too. We wouldn't have had so many if we had figured yours out ourselves that time.

Had to leave you for a couple of hours then. My brother's friend came. He's home on indefinite leave. Here's more trouble for me. He's one of those persons who doesn't know when he's not wanted. He could see I was writing, and there's no one else at home. He's ignorant, I guess. I'm rude to him too. When he came in, I said, "You again?" but I can't be bothered by people like him. He's an officer and keeps reminding me of that fact. I was never so glad to see Mother come home in all my life. I came to bed then, so I can think and write in peace. We've put up with him for a few years, coming here when he's on leave, almost every day, as he was my brother's friend. But it's too much now. My brother is away, and the rest of us don't like him. Wish it was you who interrupted this letter. I was thinking about that when I was bored to tears being nasty to him. It would be so different and so wonderful having you to myself. But it will happen to me one day, won't it? I love you so much, Darling, that continues. Like now I feel I can't wait, but I always will.

Keep loving me, Honey. I'm all yours, and dream about me. Anything you like to. Be good?

All my love,
Mary

February 12, 1945

My Darling,

No letter today. I know you must be busy and that's the reason I tell myself for not hearing since Tuesday from you. You knew I loved you when you didn't get mail from me for a few weeks. I know you love me too. I'm worrying if you're all right though. Don't let anything happen to you, Darling. I'm praying hard for you all the time and loving you so much. That's the only way I can help to keep you safe. This would be a very cold and empty place without you and your letters. I worry more now after hearing what you went through a short while ago. We at home don't really realize what you boys are doing for us, but I hope I can express my thanks to you personally very soon. I think you're wonderful any way you are. Are you getting my mail, now? Maybe you aren't and just think I've forgotten about you. Don't ever think that, Darling. Letters are the only means of me letting you know how much I love you. There's nothing else I can do except trust the postal authorities to let you have them. It's a wonder they don't find some way, like cables, so if I wanted to tell you something special you'd get it in good time. I know what you're saying. That I should be satisfied with things as they are. OK, Darling, I won't complain, as long as you don't, but I do want you to know that I'm missing you and loving you more and more every day, so I dread the thought of you forgetting me. Then I wouldn't have any right at all to love you.

We had a party at work this afternoon. One of our men celebrated his twenty-fifth wedding anniversary. His wife sent some of the chocolate cake for us that she baked for the occasion and half a bottle of sherry. They weren't satisfied with that. Had to get ice cream and oranges as well. When I got home after all that, Mother said she had something extra for tea, more chocolate cake. As she was telling me, I didn't feel so good. I couldn't possibly have ate any more. So I told her to keep it until tomorrow. I might want it then. My brothers have nagged me more than usual tonight. They finished up blackening my legs, arms, and face, with soot. You should have seen me. I couldn't help laughing when I saw myself. I was putting my final work in before taking a bath, when my brother's unwanted friend came in. If the sight I looked then doesn't stop him visiting us, nothing will. I had my bath and came straight to bed. It's only nine fifteen now. See all the sleep I've saved up ready to have some sleepless nights when you're here. How's my account? I'm supposed to have a statement every year, telling how many kisses I have to my credit. I'll let you have one, as soon as I total your credits up. You're a millionaire, though, I know that without looking at the records.

I'm going to finish this book I've started now unless I fall asleep thinking of you first. I'll be in your dreams tonight. Love me lots, won't you? You know how much I love you.

All my love,
Mary

February 13, 1945

My Darling,

Lucky me. I had a nice letter from you today. It seems my hunch about you being too busy to write was correct. You're wonderful to remember about me as often as you do when you have so much work. Wish I could help you. Maybe I'd hinder you too much though. Well, I would try for the job anyway. I have some good references. Mr. Clement will tell you I don't speak a word while I'm working, and there's a letter to the editor of the local paper published today thanking the indoor staff of Swansea's leading taxi company for being so polite and tactful. Think I'll have a few medals now. A lady came to the office yesterday and gave me some silk stockings in appreciation of being nice to her. As she said, kindness was so rare these days. Now, Mr. Deems, can I work for you?

What do you need a stove in your bedroom for when all those French girls are waiting to entertain you? Just let me hear about it and I'll break your neck. So you knew all the time that I loved you. Well, I did. I couldn't fool you, I know. My eyes would tell you how much I loved you. Don't you ever say "Wifie, dear, do you love me?" to me. It sounds as though I'm a big fat woman, and you're my henpecked little husband. I'd rather you said, "How much do you love me?" then I could show you. If I wasn't in a good mood, you'd get two black eyes. Otherwise, I'd love you so you wouldn't go to work for a few days. I'd better not tell you anymore or I won't hear from you again. You'll be thinking I'm too strong for you. You'd make me prove those words if you were here. I know, I didn't mean it. Honest, Irwin.

Gosh, I'm proud of you after reading about the 28th Division in that write-up you sent. It seems a miracle how you got through it all, but you did, and I have a lot more faith in my prayers since then. I can't explain things on paper as I want to. I wish I could talk to you. I've been wanting to do that more than ever today. I imagine I'm talking to you most of the time. Perhaps I am going crazy. I don't quite know, but it's a nice feeling.

Went to see Nancy tonight. We've been thinking of nice names to give a boy or a girl. Didn't come to a decision though. This time last year she was deciding who she'd go out with. It seems funny to me, but Nancy says her husband doesn't think it's so funny. I walked all the way home. Three miles from her house tonight. Now I don't feel a bit like sleeping. I'd like to pester you for a few hours until you'd get mad with me and say "For Pete's sake!" Then I'd be scared of you. I'm afraid of you, Darling. You know that, don't you? Now, I am kidding. You're so wonderful that you could be nasty as you wanted to me, and I'd love you just the same.

I don't have a fire in my bedroom or hot bricks in my bed, just get warm thinking about you. Try it sometime. I love you and love you all I can, Darling, so please keep loving me. Be good and miss me.

All my love,
Mary

February 16, 1945

My Darling,

Today I received the letters you wrote on the second and the fifth, letting me know you got some mail from me at last. I'm awfully glad about that. I wouldn't want you to think I'd forgotten about you.

You do seem to have a great deal of work on your hands these days. Hope they find a few people to help you soon because I want to see you badly too, remember? It's been so long, Irwin, and tonight, especially, I feel more miserable than usual. Been wondering how I've been lucky enough to love you and have your letters. The way things seem to me right now, those things aren't meant for me. I'm in a terrible mood. Had to come to bed early, thinking I'd feel different, but I just miss you more when I can think without people disturbing my thoughts. Missing you as much as I do is bad, but I can't do anything about it. Seeing you again is the only cure, but there is that question about how I'll feel when you leave again. I don't want to think about that right now though. Would much rather think how heavenly it will be waiting to see you again, whenever our next meeting will be.

Your present home sounds nice and comfortable. I could make things more comfortable though. Honest, you wouldn't need any lights or the heating system, and I'm not scared of sucker bites either. You just can't scare me. I don't have to get a sucker bite, you know. I'm tough, or am I? It seems years since I talked you out of the last one. My writing is all over the place tonight, but I can't get in a comfortable position. My body seems in the way, but it isn't a bit cold tonight. Isn't that a shame? That means that I won't need you to keep me warm tonight. I'll have to find another excuse for wanting you near to me. Have you any suggestions?

What do you mean by a snazzy calendar? If you mean they were funny, you're right. Captain Evans designed them. He's really crazy but thinks he's wonderful. I told him country scenes were all wrong for advertising our business, just to argue with him. I wouldn't like to tell you what he told me about the advantages one has when out in the country. He's a wicked old man.

Didn't I meet that sergeant whose wife is my twin at Sennybridge? I'm sure I did when we were waiting for the bus one time. He told me then that he had a lovely wife. Don't let him laugh at that calendar though. I don't want everyone to know what a crazy firm I work for. I don't mind you knowing because I love you and am willing to put up with all the cracks you might make.

Tonight I'll pray hard for the colonel to be a good, understanding man so he'll grant you a pass to England. Is it still the same colonel you had when you were here? He's not to know that I think he's horrible, and I'm ready to change my opinion if he's nice to us. I'll keep my fingers crossed until I know you're on your way here. I have a huge account waiting for you. Hope mine is big too. You're still wonderful, and I love you more than ever, Darling. Keep loving me and miss me lots.

All my love,
Mary

February 17, 1945

Irwin Darling,

Saturday night seems to come around so quickly. I hate them now, but maybe I won't have to spend too many of them this way before seeing you, and even if it will only mean one Saturday night with you, then that will make up for all these lonely ones, like tonight. Went to see "Bathing Beauty" after finishing up work this afternoon. It was quite good. No mention of war in it, and that's something different. What am I complaining about anyway when this morning I had two wonderful letters from you and enough magazines to keep me occupied for the next few evenings. You're certainly a darling. The best one in the whole world. I like you a little too. I can't kid you, I know. So I might as well tell you, I love you all I can.

Sorry about that letter I wrote on Dec. 22 which you answered in this letter I got today. I remember how I felt that night, though, wondering how things were with you, as though I knew something was wrong. Maybe it's a good thing I didn't really know what danger you were in then. I don't know what I would have done. Thanks for understanding my mood at that time anyway.

Can't understand why you didn't get the letter thanking you for the lovely flowers you sent me. I had them on the twenty-third, that was Saturday, together with a very, very nice note from you, and wrote you right away. That was the least I could do, after a lovely present like that. I also wrote on Christmas Eve, but you don't seem to have had either of those letters yet. When I saw those flowers, Darling, I would have done anything to have been able to give you my thanks personally, but that means a super kiss I have saved for you instead. But all my kisses are yours. I hope you'll manage a withdrawal this year.

I'm glad you trust me, just as I trust you, and I do, Irwin. I wish I could prove to you how I've been since you left here. Sometimes when I'm not feeling so good, I tell myself I'm crazy for being this way. But all the time I know how good you are being too, and you don't think I'm crazy, do you? I meet different people I know on my way to work. They were always at Langland or the Pier, and they don't believe me when I tell them they don't see me now as I haven't been to those places for quite a few months and never go anywhere except to an occasional show in the evenings. It's nice being like this though when I have you to love. What I can't understand is that when I came home very late, not getting much sleep, I felt a lot better than I do now. Maybe I'm sleeping my senses away or something.

One of our supervisors, or I should say, the undermanager, stamped "Glamtax" all over my arms and neck this morning with a rubber ink stamp. I had an awful time getting the stuff off. I was nearly in tears when he was doing it, it annoyed me so much, and I couldn't stop him as much as I screamed and kicked, but after he gave it up, I threw a bottle of ink over him. I've never done a thing like that before, but I hate the sight of that man. I don't think he'll fool around with me again.

Have to go now. I'm leaving my heart with you, as you already have all my love. Miss me and love me lots.

All my love,
Mary

February 19, 1945

My Darling,

Missed writing yesterday. I went to visit my brother in the afternoon. It was raining so much when it was time for me to leave that I stayed the night there. It hasn't stopped raining yet. I have a wonderful cold too. Do you want half of it? You can. I'm not a bit mean. I shared yours one time, so you should have it back. I'd like to hear you snoring then. I bet I'd never get to sleep. But maybe I'd get used to it after the first few years. Certainly wish I had the chance to put up with it. I wouldn't want to sleep. What's the matter with me? I'm not supposed to tell you things like that. Oh, but I love you, Irwin, and thinks all sorts of crazy things. Do you mind? I thought you wouldn't.

My young brother's birthday today, so we had a special tea. A few of his friends came and stayed for a few hours. Mother went to a show, so I was left with them. I sent them to buy ice cream. They bought twice as much as I had told them to, and I ate twice as much as I should, but we all had fun, even though we weren't feeling so good. I looked a real mess after they had finished playing their wild jokes on me. They all wanted to know if I'd come to their parties. I didn't like to tell them that once a year is sufficient for that sort of thing. I've got a date tomorrow night. My brother is taking me to his youth club to see a play. The last words he said before I came to bed were to remind me that he's taking me out tomorrow night and not to make any other arrangements. He thinks he's a man now, but I have to go just to please him, as all the other boys are taking their sisters. I do some crazy things too, but this is war, I guess.

What would happen if I decided I wanted to see you this minute, just couldn't wait any longer? Nothing, I suppose is right, but that's the way I feel right now. It seems as though I've waited too long already, but I know how very much longer I could wait, so long as I could see you at the end of that time. This parting has one good point. We've both been able to think carefully about how much we mean to one another, as when I could see you quite often, I didn't know I loved you as much as I know now. I'm missing you so much, though, more than I ever imagined I would. That's not hard to understand when you're on my mind all day and in my dreams almost every night. You've been so wonderful to me too, writing as often as you could and loving me too.

Had quite a hectic day, so I think I'd better start dreaming now. Mair, my sister-in-law, told me I was talking in my sleep about you last night, but I think she was kidding me. I love you lots, Darling. Dream about me and love me all you can.

All my love,
Mary

PS: Would you like to buy a house? Mr. Harris Jr. is selling the one we visited for the small sum of eight thousand pounds. I think it's a little too large for me, so I won't bother.

All my love,
Mary

February 22, 1945

My Darling,

Are you busy? Have I done anything wrong? Do you still love me? Or maybe the mail is just held up. I hope that's the only reason why I haven't had a letter this week. Here I go complaining about no letters when I haven't written for the last two nights. I'm sorry, Honey. Tuesday night I went to see that play with my kid brother. He wouldn't let me out of sight all night, and when it was time to leave, I told him to go with the boys. He didn't though. Told me he took me there, so he'd take me home. Of course, I had to say I'd had a lovely time. That pleased him. When we got home, for some reason or other, all the family decided to play cards, so I didn't get to bed until twelve thirty. And I felt sleepy by that time. I talked to you instead of writing. In my thoughts of course.

Mother says I'm staying in too much, and it's not doing me any good. I never thought I'd ever hear her say that, but that's her opinion these days on how I'm behaving myself. I never want to go out though, as I've told you before. At least, I do know what's wrong with me. I'm very much in love with my Irwin. No one can ever take his place in my heart. Yesterday my brother called me. He had tickets for a dance at the Brangwyn last night. I told him I didn't want to go. Of course, I couldn't give him one good reason why. Mother had arranged all this, I've discovered since, to make me go to a dance. I had to go. It was terrible. All old people, the people of the town, and a few horrid boys. In quite a number of the dances, the lights went out, only an orange colour light left near the band. It was in one of these dances that I really lost my temper. I was dancing with a young boy who thought the dim-out was a wonderful opportunity to get fresh. I was so mad I slapped his face harder than I thought I could and made a dash back to my brother and his wife. After that, I refused every dance and sat like a dummy until it was time to leave. My brother had arranged for a car to take us home. We waited in the cold for forty-five minutes, and then no car. We had to walk to our garage, and it was pouring with rain. My cold is twice as bad as it was, and that's the end of my nice evening gown. I'm still in a terrible temper with them all. I could have written you instead of wasting all that time. If only people would leave me alone, when I'm good, I'd appreciate it a lot more.

Irwin, when do you think I can see you? Say it's soon. I'll burst if I have to keep all this love to myself any longer. This account is getting too much for one person to handle. I'm so scared in case you'd want to forget about me. I don't know what I'd do.

This morning, I got a *Yank* dated October. Thanks a lot, Honey. I love reading them, but you must have sent it quite a while ago. I was disappointed when the postman called my name, and there was no letter. You must be awfully busy though. I think some silly things too, you know, wondering if you've met anyone else, because you're very easy to fall in love with. I know. I love you so very much, Darling.

I'm liable to write anything tonight, so I'd better end this soon and dream instead. See the way this writing is going? I'm writing in bed again, so excuse, please. Love me please and miss me lots. Don't tell anyone I'm crazy about you, as though it would make any difference. I don't care who knows, because I am.

All my love always,
Mary

February 24, 1945

Hello, Honey (only because it's Saturday)

Love us? You and me, of course. Don't you dare say no, not tonight or any other time. I feel good right now, ready for all the love you have to spare. It's all right. I know you can't do anything about it right now, but I can wait. Well, I'll have to I guess. It was a big relief to get two lovely letters this morning, the ones you wrote on the ninth and the eleventh, though I was a little scared to read them as I had some crazy notion that in one of them you'd tell me to forget about you. I'm not kidding, that's just what I thought, but I was wrong. My Irwin still loved me. You do, don't you, Darling?

Who holds your hand in the show, Irwin? Must be French. You're lucky. I have to hold my own. Would I make a good job of pretending I didn't care? I know I would, until you'd see my face change colour. I realize though that everyone gets hurt at least once in their lives, and who am I to be different. So don't be afraid of telling me anything. I can take it. If this war goes on much longer, I'll be a real cynic. But I'll never stop loving you, whatever may happen.

You've got some nerve to ask me why didn't I get some heat from the stove at Bryn. You should know. Funnily enough, there are American officers staying at our house in Bryn Road, I mean. Mr. Humphries came to the garage today with them. I suppose they're staying there anyway, as that's where they were going.

You must be in love or something. You told me the most recent letter you had from me was written on Sept. 17. I know you made a mistake, and I'll excuse you, only this once though.

Sorry about your brother-in-law. I can understand how your sister feels. It does seem hard to believe that anyone you love very much can be taken away from you. I know how I'd feel if something should happen to you. Part of me would go too, and you're not mine. People living around us who have lost sons, husbands, and all the boys dear to them refuse to give up hope too. It's when they see other boys returning from abroad they realize most their loss and how useless it is to go on hoping. It's going to be a wonderful world when people can live without the fear of receiving those few official words which can alter their whole lives.

I'm sorry I have to disagree about enjoying that evening at Mrs. Blewett's. I didn't, Irwin. That's the most I want to say about it. Maybe you don't remember what I asked you that night, but I do. I didn't get a shock about what you told me, but I didn't like asking you. I'm glad I did though as before I didn't feel at ease when I was with you. That also helped me realize how much I loved you. It isn't our fault that we love one another, is it? I don't want to stop loving you ever.

Have to go now. All my kids are waiting to go to bed. Their father's useless. See you in my dreams, around one o'clock. That's when it gets too warm in bed. Can't love you any more, Darling. Miss me and love me lots.

All my love,
Mary

February 26, 1945

My Darling,

Went to a show tonight, *Old Acquaintance*, with Bette Davis and Miriam Hopkins as the stars. It was super. Don't miss it if you ever get a chance of seeing it, though being a man, you might not think it so good. I wish it had a happier ending, though. Bette Davis never seems to get the man she loves, and it's shameful the way she falls in love with married men. Her theory is that you want a thing more when you can't have it. I agree with her too, but as the RAF say, it was a wizard show.

I'm glad you are able to see some shows too. Wish I could be with you, even though I'd have to watch jugglers. I don't like those people even though they may be clever. Jessie Matthews, I don't suppose you've heard of her, but she's quite a famous British star, is in our town this week. I'm going to see her tomorrow night. She'd better be good.

You must be proud of your brother. Wouldn't it be nice if you could meet? Then you could tell him what really happened to your outfit. He sounds like a nice, happy-go-lucky boy to me. I'd like to meet him. Maybe he'll come to England one day and I'll be introduced to him some place. It's all right. That's my crazy imagination again.

Bet you would be a hard employer too. I can see you waiting for me when I got to work late with a scowl on your face, and when I gave you a reasonable explanation, you'd just look at me and shake your head. Then you'd tell me to go, but I wouldn't. I'd stay, just to annoy you. You'd never get rid of me. You never will. I'd stay in bed late every morning, just to have you drag me out.

That bed of yours sounds interesting. Too big, though. Half that size would be sufficient for us. Of course you can sleep on the floor or we'll have twin beds, if you'd rather. I know what you think about twin beds, Darling, so you'd better not say any more about them. Just put up with things or I'll nag you to death.

I don't blame the mayor's wife for crying when you left. I'd do the same thing. Guess she liked you though, and you know I don't. I love you with all my heart instead, and I couldn't say goodbye to you properly even, just have you get mad with me on the phone, because I couldn't visit you. I certainly wish I had the chance again. I'd get there as quick as I could, without asking permission from anyone. I envy Eva for seeing you after I did.

We have a new driver at work now. He's been in the Army for a couple of years, but you should hear the way he speaks, real county, as though he's just graduated from Oxford. I was too busy to go to lunch today. He was quite perturbed about it too. I was tickled pink when he said, "I say, you must be frightfully hungry. May I get you something nice to eat?" The men were grinning too. I said, "Actually, I'm not at all hungry, old boy." We had lots of fun all the afternoon. The whole staff are talking that way. He'll get wise to it in a few days and give his accent up. I've never heard anything like it before.

My brother's friend was recalled to his squadron today. He came to tell us the bad news at eight o'clock this morning. I don't mean to be nasty, but he has made himself a bit of a nuisance. Last night we were ready to go to church, when he came, so we took him along too. It was a strange thing to hear the vicar talking about the prayer meetings to be held on Armistice Day. Most of the people were almost in tears. Ray, that's my brother's friend, came back to supper and talked our heads off until twelve o'clock. Mother told me I wasn't to go to bed until he left, as she couldn't suffer him on her own. While he was telling us his experiences, I was reading your Omnibook. Much more interesting. Have you read *Leave Her to Heaven*? It's good.

Bought a new record today. The Ink Spots singing "Someday I'll Find You Again." It's nice. Have you heard it? On the other side is "Bless You." That's what I'm always saying for you. There are lots of nice new numbers out now, though all make me think of you, not that I need anything to remind me how much I'm missing you. I know too well, but sentimental tunes make me miss you more.

Have to go now, but I'll be around. Until then, dream some nice dreams about me, and love me all you can. You're all my dreams, and I love you more than you'll ever know.

All my love,
Mary

Part Two

MARCH 31, 1945–MAY 3, 1945

Mary turns nineteen on March 8, 1945.

What makes things worse, I can't think of any explanation for not writing all this time.

March 31, 1945

My Darling,

You must think I'm pretty horrible, and I guess I am. What makes things worse, I can't think of any explanation for not writing all this time. If I had been out late almost every night, then I could tell you the truth and hope you'd understand, but honest, Irwin, I've spent almost every night at home, reading and thinking about us, and the more I think, the more I'm convinced that I'll never stop loving you. What am I going to do about it? I pray so hard every night that one day my prayers will come true so I can be with you for always. I know there'll never be anyone but you. Sometimes I think I've been cheated loving someone when I've no right to. But that's a thing no laws can ever control. I'd just like to know how everything will turn out. That because I'm impatient. I am too. Here's me, writing all this, when I don't even know just what you think of me, when I've been so mean. Forgive me, Darling, please. I know how you feel about people who can't take a little of their spare time and write the people who are dear to them, so it's expecting a great deal when I ask you to forgive me. I want you to know that I'll always love you. Irwin, for this part of it, it has to be good. For all I know, you may be a chief warrant officer now. You deserve it, Darling, and I know how much you wanted that promotion. So when I know about it, I'll be thrilled too.

Gwenda has come to see me a few times lately. Of course, her people mustn't know anything about it. She's changed quite a bit. I believe this engagement of hers means everything to her now. I think she'll be happy too, even though she's going to live in the heart of the country. I think I surprised her quite a bit by not mentioning the way she acted when her father discovered the scandal attached to me. Those things never bother me much, though, and I'm sure of one thing. That Gwenda isn't any sort of a girl to have as a friend, though I'm pretty lonely these days and it is nice to have tea and go to a show with her, just to have company and to be able to tell someone how much I love you. One day I'll tell you personally. That's my ambition. In the meantime, it's hard to keep the fact to myself.

It seems as though we're very near to that wonderful day when the war will be over. It's been a long time now. Seems much longer since you left here, and I've read and listened to every bit of news to keep track of the 1st Army and keep wondering exactly where you are and what you're doing. I know you'll take care of yourself, Darling, even though you haven't had letters from me for a while. You must feel me thinking of you and loving you all the time.

We've had quite a busy time at work today. I've almost lost my voice answering people so I won't be sorry to get to bed tonight. Our date will have to be earlier too. Can you make it? Don't bother to get a shave. That will save a bit of time. You know I don't mind much, and I'll love you just the same.

Thanks again, Darling, for being so wonderful and sending those flowers. I wish you could see them, Irwin. They're beautiful. I'm crossing my fingers until I know you've forgiven me for not writing. I want you to love me all you can always. Take good care of my Irwin. I love you with all my heart and miss you so much. Don't be late in my dreams. I'll be waiting.

All my love,
Mary

April 4, 1945

My Darling,

Seems as though I'm making a habit of not writing, doesn't it? I'm sorry, Irwin, but I actually had Easter holidays and couldn't think of anything to do with myself here, as dancing holds no interest for me without you to hold me close, so I went to that farm in Carmarthen where my kid brother was evacuated to, came back this morning. I had quite a nice time but could have been so much better if you had been there with me. It's that way wherever I am though. The weather was nice too. I went for long walks in the mornings, all alone, wishing and wondering about us. You don't know what you've done to me. It's wonderful loving you. Can I have you all my life, please. Spent the rest of the time making myself useful. Farmers' wives work terribly hard. I don't envy Gwenda one bit.

The best part of the week was coming back and finding sixteen letters from you, all of them wonderful, and stacks of magazines. I won't have to look for anything to do for a long time to come. I had, amongst other letters, the one written on March 25. You were worried about having no letters from me. I know how you felt, Darling, and I feel such a big meanie. I don't know what happened to me. I loved you and missed you more and more each day. It's something I can't even explain to myself. I don't deserve to have you loving me, but please don't ever stop. I love you so much. All those excuses you made for me not writing aren't true. If someone should find out about you now, it wouldn't make the slightest difference to me. I know just what you are, and nobody could ever convince me that you were handing me a line. I'm so happy that lawyer is on our side this time. You going to all that trouble for me, and I didn't write you for a few weeks. I hate myself when I realize that you have written when things have been very tough.

That card you sent me tickled me pink. I'll pass it on to Nancy, after the happy event, or shall I keep it so you can give it to me one day. I know it could happen to me, but not yet. Well, I don't mind. But think what the neighbors would say. I haven't seen Nancy for a few weeks. Think I'll pay her a visit tomorrow and drink her orange juice for her again. She won't drink it, and it contains all the necessary vitamins. It's doing me a lot of good. Her husband wants to know who's having the baby. We tease him, poor boy, but he doesn't mind a bit. I like him a lot. He's always in the same mood, and it's easy to see how much he loves Nancy.

I like the brother I'm going to have. Jack looks nice by that cutting you sent me, which, by the way, I'm enclosing in this letter. Thanks, Honey, for sending it. I bet you're proud of him. He must have done some good work to earn that award. I remember you telling me all about him one night. Do you remember? He's your adopted brother, isn't he? I love to dream about the day I can be one of your family and meet all your people and you can join our family. I want so much for them to meet you. I know they'd like you. Mothers are wonderful people. I know you think so too. My mother seems to understand that I love you very much and never asks any questions about my staying at home every night, like she did when you first went away. Waiting for you is a very easy thing for me. It doesn't seem like waiting at all, as thinking about you is the next best thing to being with you, and I'm always thinking about you. The thought of you in danger is the biggest worry I've ever had in my life, but I pray so hard every night for my Irwin.

That boy from your outfit who came to Wales for his leave didn't come to see me. I suppose seven days go so quickly that there's no time for visiting, but I would have been awfully pleased if he had. Darling, when I think of being in your arms again, the world is a wonderful place. I pray every night too that you'll get your leave soon. Oh, I want to be with you again so very, very much. I've missed you more than I ever thought it was possible to miss a person. Life just doesn't seem anything without you. We'll make up for all this time we've been apart though, won't we? Even though it may be only seven days. I'm sure in my mind, now, that one day we'll be together for always. I love you so much and know how you love me too. Have you heard some of the new song hits? They fit in with my feelings perfectly. "I'm Making Believe that You're in My Arms" is a typical one. When I hear "Jealousy," I'm right there with you, not because the words express my sentiments so much, but the number of times we heard it played when we were together, I guess that everything reminds me of you, because you're always on my mind.

I'm glad you didn't go to Paris with Smiley. Maybe I'm selfish, wanting you to center your thoughts on me. Well, I am. You have so many more assets to become a wolf than Smiley has. It would be easy for you. I don't want you to be a wolf, only where I'm concerned. I think it was in one of your magazines that I read the definition of a wolf. I think it was in one of your magazines that I read the definition of a gentleman. He's a wolf, with patience. When I got home from work this afternoon, the family was sitting around the fire, each with a magazine in their hands. It looked like a library. I came to bed at eight o'clock, not to disturb them. After I finish this letter, I can start dreaming about your leave. I hope you don't change your mind about coming here, since I haven't written. You won't, will you? You must feel my longing to see you again. You won't have to follow me up steps like you did in your dream, either, and I certainly would run to meet you when you called me. I told you, though, that I'd be up those stairs before you.

Well, Darling, this position I'm writing in is getting more than uncomfortable. I'll write again tomorrow, but don't even imagine that I'll stop loving you. I'll just go on loving you more and more every day. Keep loving me, Irwin. You're wonderful.

All my love,
Mary

April 5, 1945

My Darling,

Seems as though I've caused you a lot of anxiety. Can you ever forgive me? You have enough to worry about without me making things worse. It seems silly just for me to say I'm sorry, but, Irwin dear, I am. It was just one of those things that I'm entirely to blame for, as I told you before. I don't know why I didn't write, but I'm hoping you'll understand because I really need your love as much, if not more, than you need mine.

Today I got another letter. Mother brought it to me, waking me from my dreams the same time. It was easy to see how worried you were about the mail situation. I thought I'd never get out of bed. I had so much to think about, trying to figure out a way I could let you know as soon as possible that everything was all right, and I love you more than ever. You mentioned in one of your letters that I could send a cable to you. I went to the Main Post Office before going to work and asked them if I could. I was informed that there's no other way of communicating with forces on the Continent except by ordinary letter. I couldn't argue, as I suppose they should know, but I wish there was a way to let you know. I want you to keep loving me. I don't want you to think I've forgotten about you. Anything but that could happen to me.

You've never said anything in your letters to offend me, Darling. Every one of them has been wonderful, even though at times you've written when you've had no letters from me for a while. And in any case, loving you so much, I'd overlook things like "For Pete's sake." That's the only way to annoy me. Just say that. I'd love to hear you say it right now, though. Then you'd have to say "I'm sorry" and give me a super kiss and a hug. Then I'd forget about it. That's how I want to forget all my worries, in your arms for always.

I too have a nightmare when I think you might refuse your leave. If I could only let you know this very minute how much I've been counting on having you here for seven days. Every day I wonder whether it will be the day I see you again. You must feel me waiting and thinking about all these things. I think so hard sometimes that I imagine I'm right by your side, not all those miles away. Things haven't changed one bit, Darling. Except that I love you and miss you more. So please don't talk about signing death warrants. We both have so very much to look forward to in the future, our future.

I know you love me, Irwin, and I realize how fortunate I am to have your love. You should know too how much I love you because I told you just how very much that was, just a few weeks ago. Do you think I could change my mind about that? I know I'll just go on loving you, and one day we'll share our love together for the rest of our lives. If it was possible for me ever to change, I'd let you know right away, Darling, but I'm telling you now, you'll never get a letter like that. I'm so sure that our love is the love that lasts forever. If I wasn't sure and I hadn't been all along, I wouldn't have written in the first place, because I know how you're changing your whole life for me, and that isn't a small matter. I do want to be yours all my life, though, to be your wife and achieve my great ambition of having you for a husband, I'll always remember that night we were walking home from Bryn. It was late, and we were talking about us. Then in a very calm way, you asked me if I'd like to be your wife. It seemed impossible then, but I cherished the fact that you had asked me. Now, when it's possible, you can imagine how I feel about it. How I wish I could live over those weeks when I didn't write. Then you'd have no fears about my love for you. All your doubts are a bad dream, Darling. But I know I'd feel the same way without having mail from you.

We've had the auditors at work today. Everything was in perfect order. I'll get a few medals when they realize how good I am. I'm kidding. They wouldn't be able to discover mistakes if there were any. They look too stupid.

I certainly hope those warrant officers are made very, very soon. You've done enough work to last for the duration. But we'll take seven days for the time being, won't we? I saw a boy with the red keystone on his arm today. I had a funny sensation when I saw it. It looked so good, and I hadn't seen it for so long. I want you to make such a big withdrawal on this account of ours. It's too much for me to handle now. It's been an awful long time since I've been kissed. If I didn't know the reason for that, I'd think I didn't have any sex appeal. But you had my last kiss, and you'll have my next. I hope my account in your hands is in the same condition too, as I want to make a huge withdrawal very soon. Can I please? You just try to stop me.

We have a nice little radio in the office. Mr. Clement likes to listen to the news, and that's all. He doesn't allow anyone else to touch it. But this afternoon, he told me he'd be away for a couple of hours. I couldn't resist turning the thing on. He came back much sooner than was expected, just as they were playing "I'm Going to Love that Guy Like He's Never Been Loved Before." All he said was the song got on his nerves, but I didn't feel at all comfortable about it.

Tomorrow night, the bus service staff and Glamtax are holding a dance at Langland. I have a ticket, but that's as far as it goes where I'm concerned as I know just how it will be. A glorified bottle party, and I'm not interested. If you were here, we could go and forget about the rest of the people. I don't want to go to a dance without my Irwin. It's no fun dancing with anyone when I hate to have anyone but you touch me.

I meant to visit Nancy tonight, but I wanted to talk to you, write to you I mean. My mind's more at ease when I know that you'll get these letters, and you'll know that I'm yours for keeps.

98

Had a nice loving letter from my brother today. He asked about you and gave me the usual fatherly advice but added that he knew I had sense and wouldn't do anything silly. He's really homesick and tired of Italy's mysteries. He meets my other brother quite often, and they write letters home telling how the other looks and what they talk about, and they read one another's letters so they won't miss any news from home. It will be nice to have them home again.

Doesn't the time go quickly when you're writing a letter. It's almost time for bed again. Last night, just after I finished writing to you, Mother brought me a cup of coffee. I didn't know whether to drink it or not in case it kept me awake. Then I wouldn't dream about you. But I did and had a wonderful dream. You weren't good either, neither was I, so I won't say anything about it. Every dream I have we're the same way, and I don't mind a bit, honest. I love you, in case you didn't know.

Do you mind if I leave you for only thirty minutes. I'll be with you in my dreams again. Then we have lots of fun, Irwin. I can hardly wait until the time comes to be with you in my dreams. Bye now, love me lots, and dream about us. Take good care of yourself, Darling. I love you with all my heart.

All my love,
Mary

April 9, 1945

My Darling,

Are you thinking about me now, Irwin? I came to bed at nine thirty and I've been thinking of you for the last hour. Almost went to sleep in the middle of my lovely dreams. You're so close to me tonight, Darling. I could almost feel your arms around me. I wish I was with you, or better still, you were here with me. My bed is only a small one but big enough for both of us. And I promise not to kick you out even if you snore. What am I talking about? If you were here,

I'd see you wouldn't sleep at all. You wouldn't want to either, would you? I wish I could wake tomorrow morning and know that I'd see you in a few hours. Time goes so quickly, and yet it seems years since I saw you. I do hope those warrant officers were successful in their examinations. I want to see you so very, very much. The weather is just about perfect here now, but it only makes me miss you more than ever. What good are these nice evenings and starry skies without the person you love to share them with you? Yesterday afternoon I went to see Nancy. It was a lovely day. Just right for walking, so we took a ride on that crazy train to Mumbles. I rode backwards as usual, and I kept thinking of all those times we made the trip together. Those were wonderful days. While I was thinking about you, Nancy was talking about Walter and how many times they had argued if it was an electric train or a streetcar, just as we used to, Darling. When we arrived at Mumbles, we walked along the cliffs a little way and sat gazing at the sea. I think that when you're in love, you appreciate beautiful scenes much more, and it was very beautiful there yesterday. Everything looked so peaceful and not many people around. We walked over to Langland and had tea there, both of us wrapped up in our own thoughts and not saying much. I was thinking how lovely it would be if you were there, and I could tell you how I loved you. I don't know who Nancy was thinking about, but I hope it was Tom. After having tea, we walked very slowly back to Mumbles to catch the train home again. I felt good after that walk and the sea air. I could have pitched lots of woo if you had been near me, but I'll save it all instead until you get here. I stayed at Nancy's place last night and was awake half the night watching all those stars in the sky. But I still can't find that little dipper of yours. You'll have to show it to me again, and I'll make sure just where it is. But who wants to look at stars when I can look at you?

Forgot to tell you I had loads of magazines today. Thanks, Honey. You don't know how they help me to spend my spare time. You'd have laughed if you could have seen me this evening. We have a very big garden, and most of it is taken up by the air raid shelter. The top of which is the only place where there's grass. The rest of the garden has been dug up for victory. So I was perched on top of the air raid shelter, reading your magazines until the sun went down. The neighbors must think I'm getting crazier. Maybe I am, but who cares?

Well, Darling, it's time to dream some more now. I hope you've had some of my letters and have forgiven me, because I want you to keep loving me. I love you so much, Irwin. Take good care of yourself. I'm always thinking of you.

All my love always,
Mary

April 10, 1945

My Darling,

I'm worried in case you think I've stopped loving you and decided to forget about me. I wish letters weren't the only way of keeping us together, Irwin, but more than that, I wish that I had written to you those weeks when I had that funny mood. I know how it must have been for you, wondering when you'd get a letter from me. I haven't had a letter since Thursday, and that's only a few days ago, but I feel miserable, thinking that maybe you couldn't see any reason to write when you weren't getting any letters from me. You loved me, though, Darling, in your last letter. Don't stop loving me, now or ever. I want you and your love all my life. You must know that. I just don't see any reason to live if you go out of my life. I knew that one day I'd fall very much in love with someone, but I didn't know I was capable of loving anyone as much as I love you. I'll never love anyone else, whatever happens, and I'll never regret loving you, you're so wonderful. Please keep loving me, Darling. I need your love so much.

An American with a keystone on his arm came to the office this morning. He's getting married tomorrow and was so excited that he got all mixed up with what he wanted to say. I'd loved to have asked him some questions, but I thought you wouldn't have liked me to do that. I envied his girl, wishing it was you and me who were getting married, but I wouldn't be as calm as she was about it. I know how I'd feel just to have you with me again. It would be more than wonderful. I hope you won't change your mind about taking your leave to England. That's a morbid thought, and I hate to think about it. Please come to me, Darling. I've waited so long, living on lovely memories. Say you want to see me too.

Didn't finish work until seven o'clock tonight, and I feel tired. So do you mind if I make this a very short letter? They're playing "Tangerine" on the radio now. For no reason at all, I feel like crying every time I hear it. I'm silly, I know. Though it's not silly the way I love you. Tell me that you love me lots, Irwin, and keep dreaming about me. Take good care of yourself. I love you, Darling.

All my love always,
Mary

April 11, 1945

My Darling,

Would you consider the task of loving me to death? Well, almost to death? I want lots of kisses and hugs right now, and the only reason I can't have them is that the Army has work for you to do, hundreds of miles away from here. They're a bunch of meanies, keeping you away from me all this time. But it's war, I guess, and I mustn't complain. If it hadn't been for the war, how would I have met you?

Didn't get a letter today. I suppose I deserve to go without mail for twice as long as you did, but, Irwin, I get so worried wondering if you're all right. Besides loving you as much as I do, I consider you just like one of my brothers. I'd feel terrible if anything should happen to one of them, so much worse if it happened to you. I don't know if you understand what I mean. I'm no good at explaining my feelings. But you're very, very dear to me. I don't know if you have any faith in me now, but, Darling, please let me know how you feel about me. All I can say is that I do love you with all my heart, and nothing can change that. If you don't want me to wait for you any longer, let me know. Naturally, I'll be more than hurt, but I won't blame you in any way. I do want to be your wife though. I've been dreaming about it so much it seemed it had to work out that way. I've been reading the last letters I had over again, tonight. You said in one letter about a ring. I want us to be together when you buy that, Darling. If you haven't changed your mind, that is. I'd settle for a piece of glass if it meant me really belonging to you. But I don't need a ring to realize I'm yours as I know why I've been so good and stayed in so much since you left.

My friend, the one that is in college, came to see me this afternoon. We went out for tea. Then to see *Janie*. It was good too. Saw it over twice. Tomorrow I have a day off. I'm going shopping in the morning and having something done to my hair in the afternoon. It's long now. I haven't had it cut yet. I'm going to leave it this way for victory. Everyone is convinced the war is almost over and making plans for celebrating. I'll be working as usual, but I can't say I'll be sorry. It's been so long that everyone will go crazy, I expect. I'll celebrate and go crazy when you are here with me. I'll have a good reason to then. I wish you were here now and I could hear you say that you love me and call me a dummy for having had any doubts about it.

How's Doc and Smiley getting on? I wish we could all meet again, then, after seeing Doc's miserable face and smiling Smiley, I'd know I wasn't dreaming as sometimes I think I must have imagined them. Irwin, you're so wonderful, Darling.

Can I kiss you good night? I promise not to bother you after. You can snore all you want. Wish you were here to turn the light out for me, that's all. I'm kidding, there wouldn't be any light on. Dream about me, Darling, and please keep loving me.

All my love always,
Mary

April 13, 1945

My Darling,

Still love me? Please say you do, if you only love me a little bit. I haven't heard you say it for a long time, but I'd give my life just to hear you say it now. This suspense, wondering if you've forgiven me or not, is awful. Before I go to sleep every night, I keep awake, it must be for hours, wondering if you still think about me and if you want to see me. I want to see you very badly, Irwin, and persuade myself you feel the same way. I'm still saving all my love and kisses anyway, whether you want them or not. I hope you do, Darling, otherwise, they'll all be wasted. You can even bite my ears and give me all the sucker bites you want. I just want to be with you again, Irwin, and live over the most wonderful days of my life. Please come and see me if you can.

Everyone is very upset today. The good war news was forgotten when President Roosevelt's death was announced. He certainly was a great man, and it does seem a shame that he isn't able to take part in replanning the postwar world when he played such a key part in bringing us as near as we are to victory. He's a man the world will never forget.

Today I got a pile of magazines from you. They're wonderful. I've been reading them since I came home from work, until I came to bed. My brother took the air-raid shelter up today. I went out to see him digging away and, being a female, gave him some advice on how to do it. The result was I got covered with earth; my nice hairstyle that I only had done yesterday is finished. I had to wash it after that. I almost killed him. Well, I thought I would have, but my weight against his only made a very slight impression. If I was only big, I'd get my revenge.

It's Friday the thirteenth today. I knew I wouldn't get a letter from you, but tomorrow, maybe I'll be lucky. I'm hoping you've had one of my letters, and you know now how things are, 'cause honest, Irwin, I love you. Can't think of any more to tell you tonight. I don't even know if you're interested in this short letter at all, but I'm keeping my fingers crossed. Please love me, Darling. Dream about me and take care of yourself. I pray hard for you every night.

All my love,
Mary

April 14, 1945

Irwin Darling,

I know too well how I hurt you. This morning I waited until the postman passed the door. No letter. I went to work feeling miserable and didn't care what happened to me, realizing that I was to blame for not hearing from you. I asked the telephonist at the office if she had heard from her brother-in-law. He's an American. I thought maybe all the mail was help up. She said they had a letter yesterday and quite calmly asked me if I had had the letter that came to the office Thursday when I had a day off. I didn't know anything about it. I searched the office but couldn't find it. Then asked Mr. Clement about it. He'd forgotten all about it after putting it somewhere safe. I nearly tore it out of his hands. Then sat down and read it over and over again. Thank you, Darling. I'll never hurt you again.

You didn't do anything to deserve that treatment. You've always been more than wonderful to me. I had no intentions of hurting you. I never want to. But how can I explain how I felt those weeks so that you might understand. I've never stopped loving you, not for one minute since I met you, but that doesn't justify me not writing you. There's no excuse for me. I had lots of spare time but spent it all thinking instead of writing as I should. You're right, Darling, nothing like that can happen to us, so please try to forget that I was so mean to you. I want you so much. You know my dreams, our dreams, are to love you all my life and to be near you always. I'm afraid to let myself even know how much I want to be your wife, but it's everything to me, and I'm sure I'll be your wife one day. I will, won't I, Irwin? It was no infatuation, and you shouldn't suggest that, Darling.

But you have no idea how great my love is and how true I've been these months. I don't like infatuations. But if it had been, I'd have gone out in the nights, looking for someone else to be infatuated with after you left here. But I knew our love wasn't like that, and I don't like going out when you're away. Nobody can ever mean anything to me. You have my whole heart and every little bit of my love. I'm glad that you knew in your mind even when you didn't get my letters that I loved you just the same. Keep remembering how I love you; nothing can change that. You wrote a PS to your letter, telling me that you'd always love me. I felt wonderful 'cause I wondered if it would change your love when I made you so miserable. One day, Irwin, I won't have to write you letters, to tell you how I love you. I'll just find my way into your arms, and then you'll know.

Nobody can poison my mind against you, you crazy person. I know all about you, remember? And have faith in you. Nobody can ever shake that faith. That makes me love you besides all those other reasons. I'll go on believing in you until our dreams come true. Maybe I forgot to tell you that the new fellow we have at work is a happily married man. He came to tell me the other day that he was going to have a baby. I told him he'd cause quite a sensation. I want you to know, though, that I don't want anyone but you, Irwin. There's nobody who'd come anywhere near you, and I feel so proud when you say you're mine. Wish the next few weeks would fly so I could see you, but knowing that you will be with me then makes everything lovely for me. How am I going to let you leave me again though? We'll be too happy to think about that until the time comes, won't we? What happens, Darling, if the war ends before you get your leave? When will I see you then? I worry myself sick when I think of you going back to the States without me seeing you. It's an awful thought.

It's strange to think of Colonel Fairchild. Major seems much more familiar. He's nice to remember me. Maybe I'll see him again too. Those were lovely days when I met him. I was with my Irwin. I had everything then. You're everything, Darling.

Why did you write to Glamtax, Honey? You didn't tell me the reason in the letter. It's set me wondering. I rushed in the house lunchtime. Mother wanted to know what I was so happy about. Then I told her about your letter. She wanted to know why it went to the office. That's something I don't know either.

Went to the football game this afternoon. I'm getting quite a fan. Swansea won. That's a rare event. You should have heard the cheers. I went with a girl in the office, and the supervisor, Mr. Clement, was there too, so the Swans just had to win. Came home about six o'clock to an empty house. It's nice to write in peace without my brother telling me what to say to you. He used to keep a list of the boys I went out with after he made me tell him their names. He's only got one name on his list now. That's yours. It's been there so long he's convinced that this is the real thing. He's crazy too, but he's got the right idea this time. Ever since I remember, he's called me skinny. It makes me mad when he says it in front of strangers, but brothers are always teasing, and I should be used to it by now.

Have to go now, Irwin. You do now I love you, don't you? I'll prove to you just how much I do. Soon, I hope. I'm missing you more and more all the time. Keep loving me and dream about me.

All my love always,
Mary

April 16, 1945

My Darling,

What are you doing now? It's only nine fifteen, and I'm in bed. It would be heavenly if you were here too, and tomorrow was Sunday. Just think how long we could sleep? I miss you, didn't you know? I want to see you take your tie off that crazy way and have you pester me while I'm trying to read. I miss everything about you. I want your love, Irwin, and you in person to tell me about it.

This morning, while I was having breakfast, the postman brought me some magazines. I don't know how to thank you for them, Darling, but they're super, and they help so much to pass this period when I'm waiting to see you. That's all I think about all day and dream about all night. The postman told me he had a letter too, but he wouldn't give it to me then as it was at the bottom of his bag. He'd call on the way back. I waited until he went to the top of the street and came back again. It was as I prayed those minutes when I waited for it, a letter from you written on April 6, making me feel that I couldn't have been so horrible. I didn't mean to be, Irwin. I hope you've had letters now, then you'll know that things are the same, except I love you more and more all the time.

You were confident you'd get a pass to England pretty soon. When you wrote that, Darling, and said you couldn't ask me to meet you because I wouldn't show up, oh, Irwin, if I couldn't be there to meet you, It'd break my heart. I know you had reasons to think what you did, but loving you as I do, it seems impossible to me that you could think things had changed so much. And then you said you knew I still loved you. I'm glad you know that, as I know you'll always love me, and our love won't be wasted, Darling. It's survived when things have been a little tough, and I'm sure we'll be together for always one day. Maybe we'll have to wait a little while, but it's something well worth waiting for because we are going to be the two happiest people in the world. If I should hear your voice at the other end of the phone before seeing you, I'd do my best to get through those wires. You'd better let me know when you're coming, or there's going to be a war in our little family if I don't get there to meet you. Don't you remember about that kiss I have waiting for you. I'm patiently waiting for the one I hope you have saved for the occasion.

When I got to work this morning, Gwenda was waiting for me. She had some shopping to do, so I went with her. The first thing she asked about was you. I couldn't tell her how mean I'd been to you. She knows how very much I love you and would want an explanation. It's so difficult to explain, and I know she'd think I'd gone crazy for a few weeks. We went for coffee and talked until it was time for me to be getting back to work. Gwenda had an aunt to visit this afternoon but said she'd come home for tea, and as it was such a nice day, we'd go to Mumbles this evening, but no Gwenda turned up. I guess she must have stuck with her relations. I know better than to rely on her anyway. The way she laughs at her troubles makes me laugh too. Her stepmother is quite a character and dislikes Gwenda very much. Last week was one of her bad weeks. Poor Gwenda had to leave home and stay with some relations until she felt better. Then her father sent for her and things are normal again. I'd hate to live like that. My mother's wonderful, and I appreciate her more these last few months. She doesn't say I'm silly staying in and is just as glad as I am when your letters come.

Was reading one of your magazines about that breakthrough Christmastime. That's the fullest report I'd ever read on it. It gave me an awful feeling to think that you went through that, but it's so wonderful to know that you want to help. I want to help you forget about all this, Darling. I know I'll never let you down because I'm so sure that I'll love you forever, and that's a long time. But I have enough love saved up to last us twice as long.

I'm more than anxious to know what the colonel said about your leave. I don't like him, but if he lets you come to see me, I won't think he's so bad after all. He'll be wonderful. He doesn't know how badly I want to see you; otherwise, he wouldn't hesitate about it. Have to go now. I have a day off tomorrow, so I can dream lots of dreams tonight, then tomorrow morning I can stay in bed and think about them. Keep loving me, Irwin. I love you more than ever. I'd like to see me in your eyes soon, so hurry to me. Miss me lots as I miss you and dream about me. I don't want to be good tonight.

All my love always,
Mary

April 17, 1945

My Darling,

It's been nice here today, better than any day in our summer. I got up early this morning, even though it was my day off, and did

Mother's shopping. Thought of going to see Nancy this afternoon, but Gwenda came full of apologies for not turning up last night. We had tea out and went to see *Laura*. It's very good, but you have to use your imagination quite a bit. Gwenda said she'd love me to stay with her for a few days, but she's afraid of what her father will say about it. I told her that even if he would forget all that, I'd never stay there after the things he said about me. But she made me promise I'd go to her wedding. It's in June, by the way. I asked her seriously if she thought she was doing the right thing. She doesn't think that there is such a thing as love, and he has money, so she's happy. I know different though. Gwenda's been hurt very badly and still loves one person, but you can't tell her anything. Lots of people say there's no such thing as love, but I don't believe they mean it. I know you love me, as I love you, and that's far better than having all the money in the world. I could never live with a man, no matter how much he could give me, if I didn't love him. I'm so lucky to be able to love you and know that you love me. I'll have my whole world when I have you with me. I could use some of your love right now. Don't be a meanie. I'll give it back.

Could I interest you in a vacation, here in lovely Wales? The weather is super, just right for walking, bathing, tennis, and pitching lots of woo. The coastline can't be compared with, so they say. And at the moment, there's a beautiful moon shining on the water. Well, I think it is, and I want to see you so very, very much. Please come.

I had a lovely dream last night. I saw you, but then I woke up. I tried so hard to continue the dream, but it was no good. I'd been waiting for your train to come in, and you looked so glad to see me. Then it ended. Maybe I'll be luckier tonight. Keep loving me, Honey, I'm all yours, and I'll tell you how much I love you soon, I hope. Miss me and be good.

All my love always,
Mary

April 20, 1945

My Darling,

Love me tonight? Sorry I didn't write last night. I went to see Nancy. We just talked about everything. She was alone in the house when I got there, and I didn't like to leave her until her people came home. I did some of her knitting. It was funny remembering Thursday nights just a year ago when we went to Langland. I asked her about eight o'clock if she'd be going there last night. "Yes," she said, "if Walter came with a jeep." Well, her mother finally returned at ten forty-five. They wanted me to stay, but I thought I'd better go home. I forgot about the long walk alone. I was scared, Irwin. I almost ran the whole way. I got home about eleven thirty, so tired. It was as much as I could do to get into bed. I thought you wouldn't mind too much if I didn't write, but I did dream about you. A lovely dream too.

It's so warm here now. People are looking nice and healthy, and swimming has begun though the sea looks too rough for it. A sixteen-year-old boy was drowned at Langland on Monday. A number of people watched him drowning. There's a terrible scandal about the affair. Nobody attempted to save him, and they could see him fighting for his life for twenty minutes, until he went under. I'd hate to be one of those people, but I suppose they didn't want to risk their own lives as well.

Even Mr. Clement had to say this morning that it was too nice to work, but he didn't tell me to take a day off. He didn't come back to work after lunch. There were two people going to Langland, so the driver asked me if I'd like to go with them. They didn't mind. Naturally, I went. They were nice people too. When we got to their bungalow, they asked me in, gave me tea, and showed me about the place. It was lovely there. Perfect for a honeymoon. No neighbors to interfere. I was thinking how wonderful it would be for you and me to be there together. It's a small place, but the view is super. The sea one side and country the other. With you as well, what more could I possibly want? I was imagining all kinds of things the short time I was there. I didn't want to come back. I had to, though.

Didn't get a letter today, and I'm awfully anxious to know what the colonel said about your leave. I wish it was Colonel Fairchild you had to ask. Maybe he'd understand better and send you to me soon. I can't wait, Darling. But you know I will. It's just that I miss you so terribly and want you to know how much more I love you than I did when I last saw you. Then I didn't think it was possible to love you any more, but I do, Irwin. You'd better be prepared for all this love and imagine the millions of kisses I've saved all this time. So don't attempt to snore when you're with me or I'll bite your ears right off. I've had so much sleep that a week without it wouldn't affect me at all. I'm going to love you to death. If I go on talking like this, you're going to change your mind about coming here. I'd better not say any more.

Take very good care of yourself, Honey. I'm thinking about you all the time. Miss me and love me lots, just as I miss and love you.

All my love always,
Mary

April 21, 1945

Irwin Darling,

No letter today. It's Saturday too, and I miss you more than you'll ever know. I don't know how I'd occupy my spare time without your magazines. Today I had some more. They're lovely, Darling. What do you do when you miss me lots? I think back on those nights when we were together. But that doesn't help any, just makes me want to see you more. Can't help it. I just love you and love you and still love you. I'd give anything to dance with you tonight. Guess I'll have to go to bed and dream about it instead. Isn't this a mean war?

Couldn't even go to the football game this afternoon. Mr. Clement didn't take the hint when I told him it was a nice day to take his wife and children to the beach. I just got more work to do. He can't do things like that on Saturday afternoons. I often wonder what that man lives for. He has no sense of humour, and his wife nags him in front of me, so I can't imagine what happens when they're alone. Maybe that's why he spends so much time at work when he's not wanted there. Don't you tell me that you'll be working late, Darling. I know all the angles on that line. I promise never to nag you though I wish I was waiting for you to come home from work now. Shall we stay in tonight? We're going to have a real coal fire, aren't we, Irwin? So we can sit looking at it together. Of course, you don't know much about fires, so I'll have to see to that. Don't get mad, you'll soon learn.

You know that group of your officers I have? Well, it's taken Tyrone's place in my bedroom, so I can see you as soon as I wake in the morning. I kiss you every time I look at it. Then I look at the colonel to see if he's human and wonder when he'll let you come to see me. I know you're busy, but you deserve a rest. Some rest you're going to have with me around. I know how you want to see me too. I wish that day would come very, very soon. I want to pitch tons of woo but only with you, Darling.

See you in my dreams. You're always as wonderful as when I saw you last. I love you more than ever, Darling. Take good care of yourself and love me lots.

All my love,
Mary

April 22, 1945

My Darling,

I'm afraid today. I felt sure I'd get a letter in answer to the one I wrote after that interval. Maybe you won't forgive me, and if you've decided that way, I know nothing I ever say or do can change your mind. But you know as well as I do that I'll never forget you or stop loving you. I don't want you to forget me ever. I'll still pray for you, Darling, and keep hoping that my love will bring you back to me. I would like to think I was quite an independent person, but I'm not where you're concerned. I need you and your love very much.

Did I tell you we have a factory on one side of our garage now? There's a terrible noise going on, but it's worth it. They make silk stockings there, and the manager is very kind to us, remembering how helpful we were to him, letting him use our phone before they were fixed up with one. It was worth it though. I watched them working this morning. It's certainly a complicated process, getting stockings made. I don't envy those girls doing that work, and they work long hours too.

The RAF Officers' Mess were giving a big party tonight. We do quite a bit of work for them, so I had an invitation. Before meeting you, I would have been thrilled at the idea, but it doesn't interest me at all now. Everyone at work told me I was crazy refusing the invitation. But I know I'm not. I'd be bored. I came home instead. Did lots of things. Then read your magazines for an hour, came to bed, and now I'm writing to you. The evening went quickly, and I know I'm more satisfied than if I'd gone to that party.

Tomorrow I have a day off. Don't know what I'll do with myself. I wish you were here, then I wouldn't have to think about where I can go on my own. I don't mind seeing a show, but I feel silly going in and coming out alone. I don't know why, but I do. If only you'd be here tomorrow. It's too wonderful to think about. I want to see you so badly, Irwin. The 1st Army is making big news. I heard on the radio before coming to bed that they had taken Dessau. You will take good care of yourself for me, won't you, Darling, and please keep loving me. I love you and miss you more every day.

All my love,
Mary

April 24, 1945

Irwin Darling,

If only I could hear you say you love me now, all my worries would be gone. I'd know you were safe and still thinking of me. I haven't heard from you since the letter you wrote on the sixth. I'm not complaining, but your letters are the only means of me knowing how things are with you. I realize how busy you must be when I hear about the 1st Army. I console myself that that's the only reason I haven't had a letter today.

This morning I got up early, and I felt good. It was a beautiful morning, and I didn't have to go to work. Then the postman passed our house. Things didn't seem good any longer. I went into town to do some shopping. Met Gwenda. She'd been to Carmarthen for the weekend. So we had lunch together. That pilot who went around with Gwenda and then almost broke our friendship up when he took me out came along. He didn't have anything to do this afternoon so asked me to go to a show with him, but I wanted to come home and see if this afternoon's mail brought a letter from you, and if I went with him, he might get the idea that I wanted to start something. Whatever it is that makes me love you so much, I don't know, but I want to go on loving you, Darling. You're so wonderful compared to people like that boy. Gwenda said she didn't have anything to do this afternoon, but all he said was "It's a pity." She must have felt small. He left us then. Said he was going to get drunk on his own. I came home. The first thing Mother told me was that there were no letters for me. I felt lonely and miserable. I was going to see Nancy this evening, but instead, I read and thought until it was time for bed.

I hope you still want me and my love, Darling. I'm all yours now, you must know that. Maybe tomorrow I'll get a lovely letter from you. Then I won't worry anymore. Have to start dreaming now, Irwin. You were as wonderful as ever last night. Love me lots. Think of me and remember I love you all I can. Take good care of yourself.

All my love,
Mary

April 27, 1945

Irwin Darling,

You love me, you've forgiven me, and you're so wonderful. Today I got two lovely letters written on the nineteenth and the twentieth. Yesterday I was worried about things, so last night I wrote a really miserable letter, but I had yours this morning before I sent it, so I tore it up.

I told that girl what a dummy she was. She agrees with you too, but she's so happy about you loving her, that I couldn't get much sense from her. She loves you an awful lot too.

I'm glad you did find those letters hidden in your basket. Otherwise those men and I would start a private war. I can imagine how you felt when you saw that first letter, as I took thirty minutes to read your letters in bed this morning. Mother brought them to me. She said I may smile a bit more after having them. Your bribe sounds good to me. I'd love to have your snaps, so I'll have to do something about it, meanie. The one I like best of you is the one in the group. You really look like my Irwin in that, complete with lipstick. Every time I look at it, I kiss you, but you don't kiss me. Maybe we'll remedy that soon.

Your present abode sounds cozy, except for the cemetery in front of the house. That would be no place for me. I'd be thinking about ghosts and keeping you awake all night, and wouldn't you get mad? Thanks for the twenty thousand marks. I've got quite a collection now. I was tidying up my secret drawer tonight. I keep your letters and everything private in that place. It's surprising the things that I have got there, crazy things, but each with a special memory attached. I'll show them to you one day.

Even if I didn't get your Easter flowers, I would have written, Irwin. I did have flowers on my birthday too. They were beautiful too, and I feel such a heel now for not writing to thank you for them then. I'm afraid it was a dismal birthday this year. I missed you particularly and cried myself to sleep that night. I had expected you to be with me, but I shouldn't think of such things, I know. They gave me a party at work in the afternoon. Mr. Clement was away. They even got champagne from somewhere, just a little drop. Hazel, the other girl in the office, took all my birthday kisses for me, the men weren't pleased about that either. We had a birthday cake, a chocolate one, and ice cream. American officers came for a car and insisted they join in the party. They were funny. Naturally, they wanted to celebrate in the evening as well. I told them I had an extraspecial birthday date but didn't say it was in my dreams. Mother thought I'd like some people in for tea, but I didn't want that. So instead I spent it with you. We had a lovely time, Darling.

How do you manage to get up so early in the morning? It must be cold. You seem to have a busy day. I suppose it is difficult to prevent fraternization, and the men don't realize how serious it can be. It's just like English girls going out with Italian prisoners and those nurses who were found sending letters to the German prisoners. After all they've done to us, I'm sure I'd kill the first one I saw. I suppose you heard about the German prisoners escaping from the camp where you were at Bridgend. It caused a great deal of anxiety. They were found wandering around in different parts of the country a few days later. Two were found in Swansea, complete with maps and food. It's amazing how they get these things.

You need have no fears about Gwenda, or anyone else, changing my mind about you. Nobody knows you as I do—well, nobody that I know—and I love you so much that even if you hurt me, I'd still love you. I have a very sure mind of my own, Darling.

I had a very good job offered to me today, secretary to a dental surgeon. I went to see him, but I don't like him. The salary is too good to be genuine. You know, it made me wonder what he expected. He told me there was very little work to do, and I could entertain my friends there. He offered me a drink, which I didn't take. He said that he only employed attractive females. It makes his wife jealous. I was glad to get away from him. That's the job I don't want. I told him I'd consider it and let him know on Monday. He doesn't want anyone to work there. He wants somebody to entertain him when he has no patients. It makes me shudder when I think of men like that.

Isn't the news wonderful, Darling? I was thrilled when I heard it was the 1st Army that had linked up with the Russians. All the prisoners of war returning home from Germany can't say enough to express how wonderful the Americans have been to them. They tell everybody about it. Quite a number of boys we know are home. They don't look too bad. I saw a piece of the bread they ate at those camps. It's almost black, terrible-looking stuff. And they used to clamour for it. But they don't say very much about their life there.

Have to go now, Darling. I'm always loving and thinking of you. Keep loving me and miss me lots. Take good care of yourself.

All my love always,
Mary

April 28, 1945

My Darling,

This is an awful way of spending a Saturday evening, miles and miles away from you in person, though very near to you in my mind. When I close my eyes, you're with me, and we're wondering about going to the dance, but I want to stay in. It's been raining all day today, and it's cold too. Coal is rationed here, so we have to do without a nice big fire. If you were here, then I'd have my central heating. Then they could keep their old coal. This afternoon I went to the football game. I almost froze, sitting there. It wasn't a good game either. It was a good thing you couldn't see my nose. It was like a cherry. What am I worrying about? Yours would have been as bad, but we would have had a swell time getting one another warm afterwards. I went to a show then, at the place where we saw the opera. It was a dirty show. The girl from the office was with me. We were afraid to laugh at the jokes they were so rotten. Then a girl, well, she thought she was a girl, but I'm sure she'll never see forty again, did a striptease. Men sitting around us were disgusted with her figure. It was pretty awful, so there were no cheers. I've never seen such a low show in my life. I don't want to see one like it again, either. I came home at eight o'clock. The quickest way to get warm was to come to bed, so here I am. You may be cold too, and here I am getting warm on my own. It's a silly war.

Thanks, Darling, for the magazines that came this morning. Two *True Stories*. I've read some of them. They don't sound true to me, though. Those problems that they ask the editor to solve tickle me pink. My mother wants me to work on a farm, and I want to go to the city. What can I do? As though the answer given by the editor will make any difference. Think I'll start answering those problems though I wouldn't have any clients after a while.

Have to dream now, special dream as it's Saturday. I love you with all my heart, Darling. So guess how much I miss you? Take care of yourself and keep loving me.

All my love,
Mary

May 1, 1945

My Darling Irwin,

Stayed at Nancy's last night, so I'm sorry I couldn't write. We're having crazy weather here. Last week people were getting tanned on the beach. Yesterday we had snow. It was colder than any winter day. My aunt phoned and asked if I'd keep Nancy company as she wanted to go somewhere special, and it was too cold and windy to leave last night. I had a day off today. At least I thought I did, but when I got home about eleven o'clock this morning, Mother told me they wanted me in work. The auditors are coming tomorrow. I didn't hurry to work. Got there about two o'clock, worked hard until seven o'clock. Everything went wrong today. I had promised to meet my sister-in-law this afternoon. I don't think she believed me when I told her I had to work. That doesn't worry me, though.

The news is super, isn't it? I want to see the end of the war as much as anyone, but I can't help worrying about when I'll see you again. All I can do is keep wishing that something will bring you back to me. It will seem mean, after waiting these months and missing you so much, if you should go farther away from me again. It will be wonderful knowing that you are safe though.

I had a nice invitation today. Would you like to go with me tomorrow night? We do quite a bit of work for a big firm here, and they're giving a dinner dance and cabaret at Langland tomorrow night. The menu came with the invitation. Sounds good too. I have to take a partner with me, so you see, I'm not going. My brother wouldn't go with me, and you just can't go there alone. Wish you were here, Darling. We probably wouldn't go to the dance anyway, but I'd have you near me, and who'd want to go anywhere?

I'm writing this letter in bed, as the family came home together, making it impossible to concentrate. We were listening to the radio when the programme was interrupted for a special news flash. We looked at one another, and I thought it was the end of the European war. Then they announced Hitler's death. It was good news, but not as good as we expected.

It's quite a job trying to tell you how much I love you. I wish I could explain just how I feel right now. Then you'd know how very much I miss you and how much I want to see you. I was wanting all these things this time last year too, when you weren't so far away, but I missed you. It seems years since I saw you, Darling. We didn't know then how long it would be before we saw one another again. I'm still wondering how and when I'll see you. I love you with all my heart, Irwin.

My hands are cold, so I'll have to go now. Show up tonight. I missed you in my dreams last night. Keep loving me lots and take good care of yourself.

All my love always,
Mary

May 3, 1945

Irwin, Darling,

You still love me, don't you? Haven't had a letter since last Friday. I guess you must be busy, though. Last night, I was just about to write you when we heard the wonderful news about Italy. My two brothers are there, so you can guess how we felt. You'd think the whole war was over the way Mother acted. We have a few bottles of wine kept away for special occasions. So last night one was opened. The neighbors paying their usual visits joined in our little celebration. I bet one of my brothers got stinking drunk last night if he found anything to drink. You'd think I was a cabinet minister, the questions Mother asks me. When will the boys come home? Will my brother in the RAF fly home? And all the other questions which I can't answer.

The Ink Spots are singing "Someday I'll Meet You Again" on the radio now. It's nice. Have you heard it? This is a programme of records requested by the forces but nobody ever wants to hear "It Can't Be Wrong." I could throw the radio miles on times when they play some sentimental numbers. I'm really love-starved, Darling. I've deposited all my points with you, so I can't go anywhere else for love. I feel like dancing to a nice band, but I want you and only you to dance with me. If I could only have realized how terribly happy I was when I was with you. I never thought then I could miss you or anyone as much as I've missed and am missing you.

Had three magazines this afternoon so spent the evening reading the trouble of the GIs and other people's worrying romances. Thanks, Darling.

I'm still hoping you'll get that leave. Am I expecting too much of the Army? I feel as though I just have to see you soon. I love you so much, Darling. You're my only interest in life. Take good care of yourself and love me lots.

All my love always,
Mary

Irwin gets leave to visit Mary. He is with her on VE Day. After the end of the war, Irwin decides to make a career of the army, and he remains on assignments in France and eventually Paris.

Mary and Irwin after VE Day

Mary and Irwin

Part Three

MAY 12, 1945–JULY 1, 1945

Is that Irwin married?

May 12, 1945

Irwin Darling,

You don't like me today, do you? If you knew how I felt about not seeing you this morning, you'd like me. I left home sure of the fact that I'd get to the station as soon as you did, get on the bus, but the bus didn't move. The driver hadn't turned up, but he was liable to do so any minute, and as I had time to spare, I didn't worry too much for the first ten minutes. Then I began to panic. I didn't have time to walk, and sitting there praying the bus would start was terrible. It finally did, and I still thought I could make it, but everything was against me. The bus crawled along and stopped every few yards. It was one mad rush into the station, and I was in time to see the end of the train going out. I can't explain how I felt then. I was thinking how mean I must have seemed to you and how much I wanted to see you, and all I could do was stand and stare. I had that picture with me. You would have liked me, and I'd have one more wonderful memory, seeing you then. Please understand, Darling, how very much I wanted to be there this morning, as I always do, and try to like me even though it's only a little bit.

Everything was fine at home before I left this morning. I told Mother you were leaving today, and I was going to the station. She remarked how quickly the time had gone. I was going to tell you about it. Then we wouldn't have a thing to worry about those last few minutes together. It's all right for you to write to the house, Darling. She didn't burn any letters. I straightened that matter out today.

I worked hard all morning trying to forget what a miserable world it is today. When I think of your love and our future, I feel good though. I'm so sure now. I went to the office below us about twelve o'clock. They're a crazy bunch of girls working there. They had seen me with you and naturally wanted to know who the nice American was. I told them you were mine and wouldn't tell them any more. They wanted me to go to Langland with them tonight, and I had to explain in great detail how it didn't interest me one bit. Then they tried to tell me a few things about not knowing what you did when you weren't here. This led to quite an interesting conversation, but I held my ground and still had no interest in going to Langland. That girl we wanted to see about that camera called me this morning. She returned to that place just after we left yesterday. She had films for me too, so I guess we made a mistake about her.

On my way home to lunch, I met Mr. and Mrs. Humphries. They asked if I had seen you and seemed terribly annoyed with me when I told them what happened. They told me you had my bracelet. That was a big relief to me. Where did you find it, Darling? I'm glad it's safe. They were going for a drink and wanted me to go with them, but I had to catch a bus, so they asked me to call at Bryn soon. It will be awful going there without you because everything there would make me miss you more and more, if it's possible. But they were nice to us, and I will go and see them. Maybe they'll talk about you all the time. Then they'll make me terribly happy.

Worked hard all this afternoon, until seven o'clock, I should say. Almost caught up on things now. I looked at the clock at two forty and wondered where you were and if being late made any difference. I certainly hope things are all right, Darling. When I came home this evening, I really started missing you and remembered what we were doing last night at the same time and every night since last Friday. I wish I had stayed with you last night. I would have had those hours more with you and would have seen you this morning. Nobody was waiting for me when I got home last night. I just sat down for an hour wishing I could get to you in a couple of minutes. But we'll have lots of time together in the future, won't we, Darling. I'll never forget any minute I was with you this time. They were all perfect, gurgling and all. I'm shameless, aren't I? I love you with all my heart, and I'm all yours, so why should I be ashamed. I'll never see enough of you, Darling. I want to see you shave every day, but I saw you twice. The things I was wishing. It seemed as though you were my husband and I'll always think of you that way. I know that I'll be able to tell the whole world that one day. Until then, I'll be terribly happy with my secret thoughts. You're a wonderful husband, Irwin.

That sucker bite you gave me last night wasn't so good, Darling. It's awfully small compared to the others, but it will last quite a while.

I didn't struggle or try to argue you out of it, did I, Irwin? I could use a lot more too.

Well, Darling, I have to get some sleep now, and I'll never tell you about my dreams again, but I hope they're nice ones. I hope you understand how much I wanted to see you this morning and know that I wasn't to blame for what happened. I'll send you a nice picture. Keep remembering how I love you. I'm thinking a lot about our house and a girl's name. You'll think about it too, I know. Love as I know you do, and take good care of yourself.

All my love always,
Mary

May 14, 1945

Irwin, Darling,

It's funny. I didn't feel so bad about you leaving until you got on that train, and once more, I was alone. It seemed as though my whole world was slowly moving away from me. I don't know if you noticed a girl with an RAF man standing near us, but she must have seen the way I felt as she came on to me and told me I'd feel a lot better if I hurried away from there. She walked with me, talking all the time. I didn't know what she was saying, and I wanted to be alone with my thoughts, remembering how you looked those last few minutes and that hurried kiss. You know how it was raining, but I didn't worry or think about it, and when I got back to work, I realized how wet I'd got. I couldn't concentrate on my work. Just sat there telling myself how wonderful everything will be in a while. I got home at five o'clock. Mother thought I hadn't had dinner and tried to make me eat again, but food was the last thing I felt like. From six o'clock I was alone in the house, and from then until I came to bed at nine o'clock, I just sat and stared in the fire. I have lots of new memories now. I can live on them for a long time to come, if it's necessary. But the more I'm with you, the more I want to be with you always. I'd like to be eating with you tonight like all those wonderful nights, when we'd wait to be disturbed, instead of being alone in my little bed.

I don't suppose you've come to the end of your train journey yet. I'm awfully tired, so you must be feeling a lot worse. I wish I was on that train with you and all our worries were over so that we'd never have to part again. Life is going to be wonderful, Darling, and it's worth waiting an awfully long time for. The fact that you won't be in so much danger when you get back there makes me feel better too.

Do you mind if I make this a short letter tonight? My eyes keep closing all the time. I'll write again tomorrow, a long letter. Remember, my Darling, how very much I'll always love you and how I want you to hurry back to me. Keep loving me and take good care of yourself.

All my love always,
Mary

May 15, 1945

My Darling,

Today I've missed you more than I can ever remember missing you. I haven't been to work, so all my time has been spent thinking of us and what I'm waiting for. I stayed in bed until twelve o'clock, dreaming with my eyes open. After dinner, Mother wanted me to go to a show with her, but I didn't want to. This put her in a bad mood again. She wanted to know if I was going to stay home for another year now. I told her I would if it's necessary. Then came the long lecture once more. Things are starting off all the wrong way, and her speaking to me like that made me more determined to continue staying at home. If I had wanted to see the show, I would have gone. But it was raining, and I didn't want to sit there in wet clothes, with my mind miles away. Mother finally went on her own. I sewed my straps. It was a pleasure remembering how they got broken, and I was wondering how long it would be before they break again. Then I used the sugar

Mr. Humphries gave me and baked a nice chocolate cake, making believe it was for you, but my dreams came to an end when my kid brother came in yelling for his tea. He thought the cake was lovely, until I told him that I made it. Then he made some rude remarks but still kept eating it. Then the rest of the family drifted in. They all kept asking me the same questions. "Haven't you been out?" "Aren't you going out tonight?" Pretty soon they'll get tired of asking me. This evening, after washing my hair, I just sat by the fire, reading your magazines until I could come to bed without someone remarking how early it was as I couldn't be tired after staying in bed all morning. I heard an announcement on the radio tonight telling men on BLA leave that they had seventy-two hours extension. Why couldn't they have said that last week? Though we were fortunate having those two extra days, and it came as a lovely surprise to me. I almost had ten days with Baby.

Are you missing me, Darling? I know you must be as I know you love me. It's cold tonight. Wish I could have my central heating right here with me. You are the best heating system I know of. I don't have a trace of a sucker bite on me now. You're slipping, Irwin. There's still a big balance left on your account. You'd have quite a job to withdraw all those kisses in just over a week. You did your best though. Good night, Darling. Dream about me and how I'm loving you always. Love me all you can and be good.

All my love always,
Mary

May 16, 1945

My Darling,

These are lonely days, especially after being with you for those days when life was so very wonderful. I worked hard again today, though, even then my mind was on you. I'd stop and think what I was doing at that particular time last week. Every minute I was with you is a precious memory to me. Maybe those memories will have to last a long time too. When I came home to lunch today, Mother didn't say very much to me. I sensed there was something wrong, but I didn't have much time to wonder about it until this afternoon at work, then I was trying to think what she'd heard about me. I didn't get home until six o'clock this evening. As I was going in, Mother was going out, so I didn't get any satisfaction from her. Then my sister said, very suddenly, "Is that Irwin married?" I was so surprised that I just stared and asked her what made her think that. She just said somebody told her, and naturally I kept on asking her who told her. She only said I'd be told about it tonight. That was why Mother looked at me the way she did. I tried to think then how she could have found out. When I went into my bedroom, I knew. The drawer where I kept my letters had been opened, and my letters were an untidy mess. I'm waiting for her to come home now. I can never forgive people who read other people's letters, and we can get all this straight at last. She's determined to end things between you and me, so I'd better warn her what a job she has in front of her. But she probably thinks it's for my own good. But nothing can change my mind now. How could I let you go when I love you so much?

Thought I'd better write while I'm waiting for Mother to come home. Maybe our confidential talk will go on until early in the morning. Then I wouldn't get a chance to write. I can hardly wait to get it over now. I'll write and tell you about it tomorrow. Whatever happens, I'll always love you as you know. Keep loving me, Darling, and miss me lots.

All my love always,
Mary

May 18, 1945

My Darling,

How I wish today was that Friday when I knew I'd have you with me for a while, and life seemed so wonderful. It still is, though when I think one day I'll have you here, not here exactly, I'm in bed now, but with me for always. Seeing you again, Irwin, certainly made me love you more. And when I can see you every day, it will mean that my love will just grow and grow. I'm glad I love you like this, because I know you love me too. And I'm sure that in time our love will help bring us together for always. Then life will be perfect.

That talk I intended having with Mother hasn't come to anything yet. When she returned home Wednesday night, my aunt was with her. It was quite late, so I went to bed. Yesterday, she went to visit Nancy, and I didn't see her until it was time to go to bed again. The whole family were there then, including my brother and his wife, who I had to put up with all evening. My brother didn't mention you, except when he asked if I'd go to the Victory Ball with them tomorrow night at the Brangwyn, and I told them I didn't want to. Then he told me to forget about you and behave like a normal person. I should have given him an answer to that, but I didn't. Brookman had a party at his place last night, and when I told him I wouldn't be there with the rest of the staff, he made some cutting remarks too. But there's no use in going anywhere when I feel better just coming home and writing to you. That's one of the reasons why I'm so sure I love you. I intended writing in bed as usual last night, but when I went to put the light on, there wasn't any. They'd robbed me. It made me bad-tempered in my dreams too.

You said our summer would come when you left here. You're right too. It's warm enough for swimming. Spent this evening pressing my dresses and tried my suit on to see if any sucker bites were in view. There aren't any, Darling. Aren't you sorry? I wish there were some too. Can I have some tonight, please? I wonder how long I'll have to wait for them again. Make it soon, Darling.

I'm going to dream nice dreams tonight. Be there. I love you, well, you know how much I love you. I'm all yours, Irwin. Love me lots too, and dream about me, but I haven't been gurgling tonight. Take good care of yourself.

All my love,
Mary

May 21, 1945

My Darling,

Missed me? The two-day silence, I mean. I've been on my travels again, all the way to Mumbles. It was wonderful here on Saturday. I was working and feeling awfully lonely, wishing I could be with you and wondering where you were. One of the drivers lives at Mumbles. He's one of the nicest men working there, and I like his wife very much. He was about to leave in his car for home, and I said, not meaning it, that I'd like to stay in Mumbles Saturday evening, then I could go swimming on my own. He said his wife would be very pleased to have me stay there. I thought it over and decided it was a good idea. He took me home so I could gather a few things together and tell Mother about it. I went swimming in the evening. I met a girl on the beach who went to one of your parties at Penclawdd. I don't remember seeing her there, but she remembered me. She knows Corporal Webb's wife very well and told me that he was safe and back in the States. I was awfully glad to hear that. This girl wanted to get very friendly. She asked me to go to the Pier with her, but I told her I didn't have anything with me to wear to a dance. That was an easy way out. She told me all about Eva, trying to get me to say something about her, but I wasn't playing. She was at that club near Penclawdd with her last Sunday, and Eva, so she said, is going about with the most wonderful-looking Scottish officer. He wears a kilt too. I was glad to get away from that girl. She talked about everyone except herself. I stayed in Mumbles Saturday night but had to get up at six thirty Saturday morning to go to work in the car with the driver. His wife made me promise to go back there in the afternoon and stay until this morning as her husband would be working late. I did. We went for a long walk, stopped at her relations for tea. Then it started to rain, and I had to play cards again with the rest of them until we could walk back. I went to bed about nine o'clock last night and had wonderful dreams about us. Don't think those things but we did have lots of fun, and you loved me all the time. I expected to see sucker bites when I woke this morning. I looked for them.

Today is a general holiday here again. I worked as usual and was thinking of an excuse to give Mother for staying in tonight. She makes an awful fuss about it, then Gwenda phoned me and asked me to go to a show with her. So that saved making excuses. Gwenda saw us together that day we sheltered from the rain, when we were wandering about going to the show. She was in a passing bus. That's the first thing she told me about. She said how wonderful and happy we both looked. So that's why people stared at us, not because I'm funny-looking, like you said. I was happy too, Darling, happier than I've ever been in my life before. I thought I was going to surprise Gwenda, telling her that you had come to see me, and was surprised when she told me first. She's been staying at Carmarthen for a few days with her farmer's people. Everything is fixed for the wedding now. It's not going to be a church affair, very quiet, but I have an invitation. I asked her what her father would say if I should show up. She said he'll be too drunk to notice me. But I won't risk it in case he creates a scene. They haven't fixed a date yet, but I hope things turn out right now. We had tea at the Albert Hall, and I heard all about the house they had in the heart of the country and how she was going to change his ideas after they're married. He's very shy, or dopey, I don't know which, has never been to a dance, and doesn't like going into towns. The perfect man, Gwenda says. We saw *A Song to Remember*, no drunken pigs in it though, only classical music that I can't appreciate. I wasn't sorry to come home and to bed to have a lovely time thinking of all the things we did together and how lucky I am to have you loving me.

I have toothache right now. If you were here, I'd wake you up to tell you about it. Then you'd get mad, wouldn't you? I'll have to visit the dentist tomorrow. The filling seems too big for my tooth. You know that joke you told me about jumping puddles. In one of my mad moments, I told the men in work it. Now they call me Puddles. I hope they forget soon.

I'm pretending now that you'll go get some aspirins for me, but I guess I'll have to get them myself, so do you mind if I leave you now? My toothache's getting worse. Hope I sleep tonight so I can keep my date with you. I love you more and more every minute.

Darling, you're always in my thoughts. I miss you so very much. Love me and miss me all you can. Take good care of yourself.

All my love always,
Mary

May 23, 1945

My Darling,

Before I start, I want to apologise for this paper. Unfortunately, like many other things, notepaper is scarce, so I hope you'll excuse me.

Just as I got to work this morning, the postman came. He handed me a bunch of letters, and I went through the usual routine of stamping the time on each one. Then my heart missed a beat. There was a letter from you for me. I just sat down and read it over a few times. It was a wonderful letter, Darling. I really didn't expect one so soon, either. You're an angel, writing before you got to the end of your journey. I love you lots, Irwin.

Your leave doesn't seem to have been. I had such a wonderful time that I have to think hard before I realize that it wasn't one of those super dreams. I'm so glad that you too had a wonderful time. The nice part about it was that we didn't have to go out and get drunk to have lots of fun. Of course, one night we got a little drunk too, and nobody could have had more fun than we had that night, could they? You told me you missed me lots and loved me in this letter. That's what I want to hear. Then nothing else matters. I certainly hope we can be married the next time you come here, but if that's not possible, I'll be more than happy just being with you again. As long as you love me, I'll always be happy.

I'm glad you had an uneventful journey as far as France, anyway, and hope it continued that way. It must have been nice meeting Reynolds like that. Couldn't you have persuaded him to change places with you? I hope he's more fortunate than we were with his camera. He should be in Bridgend by now, shouldn't he? I'll be awfully pleased if he calls me. Doc should be here before long too. Mrs. Humphreys will be awfully thrilled on Saturday when I tell her that, and that I've had a letter from you. She'll have a good excuse for getting drunk too. It seems as if my fears of you going to the Pacific were unfounded, if these people are having leaves to England. I certainly hope it's that way. I don't want you to go that far away from me, Darling. You know how close I want to be to you, don't you? So I'll keep my fingers crossed about you coming to see me again soon. I'll never see enough of you, even if I could see you every day for the rest of my life. Do you know how wonderful you are, Darling? I'll tell you one day.

We had a storm this afternoon. I was scared, but you didn't come to hold me in your arms. Instead, I had to sit there, afraid to run into the other office where all the people were, in case Mr. Clement thought I was crazy. I'm a sissy, aren't I?

It's all right to address letters home now. If I should find out that any letters are destroyed, then I can do something about it, but I don't think I'll lose any of your precious letters that way.

I feel so mad when I think how that train fooled me like that. I thought it was leaving rather early too and asked that girl if it was just moving on to another platform, but she said that her husband went away on that train once a week, and it always left early. I missed a super kiss too, but that's another for my account. I know you would have called me if you'd had sufficient time at Cardiff, so there's nothing to forgive, Darling.

When I'm at work, I do think of you sitting opposite me, then I turn around to find Mr. Clement instead. What a difference. He's a misery to himself. I left work after the storm was over this afternoon. Since then I've done lots of little things that needed doing and counted all the letters I've had from you. Guess how many? 199, isn't that lovely? Can I take them with me wherever we go after we're married? They're all wonderful letters. I don't ever want to part with one of them.

Bye, now. It's dreaming time again. I love you more and more all the time, Darling. Keep loving me and miss me lots.

All my love always,
Mary

May 24, 1945

My Darling,

Just getting ready for work this morning when I remembered that I had a day off. It was a wonderful sensation, getting back into bed again though I didn't go to sleep. I thought some lovely things about us, wishing you were there with me. I haven't any straps on my pajamas to break either, isn't that terrible? Of course, I should have gotten up and gone for a long walk in the fresh morning air, but I couldn't tear myself away from my thoughts. You were too wonderful as usual this morning, and we had lots of fun too.

This afternoon, Mother wanted me to go to Llanelly, that's about ten miles from here, with her, but I didn't like the idea of waiting a couple of hours for a bus to come back, so instead I sat in the garden sunbathing, almost in the nude, until I saw the man next door gazing intently through the window. I didn't know he was home before. Then I went shop hunting for cigarettes. They seem to have disappeared again. When I told my brother I couldn't get any, he said the German prisoners were getting them all. They've cut our food and clothes rations down. I'm sure there'll be a revolution here if things get much worse. I think I'll visit Mrs. Humphries now and again. She might help.

This evening, Mother and I went to see my aunt. She was awfully pleased to see me too. The three of us went for a walk and called at my brother's house. He was busy in his garden, so we didn't stay very long. We went back to my aunt's for supper. My cousin was home then. Do you remember us seeing her one day? Her husband's in Germany somewhere, and she's worrying in case he's sent to the Pacific. She's hoping he'll be in the Army of Occupation so she can go to him. She made me laugh when she said she had everything packed ready. I've done quite a bit of walking tonight. I feel sleepy now. I'd like to find my way into your arms and forget the rest of the world. I did that one night, didn't I? I asked Gwenda if I snored all those times I slept with her, as she wanted to know if I could take a few days off soon and stay at the same place together as we did last year. Do you know what she said? She used to wake up in the morning before I did, and I wasn't snoring. She just wished I had been a man, then I wouldn't have slept at all. If I did snore, Darling, it must have been the whiskey. I'm sorry, I promise never to do it again. I think you're just as wonderful sleeping, as you are awake. Well, almost. Wish I had a chance to wake before you again tomorrow morning and just look at you until you opened your eyes. It was wonderful finding you there. Seems like one of my special dreams now. I can still remember, though, how I felt when I got out of bed. It was terrible, as though I was half-dead. I think I was too, and then all that water you gave me. You just laughed at me too. I'll have my revenge one day. You'll be asking for water, and I'll be laughing at you. No, I wouldn't be so mean. You were nice to me when I was so terrible. Nobody else would have done what you have done for me. Thanks a lot, Darling.

My brother and his wife went to a dance at the Brangwyn Monday night. John, that bore I told you about, was there too. My brother said he stuck with them all night until they felt like screaming at him. I'm glad he affects everyone else the same way as he does me. My brother told him that you had been here, and John said he saw us together on VE night, so that's why he doesn't bother me on the bus anymore. He must have some sense after all.

If you are where you were before, you're thinking about me now. I hope you are because I'm about to think hard too. Miss me, Irwin, lots, as I miss you. You're wonderful, and I love you very much. Keep loving me, and take care of yourself.

All my love,
Mary

May 25, 1945

My Darling,

Friday must be my lucky day. I had two extralovely letters from my Irwin today. Wish you were here so I could answer them in person, with a few super kisses and hugs that almost hurt you. I have quite an account waiting for you already, so be prepared for our next meeting. The sooner that better.

I'm happy because I know you didn't barter your cigarettes in Paris. I don't give it a second thought because I love you very much and trust you the same way. Can't think how I'm so lucky as to have someone like you to love. You're as wonderful as anyone could be, and to think that one day everyone will know that you're mine. I feel awfully self-satisfied when I think about it, as I know how I felt when I had you here with me.

I'm catching up fast with all the sleep. I'd much prefer to do without it though. As you say, we won't get much sleep later. That doesn't worry me. It sounds heavenly. What do you think? Those sucker bites you inflicted on me haven't shown any results, and I didn't yell either, except when you gave me a good bite. You must be slipping, Darling. I hope you liked the picture. My brother says I look the perfect picture of innocence in that one. He gave a sarcastic grin when I told him I was. I told you I brought it to the station that Saturday, if I remember correctly.

Love is wonderful, Irwin. I'm glad you're so sure about me and us. Please don't talk about anyone taking me away from you. I could have the same fears about you, but I don't want to think about those things. You know you have all my love, and there'll never be anyone for me but you. After knowing and loving you, who else could possibly interest me. That's the last thing you need to worry about. I'm all yours, Darling.

It didn't take you long to get back, did it? When I think about it, I tell myself you can't be so far away from me after all. All I know is that it's every yard from Swansea to where you are, much too far. I think I'm one of the most fortunate people in the world, though, having you come all this way to see me.

Doc is doing good work, isn't he? So he has reason to be pleased. I can quite understand how he feels about Eva, almost ignoring that letter. I've thought about it since and wondered if she got it. Her husband might have seen it first. It isn't like her to do a thing like that. She always wanted to know everything about Doc when I went to Sennybridge those few times without her.

Thanks, Honey, for getting the perfume. If you like it, I'll like it too. You'll be the only one, and me of course, who will come close enough to know how good it is. I'd like to have seen you buying it. Good perfume doesn't smell its best when it's in a bottle, and how is a man to know that? You know the dress you said you like in the window that day? I went there and tried it on. It would have been swell if I was twice the size I am. Somebody else could have come in it with me. The woman told me she didn't have anything like that in a junior miss size. I've never been to that shop before, and after that crack, I won't go back there, either.

So I'm a chief before you. Aren't you mad? Gosh, I was proud of you when I read that order awarding you the medal. I'll save it and show our children, Darling. I'd love to have the medal too. I agree with your award being much better than Johnny Monson's. You know I agree with everything you say, my darling husband. Don't call me wifey, either. You sound like Dagwood. "Remember, I love you Charles, get up them stairs." Mother saw *Constant Nymph* too. She thought it was terrible. Charles Boyer gave her the horrors. She likes Tyrone best.

Maybe your lawyer is a very busy man, Irwin. I hope he fixes things soon too. It's wonderful knowing that you are looking forward to that day as much as I am waiting to be bothered for the rest of my life. Though I can assure you, it won't be any bother to me. We're going to have lots of fun, Darling.

I feel mad when I think you are there making your bed and then sleeping on your own, and here I am, making believe that after I finish writing, your arms will be waiting for me. But we have all those things to wait for. With those wonderful things in my mind, I could wait forever, but I don't want to, Irwin. I miss you so very, very much.

It's getting late, almost eleven o'clock. Past my dreaming time. If I don't hurry, you'll think I'm not going to show up tonight. Keep loving me, Darling, and take care of yourself.

All my love always,
Mary

May 26, 1945

My Darling,

It's been some day. I still feel awful. After going to the bank this morning, I called to that place where Mrs. Humphreys made me promise to meet her. She had a bunch of people with her, including two RAF pilots. I returned the drinks Frank bought me last time, and that started something. Drinks came from everywhere. I don't like beer, and I tried to tell them I wanted to go, but you know the things Mrs. Humphreys says after she's had too much. I felt more uncomfortable. I only had three glasses of beer, and I felt as though I was walking on air. I told her I'd had a letter, well, three letters from you, and they were quite disappointed because you hadn't written to them. And of course, she was quite thrilled when I told her that Doc was coming here soon. She was more than drunk by this time and said I'd have to come there too if Doc was staying with them. I said that I didn't think that it would be right. I wouldn't like it, and I'm sure Eva wouldn't, or Doc either. She really doesn't like Eva, you know, told me in quite a blunt manner this morning. Though Mrs. Humphreys was more than good to us, I don't like her, Irwin. Sorry, but I don't. I think she talks an awful lot about everyone. She knows all my history too. I'd much prefer the old boy. These RAF boys were getting on my nerves, the type who'll do anything to attract attention. I wouldn't mind visiting Mrs. Humphreys at Bryn now and then, but I don't want to meet her the way I did this morning again. She kept on about us getting married from her place. I told her we couldn't make any plans as we didn't know where you'd be, but I thanked her anyway. Her son has been posted here too. She certainly knows how to wangle things, and she's awfully pleased with herself. You know the way she talked about the things she could get. Well, this morning she asked if I could get her potatoes and cigarettes. I told her I'd do my best, but it amuses me when people are like that. She told me too you'd be a wonderful husband, as though I didn't know. Asked me if I realized that. Honestly, Irwin, it was like a cross-examination on my thoughts. When she was asking me all this made me believe she was trying to tell me something she wasn't sure about. She's a crafty type. If Doc hasn't left before you get this letter, warn him to be careful what he says please, as she evidently knows someone who knows me very well, and I'm sure it isn't one of the drivers, either. That beer affected me very easily. I saw a grin on one of those boy's faces after I'd drunk it, so I have my suspicions. I finally got away from them, had to go without my lunch too. When I got back to the office, I felt hot and funny. They all wanted to know where I'd been. Mr. Clement and his wife came in when I was trying to concentrate on my work. They started to argue about clothing coupons. She said he couldn't have any to buy pyjamas, and I told him to go without them. You can see how I felt. I'd never interfere with them or say a thing like that when I was in my normal senses. I almost said something else too but remembered just in time. I was thankful to see them going. Then I didn't try to work. Sat there wishing I'd been gurgling with you, and you had to put up with all the crazy things I said. If you had been with me when Mrs. Humphreys was talking to me, I wouldn't have minded her one bit. But as it was, I felt mad when I left her. The only thing I like about her is that she likes you very much and was nice to us both.

When I came home, I felt all right. Mother was here and, as she never drinks, has a very keen nose, but she didn't notice or smell anything. I kept as far away as I could. She's gone to a show now. I'm all alone, Saturday night too. But that one Saturday night I spent with you makes up for all the lonely ones I may have to spend in the future. I certainly hope they'll be very few. I had to answer the usual questions before Mother went out tonight. "Are you staying in again?" "Why don't you go to a dance?" and all the other remarks that make me mad but never make to want to go out anywhere. I love you very, very much, Darling, and know that you love me too. So what better way could I find of having a good time, when I'm not with you, than writing, making believe I'm talking to you. I miss you so much, Darling, nobody could ever take your place. I don't tell myself I'm crazy for missing you, either, as I understand perfectly why I do.

Time flies when I'm writing to you. I have to get the supper before my family come home now. Love me all you can, Darling, miss me lots too. I was thinking of you at eleven o'clock this morning, as well as the rest of the day. Dream about me, and take care of yourself for me.

All my love always,
Mary

May 27, 1945

My Darling,

Well, I've read all the Sunday papers. Now what do I do? Sunday could be such a heavenly day if you were here with me. I'd have you to myself. You wouldn't have to work, and wouldn't we have fun? We could take a trip in that small car you were talking about, but there wouldn't be any need to get lost then. Instead of all these lovely things I could do, I went to work this morning. That nice driver came for me. I was in bed as usual. He was making an awful noise. I ran downstairs to tell him I wouldn't be long, still had my pyjamas on, opened the door a few inches, thought he'd be in the car. Instead, he pushed his way into the house. I felt more than silly, standing there like that. But he's all right. Just apologized and asked if he could make himself some tea while he was waiting. So when I was dressed, I had tea waiting for me. Any of the other drivers would go back to work and tell the men what they'd seen me in, but he didn't. Did I tell you that Brookman smashed one of our cars up the other night? He's left our place now. I'm thankful that I won't have to put up with him and his sarcastic remarks anymore. He's still a taxi driver, one of those that wait at the station. We might use him one night, who knows? After finishing my work, I walked home. It's been nice here today, and I had lots of spare time. I also worked up an appetite for dinner. The rest of the day, I've spent reading and did some cooking, by the way. Life is very exciting these days. I just don't know what to do with myself.

You were right when you said some of those articles in *Reader's Digest* were crazy. I've just been reading how to choose a partner for life. According to that, we have no chance of being happy together. There's too big a difference in our ages, and it also states that a divorced person hasn't much chance of a happy second marriage. He or she will always be waiting for the slip-ups. How can anybody, however much they know about people, make set rules like that about marriage? I can't see how any two people could be happier than we could. I love as much as any woman can love a man, and I know you love me too. We like doing the same things, and I've spent quite a bit of time with you. I've loved every minute, just wanted to be with you forever. I'd certainly like to meet the person who wrote that article. Don't suppose he or she has ever been in love.

Everyone can use the cars after June 1. My brother's trying to buy one, but they're very difficult to get. If you hear about the number of road accidents increasing, it's only me, though I've been warned I'm not to drive it. He told me to get one of my own, but he'll change his mind when he gets drunk one night. I can talk him into anything then. Like saying it was one thirty instead of five thirty that morning when he'd been celebrating, and we forgot about the time. It will be wonderful when I won't have to ask you the time, every hour or so, and you won't have to wake me at five o'clock in the morning for us to decide it's too late to go home. What a difference in Sundays. We had just started to drink that whiskey this time on that eventful Sunday night. I can remember laughing at that poor boy's picture when it started to take effect. Then you remember the rest better than I do, except for one thing you don't remember at all, but I do. You didn't seem to be the least bit drunk either. I think I had all that whiskey, or you can certainly take it. I'll always remember how wonderful you were to me, though. You must love me an awful lot, Darling, and I'm awfully grateful for the way you treated me. I don't think I would have drunk so much if I didn't have the idea that I could trust you. I know I can now. When I think about if it had been anyone else, I feel terrible. But I really know how irresponsible I could be for my actions if I got drunk again. You know I never will with anyone else. It was lots of fun with you, but you're different, so very much, from the rest of the people I know. I do love you lots, Darling, and I'm sorry for being so awful that night.

Must get some more sleep in store for the time when I won't get any. Wish that day would hurry. I can hardly wait. Dream about me and keep loving me. I love you with all my heart, Irwin, and miss you lots.

All my love always,
Mary

May 28, 1945

My Darling,

Still have my toothache. Didn't have enough courage to visit the dentist this morning. I wish I had. Then I wouldn't feel so bad now. If this letter is a miserable one, you'll understand, won't you?

I woke this morning to hear the news on the radio. The first thing I heard was that the American 1st Army was on its way to the Pacific via the States. Oh, Irwin. I've done some worrying today, not knowing how long it may be before I see you again if you're sent there is enough. But I wouldn't mind that as long as you weren't going into danger again. I hope you go back to the States. You know where I'd really like you to be, but we can't expect too much of the army. I've thought very hard today about how long I may have to wait for you, and I know that, if necessary, my love for you will help me to be patient for a very long time. Yes, as long as you want me, I'll be waiting. Went down to breakfast, and Mother asked me if I thought you'd be going to the Pacific. I told her I didn't know. She agreed that they should send you boys home for a long rest.

Went to the bank this morning. We had more money than usual, so Hazel's Eddie took me in a car. We were a long time there, and on the way back, Eddie wanted a drink. I went in with him. I was thirsty too. Who should be in this place but Mr. and Mrs. Humphreys. They were awfully pleased to see me. Asked right away if I'd heard from you. They had expected a letter. I told her I didn't expect a letter for a couple of days yet. They couldn't understand that at all. Frank, the old boy, bought me drink. It's all right, I wasn't gurgling, just beer and lemonade mixed, and they acted the same way they do at home. Him making funny remarks when she's telling her experiences. They told me to tell you that the rabbit has a family now, and you can imagine how she laughed when she was telling me. They both want you to write to them, Darling. You will, won't you? They kept me there for an hour. You were the main topic of conversation, as well as Doc. She was laughing about the night she went to sit on the chair and sat on the floor instead. They made me promise I'd meet them again on Saturday morning, so I'll have to go. But it's a bit of a strain to laugh at what she thinks is funny. Through meeting them this morning, I had to go without my lunch, so I worked hard when I got back, then I finished early. Had to go to the other offices below on my way home. Those girls. I had to listen to what they did and who they met over the weekend, and they want me to stay at their bungalow with them the second week in July. They were going to Langland tonight, getting some men to help them have a good time when they're on vacation. I don't envy them one bit. My Irwin is all I ever want. They can have all their so-called good times. I'm happy.

This war is getting worse. I haven't had any more notepaper now and didn't know about it until I started looking for some tonight. I'll have to leave you now, Darling. Wherever you are and wherever you go, always remember that you have all my love, and I'm waiting for you. Think about me and miss me lots, Darling. Please keep loving me. I need all the love you can spare. Take good care of yourself for me.

All my love always,
Mary

May 30, 1945

Please excuse the lines, that's all the notepaper I could get.

My Darling,

Sorry I missed writing two days. Couldn't help it, honest. Nancy phoned me on Monday morning. Asked me if I'd stay the night in her place as her people were going away. I didn't mind a bit. I like staying there, if they'd understand about me wanting to write.

On my way home to lunch Monday, I met Mrs. Humphreys. She asked about you and wanted to know how soon Doc would be coming. Her boy hasn't arrived home yet, but she said she's let me know when he did, as he's lots of fun. If she only knew how much fun you and I had laughing at those elegant pictures. I'd like to see him though. Maybe those flatter him. I told her I was in a hurry so I could get away from her. She said she'd see me again soon.

Monday evening, Nancy wanted to go for a walk, but just as we were leaving the house, it started to rain. We stayed in then. I helped her with the knitting and we went to bed about nine o'clock. I had a day off yesterday, so in the morning, we went into town, did some shopping, home for lunch, and then went to see "Since You Went Away." It was terribly sad. Couldn't help crying. A nice show to see if you're feeling miserable. Nancy didn't like it. She said if the Americans are anything like they were in it, they're all crazy. I didn't think that though. What the wives and the sweethearts put into words when their men were leaving is how I feel about you being away from me. I was tickled pink with one part of the show. Claudette Colbert going into her bedroom the night after her husband leaves, there are twin beds. She gets into her own, looks across at her husband's, then makes one dive into it and starts crying. That's when she misses him most, I guess. I couldn't be bothered getting out of my bed into another one like that, so if you don't mind, we'll have one bed. I don't care if it's big or small, as long as it's only one, then I won't fool myself one bit.

After tea, Nancy and I went for a walk through that park where we went that day. She was talking to me, and my mind was far away,

145

thinking about you as usual and wishing so hard. We went home when Nancy felt tired, had something to eat, and to bed again. I didn't feel a bit like work this morning, but I wondered if there'd be a letter at the office for me, and that made me hurry. I was glad I did too. There were two wonderful letters from my Darling. The airmail letter took six days to get here. It's no different from the ordinary mail. These letters were written on the twenty-second and the twenty-third.

You wanted to know what I was doing at ten fifteen. I'll give you three guesses, and the first one's right. Thinking of you as usual, only extra hard. I miss you in the worst way too, Darling. You know that, though. But we have so much happiness to come. Missing you now only helps me realize how wonderful things will be in the future. They will be too. I know.

Almost forgot to tell you. Betty from Bridgend called me today. Reynold's friend, I mean. They couldn't get me last week when they tried. She sounds awfully nice, Irwin. Told me that Hap met you on his way here and wanted to know how soon I had a letter after you left here. She was surprised when I told her. She's looking forward to seeing him again in three months' time, so I can look forward too. Life's wonderful. Thank Hap for me, won't you. I thanked her, but she said it's only what you did for her.

Don't be so impatient with that lawyer, Darling. Well, that isn't what I mean exactly, because I'm just as impatient, but you're not giving him much time to answer your letter, are you? I'm glad your wife feels the way she does about it and wants things cleared up as quickly as possible. I hope she'll be satisfied sooner than she thinks.

It's wonderful news, you being in the Army of Occupation, but if you had gone to the Pacific, I'd be waiting just the same, however long it may be. Now I don't have to think about that. I certainly hope I'll be able to be there with you and help you study for that examination. Maybe they'll give me a permanent warrant too, if I study hard enough with you. What do we have to learn, Darling?

Why did you think that telling me you were leaving part of you behind when that train left here would make me think you were silly? We're very much alike in lots of things though, Irwin. Often

I've wanted to say something to you, then don't say it, because you may think I'm crazy. But I want to hear you say all those things to me as long as it's to do with you loving me. And I'll tell you my secret thoughts too. Did you know that I loved you lots?

You and Doc are back together again then, just like old times. I'm glad you think I'm right about Doc, but it makes me shiver when I think about him talking about my body, that's mine, yours, I mean. Nothing to do with Doc. Let him talk about his Eva, and then I won't mind a bit. Mrs. Humphreys told me something that Doc said which made me like him less too. I'll tell you when I see you. Remind me. It will be easier to tell you than to explain in a letter. He's a queer person.

You had a busy day on the twenty-third, didn't you? I'm glad your sister-in-law is looking after you. I hope to thank her one day. You must be getting a big mail, all these letters you have to answer. I'm glad too that Modorno's all right now. I suppose his mother will be more than happy to see his army career finished with.

Haven't broken any straps since you left here, Darling. It's funny that. I can't understand it. We certainly did find a solution to put a stop to that. Why didn't we think of it before? Don't bother to bring your sewing kit next time. You won't need it, not that you'll think I'll sew my straps safely.

I'll be just as proud as you, if not more so, when I can introduce you as my husband. Then we'll really have fun, Darling. We won't have to worry about what Mrs. Humphreys thinks of us, or anyone else. Not that I worried very much before, but I won't have to go home when I want to stay. Isn't it going to be wonderful? You calling me your wife too is going to be music to my ears. I have lots of things to dream about.

I hope your sister approves of our plans for the future. Now that you've told her, I want her to like me. I hope she will. I remember how small I felt that day we met her husband at Sennybridge. I was wishing the ground would open and swallow me up. I loved you then, but I wasn't very sure of you, so I was wondering what he thought about me. Crazy, wasn't I? I'll do my utmost to make you a good wife, Darling, then maybe your sister will like me too. I know how I feel about my brothers' wives. Little things they say and do, now and then, make me dislike them intensely for a few minutes, especially if it's something about my brothers.

When I came home to lunch today, Mother was in a good mood. Everything was fine. They must have missed me not being around the house. John, the boy Mother likes, has finished with me. I told you, didn't I? Now I don't get a seat on the bus. He's mean. He has another girl too. He's walked her up and down in front of our house a few times this evening. I'm green with envy, as you can imagine. I wish he'd grow up. My sister stands behind him at the bus stop and makes rude remarks about him aloud. She makes me laugh.

Hazel asked me to work for her until seven o'clock tonight as her Eddie was taking her to a show. I didn't have anywhere to go, and it's no bother answering the phone, so about four o'clock, I sent her home. I was sorry afterwards, as Mr. Clement wasn't around, and those men almost murdered me. My face was black, and I don't know what my hair looked like. I tried to get annoyed, but every time I saw myself in the mirror, I started to laugh. I saw three Army officers coming across the garage and tried to run into the other office, but the men made me sit there. I had to wash my hair before doing anything else. Then I wrote a long letter to my brother, in reply to the nice one I had this morning. So I've had quite a busy day.

I think you'd better keep writing to the office, Darling. You have more sense than I to see that. It's getting late. I'll be missing my date with you. Keep loving me, Darling, and miss me lots.

All my love always,
Mary

May 31, 1945

My Darling,

Another wonderful letter from you, today. I love you and love you more all the time. You and us are all I think of, and it's different since I saw you again, as now I have no doubts at all in my mind. I'm quite sure that one day, you'll be all mine, so all the world can know. We already know how much we belong to one another, though.

I think my fears about Mother finding out about you were unnecessary. She hasn't mentioned a thing about it. What I think now is that my sister read those letters. I don't think she raided my drawer with that intention, but she couldn't resist that temptation once she saw them. She's always snooping around my bedroom, seeing if she can find anything she'd like to borrow. I'm sorry I made you worry about it, Darling. One thing I'm sure about, and that is, whatever happens, I'll always be yours.

I do know that we are doing no wrong, Irwin. I used to have a guilty conscience about things. I used to worry about it in times and try to have enough courage to tell you that I wanted to finish everything. But luckily, it never worked out as I planned. Even if it had, and you never bothered me again, I know I'd still be thinking of you and comparing everyone else I'd meet with you. There will never be anyone but you for me either, Darling. You know I have a mind of my own, and nobody could make me do anything I didn't want to do, so please don't worry about that, Darling.

When I said our lovely memories might have to last a long time, I was thinking of you having to go to the Pacific, nothing else, Irwin. Did you really think that I meant I'd have to forget about our wonderful future because other people don't approve? If so, I'll have to start telling you all over again about how very, very much I love you and how much I want to be your wife. Any trouble that might come right now, I'll be more than compensated for the day when I have you by my side for always.

If Mother should find out, she'd tell me I was more to blame than you for seeing you when I knew that you belonged to someone else. She wouldn't understand that I just couldn't let you go. You told me you had seen beautiful women and you looked and that was all. Maybe people would say it's funny, why I believe you, but I do, as I feel the same way. I've been to dances, and Nancy has pointed out a good-looking man coming in, and she'd be thrilled for me when he asked me to dance, but I never pretended to be interested because all the interest I have in men is centered on you. Nancy would get him in the end. That happened since the first time I met you. I remember going to Langland and hearing Nancy talk about her Walter all the way there. I hadn't seen him then. When we got there, Walter came over and asked me to dance and wanted me to stay with him the rest of the night. I took him back to our table and did a disappearing act so Nancy could have him to herself. I wouldn't have done that if I hadn't met you. It's things like that that convince me that we were meant to belong to each other, Darling.

Don't worry about losing me. Nothing can happen to make that possible. Just love me all you can, and remember how much I love you. You're wonderful, Irwin.

All my love always,
Mary

June 1, 1945

My Darling,

Met the postman on the way to work this morning. He handed me the letters to save him the climb. All the envelopes were the same size, but in between bills and complaints, I found a letter from my darling, an extra lovely one. You're a real honey. I love you so much.

On my way to the bank this morning, I met Brookman. He asked about you. I told him you were wonderful. He told me he was with a friend of mine last night. I couldn't think who that was. Then he told me Eva and said I'd never guess who she was out with. I wouldn't have either. I've decided there must be something wrong with that girl. The man she's running around with is the most notorious person in the town. He's horrible, besides being a little mad. Brookman spent some time with them, of course. He got a kick out of telling me all this and remarking what nice friends I had, as though Eva was anything to do with me. She told him she writes Doc every day and that she intends marrying him. She'll never be satisfied with one man. I'm sorry for her. It must be awful to have her complaint. Brookman said he'd be driving them again tomorrow night and thought I'd like to go along with them. I wouldn't be seen in that man's company for anything. My Irwin is all I want, and I know he loves me, so what would I want to go out for? I have everything in the world just thinking of you. You can't think how I felt after I left Brookman. Don't know why I was so disgusted, but I was. It's good Doc is the way he is. It could be somebody who thought she was perfect because they got a letter every day. She's quite a girl.

Hazel picked up the phone this afternoon, and the next thing I heard was a yell and "Steve." Her sister's husband, the American, was on his way here. I thought she'd gone crazy. She was going around with him until he met her sister, so he's a little more to her than just a brother-in-law. I envied her sister, wishing it was me, all excited again, because you were coming to see me. It's a wonderful feeling. Nothing else matters. I'm sure I'll be like that every day after we're married, waiting for you to come home from work. It's going to be wonderful. But I'll just have to think of other things as well. Like getting you meals so that there won't be anything for you to complain about. Then we won't have quarrels, will we? If we ever do, I know they won't be serious ones. I'll refuse to get mad at you. I already know you have quite a temper, haven't you. It's the Irish in you, I guess. I'll understand that as long as you don't try murdering me. You wouldn't do that, would you, Darling?

That man we have working with us who likes me told me today I could borrow his car anytime I liked. It would have been nice if we had been able to use it when you were here. Now, I don't know when I'll want it. It was nice of him to suggest it though. See, somebody would trust me with his car, even if you wouldn't. You meanie. I love you.

Your letter today had been opened by the censor. I wish he'd mind his own business. I suppose he was curious though, as those coins were in it. Thank you, Darling. I have quite an interesting collection of coins and paper money. If you're a good boy, I'll let you see them one day. We'll never be really poor as long as we have them. We'll be able to show our children them too. Those kids will never have a dull moment. You can tell them all about the places you've seen, and between us, we could help to educate them in lots of things. Love would be the subject we know most about, I know. But they'll soon learn about that themselves. You were my teacher, Darling. I was a good learner, wasn't I?

You know, Darling, that I want to marry you as soon as possible too, so you certainly can let me have those papers to sign right away. I get all excited when I think about it. Have you any idea when your affairs will be settled? I want to go to London and get something wonderful to wear for the most important day of my life. You ask me if I think you're too impatient, when all the time you know how much I want to be Mrs. Deems. That sounds awfully good to my ears. After telling me all these lovely things, you say, "Don't let John steal you away from me." Will you ever understand that I'm all yours now, just as though I were your wife already? I am, Darling. Please realize that. Lots of people would like to steal you away from me too, like that girl at the dance we went to. I could have killed her for even trying, but I'm sure you're mine, aren't you?

I'm glad most of your boys are safe now. It was right what that girl told me about Corporal Webb then. His wife is going to the States very soon, so I imagine she must feel pretty good about everything. It must be terrible waiting and wondering as long as she did.

Your swimming pool sounds super. Wish I could go swimming with you. You're a lot better swimmer than I am, I suppose. I like to fool around in the water. I wish it had been warmer when you were here, but we had lots of fun anyway. As long as I'm with you, I always have fun.

I don't think there's anything wrong with you, even though Smiley does. To me, you're perfect. There's something wrong with him, though, for being surprised at you not acting the way he did in Paris. Eva and him should get together some time. They have a lot in common. Don't change, Darling, whatever they say. I love you so much that I don't want to think of you being any different.

If you hadn't known me, you'd be going home this month then. You aren't sorry, Darling, that you had to throw that chance away, are you? I realize that you want to get back to the States and do the things you've missed doing and see all the people you've thought about since you left there, so I appreciate all you are giving up for me, and I'll do my very best so you'll never regret it, Irwin. You're wonderful doing all this for me. The colonel is getting nicer in my mind, as he's going to do what he can about you getting a permanent warrant. That will make everything lovely, won't it, Darling?

Say hello to Sergeant Cummings and Walt for me. (Who's he? I've never heard of him before.) It was quite nice of them to want to say hello to me. If I had any love to spare, I'd send it to them, but as you know, you have it all. How's my twin these days? I hope her husband gets home to her soon.

On the local paper tonight, there was an article describing how part of the American 28th Division invaded the outlying districts of Swansea. It described the artillery range at Penclawdd too. I was thrilled when I read it. Would you like to see it?

It's late, Irwin. You're sleeping by now, I suppose. Wish I could be in your arms, but it won't be very much longer before those nights when I can hug you all I want. I love you with all my heart, Darling, and miss you so much. Love me lots and dream about me.

All my love always,
Mary

June 2, 1945

My Darling,

It seems years since that wonderful Saturday night when I danced with you. Remember how we'd wait for the slow numbers before we'd get into the crowd? I just wanted to sit there looking at you. I did, most of the time. Neither of us said very much. I was so happy. Just couldn't believe it was true. I wish that day would hurry when I can be with you for always, Darling. Until then, I'll be contented with all those precious memories I have of you. Instead of doing all those things I could do if you were here, I came home after work, listened to the radio while I studied the clothes situation. I only have seven clothing coupons left. They have to last until August, and I want so many things. But there's always my dear brother Walter to rely on. The things I have to do for them, though. Press his clothes and supply him with cigarettes for a few months. It's no wonder he never wants to get married.

Went to Hazel's place for dinner today. I didn't have time to go home. I intended going out to eat, but she wouldn't go home without me, so I just had to go with her. I didn't want to go as Steve, her American brother she calls him, was home on leave, and I imagined they wouldn't want any visitors, but everything was all right. Steve is a very nice boy, or man I should say, has time for everyone. Told me all about his travels and his hometown. Couldn't understand everything he said, though. He has a funny accent, mixture of American and Yugoslavian. His hair is grey, and he looks a lot older than what he really is. When I saw him, I thought how wonderful you were. But he has a nice personality to compensate him. Why do you have everything, Darling? I'm so lucky, having your love. I don't love you just because you're good-looking, though. I love everything about you, but I love staring at you, do you mind? Did I tell you about the nice compliment Gwenda paid us? She said we looked as though we stepped out of a magazine the day she saw us. Do you like Gwenda now?

You nearly got rid of me this morning. I'd forgotten about all the extra traffic on the road now that people can use their cars and started to cross the road in front of a stationary bus, when a car came along. I missed it by a few inches. Shook me, though. I'll know better in future. Imagine me risking my life, when I have so much to live for now. These days are going so slowly. So different from those days when I was with you. Remember how we'd be on edge after ten o'clock waiting for Mrs. Humphreys to interrupt us with sandwiches? She wasted a lot of our time if she only knew. But she didn't think we could have fun, being alone so much. Only you and I understand that. We'll have to go out a lot after we're married. Otherwise, after a year of us together every night, we'll be total wrecks. We'll go dancing and get tired, and then you'll only have time to kiss me good night, before we'll both be sleeping. Can you imagine us being like that a few nights a week? It was wonderful sleeping with your arms around me. I'd settle for less than that right now. It's such a waste of time getting into my bed without you being here too. I'll just have to dream the rest for now, I suppose. That's too bad. I'm love-starved already, and you haven't been away very long. I know I'm terrible. It's your fault though. You shouldn't be so wonderful. I miss you so much, and I have so much love saved for you already.

Do you mind if I go now, Darling? I want to start dreaming so I can be with you. It's ten thirty now, so you must be thinking of me. I hope they're extra nice thoughts tonight. Love me lots as I love you and miss me all you can.

All my love always,
Mary

June 4, 1945

My Darling,

Had a nice little trip yesterday, quite unexpected too. I was just finishing work when Hazel came to the garage. Eddie was borrowing one of our cars for the day to take her and her sister and husband out. She ordered me to go home, have something to eat, and they'd pick me up. I didn't like the idea of spoiling a foursome, but she said she wanted me to come, and I wanted somewhere to go. We had a nice time. Went to a place about twenty-eight miles from here, Porthcawl. I believe you and Doc went there once. There's quite a good fairground near that place. They call it Coney Beach. I don't know whether it resembles Coney Island in any way, but it's lots of fun. We had something to eat at a nice place, then Eddie and Steve wanted a drink. The bars are open on Sunday there. That's why Eddie took us all that way, I suppose. We found a quiet place where you could have anything you wanted. I had one cocktail. It was good too. I felt funny after it. So I was afraid to drink any more, but we stayed there for quite a time as there was nowhere else to go after it started to rain. And it was too early to go home. When the place closed at ten o'clock, Eddie was quite merry, so I persuaded him to let me drive, so the four of them could sit at the back, and I'd be happy too. I'd liked Mr. Clement to have seen us. He'd have a fit if he knew that I was driving the best car in the garage. I was dreaming about us, wondering what it would be like to go for miles and miles in a car with you. You'd be driving, but I'd be so close to you. Maybe that's why I took the roundabout road home. They were singing sentimental songs all the way, and I felt so miserable and lonely. Eddie took over when we were nearing the town. I felt like driving for hours, but we had to consider Glamtax a little. I was quite tired when I got home, and though I'd had a nice time, I missed you more than ever. I imagined you had been with me all day, and we'd go to our home, then I'd fall to sleep in your arms. It's going to be so wonderful, Darling. Hazel said when we started out, "Wouldn't it be lovely if Irwin was with us." Lovely wouldn't be half of it. I talked to you instead of writing last night. I hope you don't mind, Darling. I was so tired.

Went to work this morning quite certain that there'd be a letter from you, as I saw a cross-eyed man on the bus. There were two wonderful letters from you. They rate a number of super kisses, Darling. I can imagine how you must feel amongst all those Germans. I feel pretty lonely on times, as I can't run around with girls who are looking for men. They'd get bored with my lack of interest. But at least I can say hello to people and listen to what they have to say. It must be terrible for you. I was reading an article on the paper about this no fraternizing rule. It was written by an English woman from Germany. She was saying it couldn't last. The British troops didn't suffer so much, as they weren't so far from home, and they had leaves quite often, but the Americans in these places who normally are so friendly with strangers are already having court-martials for more than just making friends. What she really wanted to say was that the Americans were so much more oversexed than the English, and that's why they suffered more. She suggested passes to Belgium or Paris for you very often as the only way out at present. I suggest my Irwin coming to see me every month, or me going to see him. I know you won't break the rule, though, because you're mine. Aren't you,

Darling? I don't mind where the Army sends us after we're married, wherever it is, as long as I'm with you, it's going to be heaven, and that's worth waiting and being lonely for. I do wish I was with you now, though.

Thanks, Darling, for the money. My collection is almost complete now. I could make a good business out of this foreign currency. Why didn't I think of it before? Besides what you've given me, I have Australian, South African, and Canadian coins that the drivers paid in, and I didn't notice until I got to the bank. I have to make good all those coins with my money, so that's a dead loss.

Why do you ask where I usually write my letters? You know. I told you. In bed, of course. That's when I get such nice thoughts, but I'm afraid to write half what I think. You might get the wrong impression, or maybe the right one.

It's strange I should be thinking of the wonderful times we could have when I was in that car yesterday. Then in your letter you tell me about going to Niagara Falls and Crystal Beach and being so happy. Don't you wish that we could start our life together when you wake tomorrow? I do, Darling.

My future husband is going to be a chief, or maybe he is now. I'm proud of you, Darling. I bet you feel pleased with yourself too. You have every right to be. I'll wear my bars and think how nice they must look on your shoulders. Wish I could fix them for you and congratulate you in the correct manner. I'll save a super kiss until I see you.

I hope by now that picture has arrived. It shouldn't take any longer than a letter as it was mailed the same way, so I can't see how it should be held up. Then Lieutenant Rankin won't take any more unnecessary trips, and my darling will like me. Why is Lieutenant Rankin so eager anyhow? Does he think I don't want you to have it? It does look that way though, but he's wrong. You know I'm all yours, so a picture isn't anything to me. I used that film you gave me this evening. Well, part of it. I could have screamed when Mother showed me a letter of my brother Ken asking for snaps of me and if my brother at home could take them indoors as he wanted to see me in the evening gown he bought. If he could only see that, he'd be disgusted with me. The top half of it is all right. There isn't much of it to ruin, so that's all he'll ever see of it. If the snaps turn out all right, I'll send them to you and have the negatives developed for my brother.

I got a good laugh out of that cartoon you sent me. I should have been mad. You thought, I thought you would expect. But I'm tickled at the big woman and the little man asking her so nicely. I'll do better than carry the tools though. I'll carry the car. Just think how nice you'll have to be to me then.

When I got home to lunch today, Mother was reading your magazines. She said they'd come this morning and made no further comment on them. I guess she was glad to have them, as I was. I've been reading my brother's books about explorers, just for something to read. I don't know what I'd do without magazines now. Thanks, Darling.

I told you about the men calling me Puddles, didn't I? This afternoon one of them was over the other side of the garage. I was in the office when he yelled, "Puddles!" Mr. Clement said, "Who's Puddles?" and before I realized it, I said, "I am." That's your fault. I felt so silly afterwards. I actually saw him smile, though.

Tomorrow I have a day off, but I have to do the housework in the morning. Mother is going away for the day, so no bed until one o'clock for me. I'd better get some sleep now. I want to dream such nice dreams. I love you lots, Irwin, and miss those wonderful kisses and everything about you. Keep loving me all you can. I'm all yours.

All my love always,
Mary

June 5, 1945

My Darling,

Wish we were eloping right now, or rather, I wish we had eloped and been married today. Then I wouldn't be here in bed on my own, listening to the rain pour down with no Irwin to hug. I'm right in the mood as I always am when I'm with you to pitch lots of woo.

I'd like to turn the light out and get so close to you and just forget about everything else. When I think of those times when we were alone with no lights, it seems just like a wonderful dream. When we are together for always and I don't have to go home just when I want to stay so much, life is going to be perfect, Darling. I'm going to be the luckiest person there is, having you for a husband and being able to see you shave every day. I had a big thrill watching you on those two occasions, thinking of how it's going to be when you're all mine. You're so wonderful, and I love you so much.

I've been busy today. Didn't have much to do this morning, though, as Mother did most of the housework before she left this morning. She must think I'm not capable or something. I cooked a good dinner after waiting at the butcher's for an hour to see if it was our turn to have meat. Luckily, it was. I would have been murdered if I had given my brother Spam. It was raining so much I decided I had to get a raincoat today. After being nice to my brother and getting the required number of coupons, I went into town and actually got what I wanted. I look like Red Riding Hood, so my brother told me. I went to a show. Was going to get a bus home, but I didn't want to go home to an empty house, and *Madonna of the Seven Moons* has been talked about quite a bit. It was really good, British too. The best show I've seen for a long time. All about a woman with a split mind living two lives. It was exciting. In one scene a man was trying to make love to a girl. She had an evening gown on, and one of her straps broke. I thought about you and wondered if that man knew of the nice remedy we have.

Came home this evening. My sister made supper for us. Then we played cards and awaited the return of Mother. I told her about my shopping, then she insisted on paying for the raincoat. I don't know what's wrong with her. She said it was a birthday present. That's about six presents I've had from her for one birthday. What I think is that she's sorry for what she said a few weeks ago. If anyone mentions Americans, she changes the subject quickly. Maybe she realizes that whatever she says about us will make no difference to the way I feel.

These are long days, Darling. I miss you terribly. Knowing you love me as I know now makes waiting much easier than it was before, though. I think that leave you had settled every doubt I had in my mind. You were wonderful to me. Those were the happiest days I've ever spent in my life. When you talked about going to the Riviera and all those lovely places instead of Swansea, I was scared in case you'd regret the choice you'd made. You didn't, did you, Darling?

British soldiers are protesting about the no fraternization now. You should see the letters written by English girls telling those men how they feel about it. My brother was teasing me about you going out with a nice German girl. I said "You can never tell," but I knew differently. I know you wouldn't have any difficulty at all in getting all the girls you wanted, but I have lots of faith in you as I know how I feel about going out with anyone else. I don't want even to think of losing you now. You're my whole world, and you have all my love. Have to go now. Miss me, Darling, and love me lots.

All my love always,
Mary

June 6, 1945

My Darling,

Happy nineteenth anniversary. Maybe I won't have to tell you by letter for very many more months. We'll be together celebrating as we should. Then when we lose count of the months, we'll still have two anniversaries every year. One on November 6, and I just wish I could say the other important date. Time will tell, though.

It doesn't seem possible that only a month ago today, we were both so happy. Even though I said such crazy things, I'll never forget May 6. It was all wonderful. If tonight could only be the same. I'd better stop dreaming right now. Otherwise, I'll never get this letter to my darling completed. I love you so much, my Irwin.

Do you know what I had on this special day? Three wonderful letters from you. You said everything I wanted to hear in those letters. Life is more than wonderful. I'm sure I'd hug you to death if you were here. Well, not to death as I want you all my life. But I'd hug you until it hurt. These letters were written on the twenty-fifth, twenty-ninth, and thirtieth. The one written on the twenty-fifth was by airmail, some air service that. I shouldn't bother with it anymore if I were you.

How can you say Charles is a piker when he makes love like that, even though he looks as though he's going to be sick. He bores me after my Irwin. I know all about love too. You taught me everything.

We could certainly do some gurgling with fifteen bottles of champagne, as well as the whiskey and gin. It's no fun gurgling on your own though. I'm glad you didn't use it all. The whiskey won't do you any harm when it has to last a month. I know, because I had half a bottle in a couple of hours, and it didn't affect me very much. Don't laugh at me. You were drunk too. Didn't we have fun, though?

I have heard "Coming Home to You." I often wondered if, when you listened to it, you thought about me. It's lovely, isn't it. Makes me feel like crying, too. There's a British number too, "When You Come Home to Me." I like it very much. There are a few lines in it that just make me ache to see you again. I keep thinking of them, all day. When you hear that song, think hard about me and remember how I'm missing and loving you every minute of the day.

You know what the Humphreys told me about service in the UK. I think they just wanted something to say. I'd want you to be as near to me as possible, you know that. But I can't imagine Americans getting those jobs when there are so many British soldiers wanting the same thing. Lots of things Mrs. Humphreys said didn't seem right, but you can't contradict her type. I'm more than grateful knowing that you're not going to the Pacific, and you know how near I'd like you to be to me, but it doesn't seem as though they're keeping even a few Americans in England any longer as last night there was a big farewell party to the American personnel who have been here since the beginning. I hardly think they'd send them home now and get new men to take their places. It would be more than wonderful if they sent you here or anywhere in England, where I could see you quite often. If you wanted to go to the States, maybe they'd send you here. The Army never seems to do the things you want them to do.

Eva gave a funny explanation for not showing up, didn't she? Even though she'd be jealous, she could have come to see you. I'd want to see anyone who'd recently been speaking to you. If Doc had come here before you did, I'd have been jealous too and excited at the same time. Then he could tell me how you were. It's a wonder Eva didn't come to see me since you left, in case I had any special news to tell her. I'm sorry for Doc if he feels that way about her. I'm glad I didn't mess my life up the way she did. It's tough getting a divorce here. I can remember Eva telling me that her husband always told her if she wanted a divorce, it would be all right by him. He must be pretty dumb, knowing how she runs around and still wanting to keep her when she has other plans. He has plenty of grounds for a divorce, but she has none as far as law is concerned. So there's nothing she can do about it. All I'm thankful for is that I'm not in her position.

If I could wish myself to you, Darling, I'd be with you right now. Then you'd know how lonely I am without you. And when you say you're missing me so much and want to have me in your arms, I wonder how much longer I can stand this loneliness. I need you and want you so much too, Darling. Let's elope tonight, but don't ask me to wait for the preacher. I can't. It's all right. I'm just love-crazy right now and feel as though I have to see you. You're going to have an awful time with me. I'm just warning you. It's going to be heavenly, though. You think so too, don't you?

It will be terrible for your sister when she gets your letter telling what happened to her husband as far as you know. Then she'll realize there's no use hoping any longer. It must be a hard thing to give up your hopes. Life can be very cruel, can't it? When I think what you went through, I'm so thankful, Darling.

Your brother must be wondering about your impatience with that lawyer. He is taking his time though. Maybe yours is one of his minor cases and doesn't think it's so important. If he only knew, he'd give it all his attention. We've waited too long already, but it's well worth waiting for a husband like you. And I know we're going to be so happy.

Wish I could take you away from that place and those Fräuleins. They're scheming females, aren't they? But they'd better keep their eyes off you, or else I'll start another war. I think they should send a few hundred British women who have worked in factories since the war over to settle those German things. I think they could do it too.

When I was reading your letters this morning, Connie, whose Canadian husband was killed, came to the office. I asked her where she was going, and she calmly said, "Canada." Then she started to cry, and I was trying to make her feel better, almost in tears myself. She was going to the station and asked if I would go with her as she felt terrible leaving everything behind with no one to see her off. Her mother died when she was very young, and her father doesn't approve of her making the trip. I felt so sorry for her. She's tiny, Irwin, and looked so lost getting on that train. She begged me to answer her letters, and maybe one day I could go see her, she said that, as Canada was only two hundred miles away. I hope she'll be terribly happy there. After losing Dutch, she needs some new interest to help her forget a little. Her husband was in the same squadron as the boy I went around with. We both knew all the boys in it, and they're all gone now. She said that if things had worked out right, I'd be going with her. I agreed with her, when I knew differently, really. They were all nice boys, and I liked them a lot, but Irwin is the only person I've ever loved and wanted so very much.

It's ten thirty now, Darling, and if the things I'm thinking are what you're thinking too, then we're going to have lots of fun in our dreams tonight. Wish it didn't have to be dreams. Love me all you can and miss me all the time.

All my love always,
Mary

June 7, 1945

My Darling,

It's still raining here. Maybe that's good as it seems the natural thing then for everyone to spend their evenings at home, and I don't get nagged about finding somewhere to go, not that it bothers me any when they do. It's just that I dislike people picking on me. I'm quite satisfied with my life and loving the best person in the world.

I had the lovely letter you wrote on June 1 today. Thanks, Darling, for being so wonderful to me. You asked me my reason for not writing from the eighteenth to the twenty-third. I remember missing the nineteenth and the twentieth. That's when I was at Mumbles, but those were the only two days, and I told you about that, so you had better keep track of your clerk, or maybe you'll think I've forgotten you, and I certainly don't want that to happen.

It's your turn to be boss in our family. I've been boss long enough now, don't you think? You can wear the pants, as the men at work say. I'll do anything you say, as long as I want to do it too. You wouldn't want me to leave my letters behind really, would you? I promise to carry them around myself, then when you get nasty with me, I'll show them to you. Wouldn't that be a mean thing to do?

I like the little bits of French you put in your letters, Charles. Reminds me of my happy days at the Riviera in the summer of '38, you know. Lashings of sunshine and simply oodles of love. Tout de suite. It's a good thing I know a little French, otherwise I'd be wondering what you meant. But in any language, I love you with all my heart, you American darling.

I know you want me as much as I want you, but I didn't know that anyone could act the way you did. That's why I said what I did that night, for which I humbly apologise, and I hope you know that I've never acted that way before, even when I've had some drinks. I've always had to do the fighting until it was clearly understood that I was no good-time girl. I have no desire to be one either, and I certainly do appreciate what you did for me, Irwin. It just convinces me more that you love me. At the time though, I didn't think that. I can't remember thinking anything except how wonderful you were. I've never been that drunk with anyone before, but I know, like I must have known then, that I could trust you.

This morning I saw those girls that work in the offices below. They kept asking me to go to this bungalow with them for a week in July, so now I'm going. I couldn't go very far away from here for my holidays, as I'll have to work a few mornings, so I decided it was a good idea they had, and they are nice girls. When it was all settled, they wanted me to go to Langland with them on Saturday and see what new men are around. I explained all over again how I spend my spare time when you're away, and I wouldn't spoil their fun at the bungalow if they invited anyone, as long as I wasn't included in the dates. I want to spend my spare time when I'm there swimming, if weather permits, and if they go to a dance, I'll go with them, but that's all. I have to go somewhere when I get my holidays to keep the peace at home. And when I told Mother what I was going to do, she was pleased about it and told me that John is staying at Langland until September. He went on Monday. If she only knew, this place is quite a few miles from him, and just what all these girls say about him, the dope. I wish it could be you and me going there. Imagine it, no neighbors. Just us to have all the fun we wanted. It's one of the beaches where very few people go. It's good for swimming too. There's a hotel about a mile away, where we can eat so we don't have much cooking to do. We were making all these plans when their manager walked in. He's great. Asked me to tell him where I'd been and who I'd met the last few weeks. He wouldn't believe me when I told him where I'd been, at home, almost every evening, reading and writing. I must have been talking there for almost an hour. Mr. Clement wasn't at the office when I got back though, so I had nothing to worry about.

Mother asked if she could meet me from work and then go to a show this evening. That suited me all right. We went to see *And So Tomorrow*. It was very good. Loretta Young was in it. Alan Ladd was her doctor. He's nice. Not as nice as my Irwin, though.

Now I'm in bed alone again. It's not nice when I know how different it could be. There I go again. I'm getting terrible, but you are wonderful, Darling, and I love you so very, very much, as you know. Be good and love me all you can. I'm missing you terribly, Irwin. Why? I'll be with you in a little while after I make myself comfortable the best way I can, alone in this bed. Dream nice dreams, Honey.

All my love always,
Mary

June 9, 1945

My Darling,

Why can't I be with you when I miss you so terribly? I'll never see enough of you, Irwin. I love you so very, very much, and it doesn't take Saturday nights to convince me of the fact, except I just think about what we could do if you were with me.

Yesterday, loads of magazines came from you. They're lovely, Darling. Thanks ever so. I read them last night until I felt sleepy. I sent to bed and started to write, but my eyes kept closing all the time, until they finally got the best of me. I'm sorry, Darling, though I had lovely dreams last night about us.

While having breakfast this morning, Mother handed me two letters from you. I was waiting for anything she may have to say, but nothing was said. Having your letters was the only good thing that happened today. I put money on a horse. Everyone does on Derby Day. It was a cert, and Lady Irwin owned it, so I thought it had to win, but it didn't. And I mustn't complain as yesterday we had a gamble between us at work, and I drew the winner, making me four pounds richer than I was before. After my horse letting me down today and spoiling my lunch hour through listening to the race on the radio, Mr. Clement asked me when I was taking my holidays. I told him the second week of July, and he calmly told me to make other arrangements as that's when he's taking off. Now I can't go to that Bungalow with those girls as they can't change their plans, I know. I haven't seen them to tell them about it yet, but I know they'll be mad. I'm not so upset about it though. I was more annoyed at Mr. Clement than anything else. Even though he's the manager, he could at least have asked me if it was convenient for me to postpone my holidays. It will be as good as a holiday to get rid of him for a week though. He was in an awful mood today. Told me to tell the telephonists to stop smoking when they're on duty. It looks bad and added, he noticed that I didn't smoke, so they needn't either. When he said that, I almost laughed at him. Can't think how I kept a straight face.

Came home tonight. Nobody to bother me, so I was going to write you an extralong letter. Just about to start when my brother and his wife walk in. I can't understand them one bit. He left her with me and went for a walk. She's going to Liverpool for a week tomorrow without him. I can't ever imagine us doing that, and they haven't been married two years yet. I had to be nice to her for four hours. She told me she never wanted any children. She'd die if she thought it would happen to her. I thought she must have been kidding, but she meant it, all right. I don't wish her any harm, but I hope she's presented with triplets one day. Her chief topics are clothes and all the select people she knows. Four hours listening to that is no joke. I was glad to see my sister coming home, to take over for a bit, so I could make supper without her watching every move I made. I thought I'd never get to bed so I could be alone with my thoughts, but I made it before ten thirty. Did you think nice things tonight, Darling? You'll never guess what my thoughts were.

I did say "Me too" once when you were here, only you were so busily engaged in biting my ear that you didn't hear it. You know I love you more than you love me, Darling, so don't lets argue about it again, but I'm sure we have enough love between us to last more than a lifetime, and that's what really matters.

Your wife isn't losing any time in getting married again, is she? It's a good thing, really. It's going to work out that way, isn't it? As long as you don't mind the thought of her wanting to get married again, I guess you don't love her as I said you did. What would you do to me if I were near you, after making a remark like that. I want to tell you, Irwin, what I thought since I met you until you came here this time. You can say I'm crazy if you want to after hearing this. Well, I had the impression that you loved your wife very much. Then she hurt you, but what she did didn't stop you loving her. Then when you came here, you wanted someone to fall in love with you to redeem yourself in your own eyes, and it had to be me. It was easy to love you, even when I tried so hard not to and made so many resolutions never to see you again. Then when you left here, I thought I'd forget about you gradually. Instead I loved you and missed you more every day and envied your wife so much for having you. Since I've seen you again, I realize how very wrong I was, and I just know that we will be together for always. I'm so glad I love you, Darling. You're just wonderful.

Do you mind if I kiss you good night now? It's getting late, and I want to see you in my dreams. Love me as I love you. Then I'll be more than happy. Miss me lots and dream about me.

All my love always,
Mary

June 10, 1945

My Darling,

It's only nine o'clock and already I'm in bed, but I'll keep awake until ten thirty so I can think hard about you and know that you are thinking of me too. Isn't it awful to think of you alone in bed there, and here I am with only wonderful memories and thoughts of the happy future in store for us to keep me company. What I wouldn't give to have you here right now. You certainly wouldn't sleep tonight. You wouldn't mind, would you, Darling?

As soon as I got up this morning, I thought it's Sunday, and it's raining. Irwin and I would have to sleep late today. I'd go after the Sunday paper for you, Darling. Then I would come back to bed again. Couldn't I ever sit on the bed and glance at the headlines before getting your breakfast? You just wait and see what will happen. Instead of all the things that could make Sunday a wonderful day, the driver makes an awful noise with his car, waking the whole family and all the neighbors, and I have to go to work. It was quite an eventful morning. (I'll leave for a couple of minutes. I can hear my mother and brother discussing me downstairs. They've said what they wanted to now. My brother asked where I was, and Mother went on to tell him that she can't understand why I should be like this, believing in you and not going anywhere, and that's all I heard.) This morning at work, Mr. Clement told me that he had some news for me. I thought it was the Cardiff proposition again, but it was worse. Our supervisor here is going to be manager of a depot we've bought at Cornwall, a few hundred miles from here. He knows very little about the office part of it and the income tax system, so Captain Evans had the bright idea of me going with him. I have to go. I can't change my job as I'm still in a reserved occupation, unless, of course, I'd like to work in a factory. I'm supposed to start work at that place on August 16. Mr. Clement told me it was a nice place, and they'd find somewhere for me to stay. I told Mother about it. She thought it was a wonderful chance for me, naturally, but I'll do my very best to get out of it.

This is all the paper I have left in my room. I'll write an extralong letter tomorrow to make up for this stingy one. You know I love you with all my heart, so keep loving me, Darling.

All my love always,
Mary

June 11, 1945

My Darling,

Lonely? Me too. But I had two lovely letters from you this morning. You still love and miss me, so I have very little to complain about but how I wish I was with you. I miss you an awful lot, Irwin. Save that bottle of cognac. I'll be with you in a few seconds. Wouldn't we have fun?

They're certainly keeping you waiting for that promotion, but it will seem better to you after waiting so long. I guess I have no option about being boss now, since I have the insignia. Couldn't I give you some orders, like come here as soon as you can?

The roads here are certainly filled with cars now. Almost every one of the men at work bring their own cars to work, but nobody lives my way so I can have a ride home. I'll believe you are the best one-arm driver in existence, though I've met people who drive without using any arms at all, but I wouldn't look for any better one than you, Darling. I'm pretty good at changing gear for one-arm drivers too, so we should get along fine, or maybe you have cars that change gear themselves, so I won't have to think of those things.

What are you going to do to help the colonel's orchestra? Don't tell me you're going to learn to play something. I often wish I could do something like that, but I'm hopeless. Before my brother joined the RAF, he was crazy about becoming a pianist. I think he had four lessons, and every time I went home, I'd either hear him finding the wrong notes, or he'd be learning Morse with his friend, and that buzzing in my ears would almost drive me crazy until I decided the best thing to do was get interested in it. That was a fine idea until I started asking questions. Then I'd be told what to do with myself, in no gentle manner.

I know the Colonel's Wren friend. She was at that party in Penclawdd, not in uniform though. That tall blonde girl. You remember. When I stay at Nancy's place, I see her a lot, and she always smiles very sweetly at me. She's a permanent fixture in a cocktail bar about six miles out of town. I think that's where the colonel spent most of his time when he was here. I hope he comes here soon so that you can come here again before very long. Please come, whether you have your divorce or not. I want to see you so much, Darling, and it seems years since you were here. It's a wonderful idea you have of buying the rings in any case, even though our engagement will be a secret between us until that wonderful day. The place I talked about in Scotland has been banned since the war, as people were taking too much advantage of it, resulting in a good many bigamous marriages. No witnesses or anything were needed. You could go there at a minute's notice, no waiting three days for the usual formalities. It would be just the place for us, wouldn't it, Darling? I don't think we should go as far as Scotland now. It will take too much time getting there. We can't afford to waste any more precious time than is necessary at a time like that. The three days that we have to wait will be too long as it is. I'll have to find a place between now and then. Every time I think of it, I'm all excited. I can't believe it's true, me having you for always. I think you'll have to hold me up, not me hold you. Talking of weddings, one of our men drove a bride to be to the Civic Centre this morning, and the bridegroom didn't show up. The poor girl almost broke her heart. I feel sorry for her. It must be an awful sensation, having to go home again. Don't you dare be late on our wedding day, Darling, otherwise, I'll go crazy, and you wouldn't like to have a crazy wife, would you? I promise I won't be late in case you change your mind before I get there.

That course you talked about for occupation troops seems a very good idea. But I looked for that place, Shrivenham, on the map, and it isn't in Britain at all according to that. So I looked up the index of all the places in the world to find out just where it was, but it doesn't exist. Maybe the map was an old one, and that place wasn't listed. As long as it's in England, I'll come see you.

You did tell me about your wife being anxious to get married again, Darling. She evidently doesn't believe in waiting for anything, even though she lives upstairs, and he lives downstairs. They say that married life is fine for people who aren't married, but I don't know. I don't care what she does as long as she wants a divorce. In fact, I don't want to think of her at all, but I wanted to be sure that you didn't want her anymore, as if we should get married, because what she did annoyed you and you persuaded yourself that you didn't love her anymore and then you'd go back to the States and meet her and realize you could forgive her. Well, I wouldn't want to take you away from her. I'm satisfied now, though, that she means very little to you. Naturally, I wouldn't expect you to forget about her altogether, but I'm sure I can make you happier, much happier, than she did.

I worked until seven o'clock this evening. They really mean business about me going to Cornwall. Mr. Clement is on my side though. He doesn't want me to leave him. I'm determined I won't go there, whatever I do. Came home this evening. My sister's boyfriend was here. We played cards until he won enough money to take my sister to a show tomorrow night, but he did offer to take me as well. Now I'm in bed again. Realizing how much I want to be yours for always, just as I am now. I love you, my Darling. See you in my dreams. I promise not to be awful tonight.

All my love always,
Mary

June 12, 1945

My Darling,

It's ten thirty, the time when you're sure to be thinking of me. Wish I could know what your thoughts are now. If they're anything like mine, they're wonderful. I'll tell you about them one day, after we're married.

I had extra dreaming time today. Stayed in bed until twelve o'clock. I wouldn't have if I had known there was a letter from you downstairs, the one you wrote on our nineteenth anniversary, a lovely letter as usual. I heard General Eisenhower's speech on the radio. He's an excellent speaker. That's all people are talking about today. Then I had good old Spam for lunch while they were playing "The Star Spangled Banner." An all American session.

We're having terrible weather here. It was raining all the afternoon, so I stayed at home and read your magazines. This evening, Mother and I went to the theatre to see some of Carroll Lewis's discoveries. It was good too. He invited a soldier from the audience on to the stage then asked him if he was married and if it was his wife he had with him. The soldier said he was married but had somebody else's wife with him tonight. There was a roar of laughter when Carroll Lewis said, "A Yank from Swansea."

I wonder why they're holding up all the English mail? I'm scared in case you think I'm not writing. But you do know that I love you for always, don't you, Darling? So don't have any crazy ideas like me being talked out of bothering with you. Whatever anyone says, I can't change my mind about you, ever. I want to be all yours so much, and as long as there's the chance of that desire being fulfilled, I'll wait, just as I'm waiting now.

So the colonel is paying another visit to England. Wish it was my Irwin coming to see me. You asked if I could stand you another seven days, as though you didn't know how I loved every minute I was with you when you were here. And you know just how willing I am to spend the rest of my life with you, Darling. You're so very wonderful. No wonder I love you the way that I do.

You must have been awfully proud when you were given the Bronze Star. I'm proud of you too, Darling, but I can't realize that you want me to keep it for you. I'd love to, Irwin, and esteem it as a great honour, especially when you went through so much for it. I'll keep it safe for you, so you can wear it when they have parades.

Your prediction for this time next year sounds wonderful to me, but I'll never get used to being addressed as Mrs. Deems. I'll always have a thrill out of it. I'll be so happy then, Darling. I'll have everything I've ever wanted when I have you for good.

I'm glad I don't have anyone sleeping with me these days, as Hazel was telling me she sleeps with her sister, and her husband's just returned to Germany. When Hazel got into bed the other night, her sister put her arms around her and kept saying "Steve darling" all night. I wonder what I say in my sleep?

Have to go now, Darling. I love you and miss you all I can. Love me lots, Irwin, and be good.

All my love always,
Mary

June 13, 1945

My Darling,

It's a beautiful night for love, a nice moon, and lots of stars. Wish you were here. Then I could appreciate them a lot more, though I don't need any stars or moon to put me in the mood for love when you're around.

There's a Victory Party at the club where I'm a member tonight. All the drinks are free. The men tried to persuade me to go with them tonight, but I knew how it would be. A nonstop drinking party ending up in somebody's house, and I don't want to gurgle without you, Darling, especially with people like Brookman around. He came to the garage this afternoon to find out, in a roundabout way, if I was going tonight. He's going down with Eva and her friend. He told me all the news about her, as though I should know. Her friend has a wonderful car, so she's going places, all right.

Heard our song, "Coming Home," tonight. It will be wonderful when you'll be coming home to me every day after work. Then I'll only have a few hours each day to wait for you. So you can imagine how I feel now, waiting for you. But I love waiting when I know it means being with you for always when things come right. I know I love you. There's no doubt in my mind about that. And one of the reasons I'm so sure is the way I'm so content with staying at home. However exciting people make a party or a dance sound, it holds no interest for me if I can't be going with you. I do love you very, very much, Irwin, and I'm so happy about it.

I should visit Mrs. Humphreys again, but she's so difficult to get along with. She's pleasant, all right, but the queer way she looks at me and little things she says make me awfully uncomfortable. Have you written to her yet? She had expected a letter from you just after you left here. You are her son, remember? You'd better tell Doc to write to his mother too.

I was going to see Nancy tonight. Her mother phoned today and said she wasn't so good, but I worked late and wanted something to eat before I went anywhere. There was nobody here when I came home, and by the time I fixed my food, it was too late to go out again. I'll have to go tomorrow night now.

Remember that American that wanted you to drive his Bewick for him? I saw him today and his Bewick. It's a wreck. It has USA WSA written on it. This it's something to do with the war shipping. So I apologise for saying he was in the Intelligence Department. You're always right anyway.

Met Mrs. Bent this afternoon. She sends her love. Her husband's in hospital here. He's in a bad way too, but she's just the same. Nothing seems to upset her. She had news for me too, but I don't think it's right. Gwenda's married. She went away without telling her people as they didn't approve altogether, and she had a quarrel with them. I haven't heard from Gwenda for a few weeks, and I'm wondering if that's that reason, but I have my doubts. She wouldn't have the nerve to do a thing like that. She's always done exactly as her father said. You can never tell, though.

When I got up this morning I was minus my pyjamas, and I did put them on last night. Wonder how this happened. Must have had a tough night. Perhaps I was dreaming again. It's ten thirty, so I mustn't think those things now, must I? Good night, my darling. Miss me all you can. You're wonderful.

All my love always,
Mary

June 15, 1945

My Darling,

It seems a lonely world, not having a letter from you for three days. I know that's not a long time and nothing to complain about, but I want you to tell me every day that you love me. I want your love so much, Irwin, as I love you, well, I just can't explain how, but I don't think of anything but you all day, and then at night I find you in my dreams. I have tea every morning at eleven o'clock, so I can sit down, and my thoughts are undisturbed. I imagine myself with you, and you're telling me all that's happened and what you've been doing. Then at ten thirty each night, I'm in bed, and I have entirely different thoughts. You're not miles away. We're in our home, and I'm in your arms. It makes no difference how I think of you, or when, you're always as wonderful as anyone could be. I keep hoping so much that the day will come very soon when I won't have to wait for letters, but I can pester you to death until you say you love me. I'm awfully impatient, Darling, when I think how happy we're going to be. I can't realize that I'm so lucky as to have those dreams in store.

This evening I had another lecture about the way I'm staying in, but from a new angle this time, as though she pitied me. My brother had to have his say too. He can't see why anyone with any sense would waste their time the way I am. It doesn't make me feel a bit sorry for myself though, only more determined that, for my part, nothing will come between us. We had a letter from my brother in the RAF today. All his squadron were sent home from Italy, except him. He's in Algiers and terribly disappointed about it. I think that's what upset Mother today, and she had her revenge on me.

Don't know why, but I'm awfully tired, so I'll leave you now, Darling. Love me all you can.

All my love always,
Mary

June 16, 1945

My Darling,

Been to Langland this afternoon. One of the girls wanted to celebrate her birthday, so we went to the tea-dance. It was pretty crowded there. We couldn't find a table for tea. That was a good excuse for them to decide the bar was the next best thing. As soon as we went there, these girls met some RAF men they knew. They joined the party. There was only beer to drink. One glass was more than sufficient for me. In any case, I didn't feel like drinking. We had tea and danced until the band took a break before starting the dance tonight. We sat around for a while. The same people go there, but it seems to be different somehow. Nobody is interested in the dance itself. One of the girls had to go back to the office. It's her night on the phones, and she was late, so we decided to get a taxi. While we were waiting for it, the rest of the girls drifted off, one by one with the RAF. They were staying for the dance tonight in any case. An American officer came on to me and said, "Hello, Mary." I didn't know who he was but wondered if I'd met him at Langland before. Then he asked me if I still heard from you. This had me puzzled, but he wouldn't satisfy my curiosity unless I stayed with him for the dance tonight, so I'm still no wiser as the taxi came just about then, and it was no effort to leave there. Every man had that certain look, lots of old men too. It seems anything but a nice place to go. I'm glad I love you the way I do, Irwin, so I have no desire to go to these places.

Didn't get a letter again today. I get worried after hearing from you practically every day since you left and then a four-day silence. I'm thinking all kinds of things. Maybe you've been sent to the States. That's much too far away from me to make me feel happy about it. Then I think about what Mother said about burning your letters, but I don't think I need worry about that. She said something about there not being any letters for me today. Is there any need for me to worry about you not loving me anymore? That's the worst fear of all. By the time we're together for always, Darling, I'll be a nervous wreck, keeping my fingers crossed that you won't change your mind. It's a sure thing I won't hear from you tomorrow as it's Sunday. Think I'll dream about the things I want to hear you say now. I love you with all my heart, Irwin, and miss you terribly.

All my love always,
Mary

June 17, 1945

My Darling,

It's been a wonderful day as far as the weather was concerned, but I've missed you terribly, Irwin, more than the usual, and that's saying something. That day can't come too soon when I don't have to rely on memories to be with you. I want you all to myself. I'm not selfish. It's just that I love you an awful lot. You know that, though.

Eddie and Hazel said they'd come for supper this evening, so I didn't bother to go out this afternoon, just lazed around in the garden covered with oil, trying to get tanned. You can imagine what I looked like. Then my brother's friend, who used to spend most of his time at our house, came with his girlfriend. She must have thought I was crazy. I didn't worry about it though. They stayed for tea and were just ready to leave when my brother and his wife walked in. The conversation started all over again. Then Mother went to church. It was only poor me left with them. I was expecting Hazel about six o'clock, but Eddie kept her waiting, and they arrived at nine o'clock. She kept nagging him all the time they were here. We had six extra people for supper. It was almost a party, except that they left around eleven thirty. I came upstairs at ten thirty, so I could think hard of you for ten minutes without people disturbing me.

My sister's boyfriend is going to the Navy next week. She's awfully upset about it. She asked me tonight if I thought he'd forget about her when he went away. As if I knew how he felt about her. I told her he wouldn't. He'd miss her more instead. She's funny too. Before today, I thought he didn't mean very much to her. But she told me she's not going out with anyone else, and maybe we could go swimming together in the evenings now. I hope Mother doesn't keep telling her how silly she is, the way I've heard it all day today. I think my sister would believe her, but I won't believe that until you tell me, Darling.

I hope I get a letter tomorrow. Otherwise, it's going to be an awful day. Captain Evans is visiting us, and I have to tell him what I think about the journey he has planned for me, and that's not good.

Please keep loving me all you can, Darling, and miss me lots. I love you more and more all the time. You're wonderful.

All my love always,
Mary

June 18, 1945

My Darling,

It's been a lovely day for me today. I had two extra special letters from you. Your bronze star came in perfect condition, and when I saw it, I realized how much you love me. You let me keep it for you when it must mean a lot to you. I was proud of you all over again, Irwin. I hope it's always in my keeping because then you'll be with me too. I also received some more magazines. You know how acceptable those always are, and this notepaper I'm using came with the magazines. Thanks loads, Darling, for everything.

I saw Captain Evans today, and my little war is over. I don't have to go to Cornwall, or anywhere else. He was very nice to me and explained that he thought I'd like a change. I was expecting something different from that, but I'm glad that's settled.

It's been terribly hot. I spent most of the afternoon with the girls in their office eating ice cream and listening to their adventures at Langland last Saturday night. I don't know if I was supposed to envy them, but I listened to everything they said and formed my own opinion. All I know is that I'm the luckiest person in the world having your love and being able to love you so much.

Came home this evening and sunbathed in the garden until it began to get chilly. Then I had a nice bath and came to bed. It's too warm for pyjamas tonight. What can I do about it? Oh, Irwin, you know I can't do a thing like that.

There's no sense in the way they're holding my letters back. I'm glad you don't think that I've forgotten you. That need never enter your head though. I'm yours for always, as long as you want me, that is. Say you'll always want me, Darling. That's what I want to hear. It would be an awful world if I had to let you go now, but I don't want to think about it. I want to be at your side as soon as I can, for as long as I can. Then life will be really wonderful. I know. I've dreamed about it, and that's all I think about when I'm awake. Don't have any dreams about going to the Pacific, Darling, even though I'd be in Buffalo waiting for your return. When you know I'm waiting though, why don't you come to me before you wake up. That would be the best part of the dream.

I thought I told you that Webb's wife was going to the States this month, so she doesn't work anymore. It was announced on the radio yesterday that no more English wives of Americans could go to the States for another year. That's tough on some of them, but there are too many people with good reasons waiting to go now, and they are paying their passage, so it makes a difference.

I'm sure too, Darling, that ours is a real match. I'll never fail you, and there's no need to thank me for loving you. I'm so glad I am able to because you're the most wonderful person in the whole world to me, and you're going to make me so happy. We'll both be very, very happy though.

That's wonderful news about them flying company grade officers to England as long as you're one of them. I have enough love, of all kinds, including hugs and kisses, saved for you already, to last forever. I just wish you could make use of it right now. I'm lonely, Darling, and I miss you so terribly. It gets worse every night when I get into bed and you're not there too. I could give you the biggest hug you've ever had in your life right now. Do you want it? Well, what are we waiting for?

Nancy isn't expecting the baby until August. What are you so impatient about anyway? I haven't heard a sound from Junior since you left, Irwin. He only makes a noise when you're around. I have our house all built now. I'll see if I can draw a plan to see if you approve of it. You'd better. I think it's super. I've decided you can name our little girl, and I'll name our son. Is that all right by you? I won't criticize any name you suggest as long as my little boy is left to me. Isn't that nice of me?

Now I've got to close my eyes and make believe all the wonderful things that could be. You know what I'm wishing right now. I love you so much, Irwin.

All my love always,
Mary

June 20, 1945

My Darling,

You're taking up a lot of room in the bed tonight. Move over or else I'll be on the floor. You wouldn't want that to happen, would you? I'm not crazy, Irwin, it's just my imagination again, nice though. I know you'd like all these things I imagine to come true just as much as I do. So we're going to have lots of fun when it's all possible.

I had two wonderful letters from you today and also the snaps. When I look at you, I want to be with you so much 'cause you're more than wonderful, Darling, and I love you so very much. Doesn't Smiley look funny? He's buried under that thing on his head. Sergeant Cummings looks nice though, but nothing like my Irwin. You're my one and only pin-up boy. I did have a wonderful feeling when I opened your letter and saw the snaps. I hope you feel just as good when you get my picture. I don't mind seeing your arms around girls as long as they're not over sixteen. I wonder if those little girls realized how lucky they were. Have you had our snaps developed yet? I know I'll look terrible in them, so I'm in no hurry to see them.

Gwenda came to meet me this afternoon. She's getting married on July 2. We had tea and then went to see *Between Two Women*. It wasn't too bad. Gwenda kept talking about her wedding all through the show, so I couldn't concentrate very well. If the weather's nice next Sunday, her future husband is taking her for a nice long ride in his car, so she said she'd pick me up, and I could go along too. I said he might not like the idea, but Gwenda is boss. She said, "He'll have to like it." She wants me to see their home. It's supposed to be a dream. The only thing that's worrying her is her father. He's against the whole thing, so she has her troubles too. Anyway, Darling, we can't take her to our bungalow and hang her on a hook as you suggested. She'll be very much married by that time, and we couldn't find a hook that strong. She's been on the farm for a couple of weeks, and it's made a big difference to her weight. I want to be alone with you with nobody to listen to the things I have to say. Just you to hear me snoring, as you say I do, and you should know, I guess. I heard you snore too as I was awake before you that wonderful morning. You had your arms around me, and my arms were around you. I could have stayed that way forever. Even though I was drunk the night before, it seemed quite natural to wake and see you there, but it was heavenly, just the same.

Do you think you could possibly get a job at Southampton? Irwin, that would be perfect. It would be easy for me to get there almost every weekend until we can get married. Then I can be with you all the time. The way the mail situation for you at present is certainly seems to indicate that they're very uncertain as to where the mail should be sent. I've been thinking that ever since you said about not having my letters, because I've written almost every day. You know that your letters telling me about that aren't one little bit monotonous. If you weren't concerned about it, then I'd start worrying. I don't know what I'd do without your letters. They're all so wonderful, and I'm so sure you love me when I read them.

Of course I'm saving all my kisses for you. You know that only you can make withdrawals on this account. I'm more than starved for your kisses, Darling, and I'm all ready to play house, but you won't play. I love you with all my heart, Irwin, and miss you so very, very much.

All my love always,
Mary

June 24, 1945

My Darling,

Missed me? Sorry I haven't written since Wednesday, Irwin, but we've all been excited at home. My brother Ken walked in on us Thursday morning, and after not seeing him for almost four years, you can imagine how we felt. He flew back to Algiers this morning, so he had a lot to say during his brief stay, and he doesn't expect to see us for fourteen months again.

Yesterday I had four wonderful letters from you and intended writing last night in case you started thinking those things that I don't ever want you to think, but after supper, my brother started telling us about his travels, and it was two o'clock this morning before any of us got to bed. It's been that way the three nights he was here. You're not mad because I didn't write you, are you, Darling? You know I love you more than anyone else in the whole world. The letters I received today were written on the eighth, fifteenth, sixteenth, and seventeenth. You're certainly wonderful, Irwin.

Don't you ever call me Puddles. They've forgotten about it at work, and I don't need any inducement to change my name to yours, Darling. That's my greatest ambition, remember? But honest, I don't like the name Puddles one bit.

Thanks for the snaps. Doc hasn't changed one bit, has he? It doesn't look like my Irwin, though, and I've stared at you so much and so hard that I should know how wonderful you really look. I felt so good when you said to take a good look at it because you're my husband. I really do feel as though you're my husband, Darling, and it's a beautiful thought. I feel awfully pleased with life when I think of having your love and you for all my life when things are settled. Until then, it's very easy for me to wait for you. I have wonderful memories, and you write such super letters that all I think about is you, and you have all my love for always too. I just wish our life together could begin right now. I miss you so very, very much, Darling.

You know I don't mind where I go as long as I'm with you, Irwin, and that clipping about wives etc. joining the men on the continent certainly means as much to me as it does to you. Tell me, Darling, do you really believe that I love you beyond all imagination and that I want to be with you always? Sometimes I have my doubts, as you ask me some crazy questions. I didn't suggest waiting a year and a half before having our daughter. You did, Darling, remember? You were quite emphatic about it. I'd like her right away. You know best, after all. I'd like to see your face if it should be a boy first. As long as you don't leave me alone in the evenings because you don't like to hear the baby crying. I think it would be perfect, don't you? Wish that time would fly so that all these dreams can come true.

Friday night, my brother borrowed a car, and he took me all around the coast, fifty miles to the farthest point. It's a little beach called Oxwich. He's crazy. I thought my end had come. He drove the car along the water's edge and then decided he wanted to swim. It was pouring with rain. I called him all the dopes, but he went in. Then I had to help dig the car out of the sand. We eventually got it out, and I fell in the hole we had dug. I've got to laugh when I think about it. On the way back, he saw an officer from the aerodrome here, so we gave them a lift. He was with a girl, and they wanted to see the church that's supposed to be haunted. It's on the cliff's edge. A tiny place hundreds of years old, surrounded with family vaults of noted families. When we arrived there it was dusk, and this girl tried to talk them out of going through the gates, but they insisted. Everything looked eerie. I was scared stiff, but we followed them into the church. It was dark inside, and the next thing, my brother and this other boy ran out and locked the door, leaving us alone. I could feel ghosts around me, and this other girl started to get hysterical. She couldn't open the door. When my brother heard us screaming, he let us out, then lit the lamps in the church so that people living around would wake up in the middle of the night and think the ghosts were having a night out. We took this officer back to the aerodrome. Then we went right through it. Saw planes landing on the runways, until I was tired of seeing them. My brother took us to see the plane he brought over, his wife as he calls it. Then we had coffee at the officers' mess before we came home. I never thought I'd get back in one piece. I told him I'd never go in a car with him again, and I meant it too. That was a night I'll never forget. It's a good thing he doesn't drink. I can't imagine what would happen if he did. He's not at all interested in girls, either, and it isn't that he wouldn't have a chance. Mother told him about the way I spend my time at home since you've left here. He said that all the Americans he knew were the best people he'd ever met and added that I knew what I was doing, so she shouldn't interfere. I could have kissed him for that.

I just wish I could put into words how I long to be with you again. It doesn't seem to be me here at all, as all my heart and thoughts are with you constantly. Without you, nothing seems worthwhile, Darling. You're my everything, and if I can hold your love for always, nothing else can worry me. I'd give anything to hear you say that you'll always love me right now. Then you'd be so close to me, and it would be just like those nights when you were here, as though you'd never been away. I dream so much about being with you that when I am, it seems the natural thing. I just hope that my dreams of being your wife will be realized, just as my dreams of you coming here for leave were. But please, Darling, if you can come here again, even though we couldn't get married, come, as already it seems like years since I saw you.

I'll keep that medal safe for you to show our son. Then he'll be proud of his father, just like his mother is. I won't tell our daughter, I promise, about what I did for America. She'll know, as I know now that I'm so lucky to have your love, and anyway, I wouldn't risk losing your kisses for three whole nights. I can't imagine you coming home in the evening without kissing me. I'll never have enough of your kisses, Darling.

It's ten thirty now, Irwin, and I'm awfully tired but ready for your love just the same. I love you and love you and love you so very much. A big kiss now, please, then I won't bother you any more tonight, much.

All my love always,
Mary

PS: Please excuse ink blots, please. My pen is leaking. I love you.

June 25, 1945

My Darling,

You know something? I think that I'd love you to death if you were here tonight. I'm right in the mood for all the kisses you have saved for me. You're more than wonderful, and I miss you so terribly.

When I got to the garage this morning, one of the men said, "There's a letter from your Irwin in the office." Before he told me, I felt good. The weather was wonderful, and everyone seemed happy. You should have seen the way I ran up that ramp to see if there really was a letter from my darling, as though I hadn't heard from you in weeks. But every letter you send means so very much to me. When you aren't here to tell me all the things I want to know. It was a perfect day after having that letter, the short one you wrote on the nineteenth, but nevertheless lovely.

What's all the extra work in aid of? I could help you. I don't have enough to do these days, and you have to work until one thirty.

That's bad. They can't do that to my husband. I started work at nine thirty this morning. Mr. Clement arrived at ten thirty, in one of his confidential moods, and kept me talking until twelve o'clock. When he's that way, I have to hear everything from the cars to the directors, and he keeps saying, "Just between us two," making everything seem such a big secret. Then I went below to see the girls. They went to Langland on Saturday and had a super time. There's a new squadron come in, all New Zealanders. They tried all ways to persuade me to go on Thursday, but they've had it. Elaine, the nicest of the girls, asked if I'd go to a show with her tonight. That suited me fine, so we made arrangements, and then I went home for lunch. Everyone at home seemed in an extra good mood, so I went back to work happy. Didn't have much to do. One of the men went out for ice cream, and I sat on the roof sunbathing and reading your letter over and over again, until it was time to go for Elaine. We went had tea at the Albert Hall. Then went to see *Here Come the Waves*. Bing was good, and there were some lovely songs in it. "Black Magic" and "I Promise You" are two I like very much. We had more ice cream in the show, so everything was nice. Elaine lives at Penclawdd, almost opposite the place where you were stationed, so she had to leave early to get her bus home. I like her very much. We're going swimming tomorrow, weather permitting, of course. Wish I was going with you, but one day I know we'll be able to do all those things together.

Did you love having twelve letters in two days? I wish I could tell you exactly how I feel about you, but somehow it doesn't seem right when I write, as if there aren't any words to express how very much I love you. I do love you with all my heart, Darling. Even when you're here, I want to tell you so much, and then when I do, I never get to saying what I mean to. I'm dumb, I guess, but you know how I love you, even though I didn't say anything.

Have to go now. After working so hard all day, a girl needs some sleep. Love me all you can, Darling, and miss me lots.

All my love always,
Mary

June 26, 1945

My Darling,

It's rained all day, so no swimming. Instead, I went to Elaine's place to Penclawdd and had quite a nice time. When I saw that camp, I was thinking how perfect it would be if you were still there, but that even would be too far away. I want you where I can see you every minute of the day. We went to the New Moon this evening. I don't like it, but we had quite a good meal there. It's surprising how all those people fill the place when it's so far from town. I know I wouldn't want to go there again.

When I came home, I looked for a letter from you. I know I expect an awful lot, but I love having your letters. I wasn't lucky today though, but I did have magazines. Thanks, Darling, you're wonderful, and I love you more all the time.

You're going to stop liking me when you hear this, I know. When I got to Penclawdd this afternoon, I looked at my wrist to see if my bracelet was there. I have to keep looking from time to time as it's so small, but it wasn't there, Irwin. I felt terrible but wondered if I'd left it at home. This time I was unlucky. I don't know where I lost it. I'd give anything to get it back, though. You must think that I'm more than careless, Darling, but I'd rather lose anything than that, and you couldn't feel more miserable about it than I do. I've worried about it all day, and now I've searched for it at home, I'm more worried. It meant a great deal to me, Irwin. I hate myself for losing it.

I'm not in the right mood for writing a letter tonight. Wish you were here so I could know what you think of me. Please keep loving me all you can, and don't think too badly of me for what happened today. I love you with all my heart. Miss me.

All my love,
Mary

July 1, 1945

My Darling,

You weren't thinking that I'd forgotten about you, were you? I love you more and more every day, Irwin, even though I haven't written since Tuesday. Althea, my friend, the one in college, phoned on Wednesday morning and asked if I'd like to spend a few days at their new house at Mumbles. We've had good weather this week, so I liked her invitation, but I had to work in the mornings, and I've traveled on that electric train too much in one week for my liking. It's a lovely house, Irwin. Tennis court and beautiful gardens, too big for you and me, though. We'd be losing one another all the time. I have quite a nice tan after swimming and playing tennis every day, and every evening we went for long walks. You can imagine how fit I am to pitch lots of woo. We met a lovely Canadian girl married to one of our airmen. She's only been here two months and can't understand why people are so unfriendly. She came around to see us every afternoon and stayed with us the rest of the day. I thought she was sweet and felt sorry for her, stuck in a place like this, but Althea said she should have thought about that before marrying an Englishman.

Yesterday, I had three wonderful letters from you, written on the twenty-second, the twenty-fourth, and the twenty-fifth. Then I wanted to come home and write to tell you how much I was missing you, but I had promised Althea to stay with her last night, and I couldn't let her down after her people had been so nice to me. One of her relations got married yesterday, and we went to the party last night. Everybody sat and looked at one another. I was afraid to move. I don't like those affairs one bit and managed to get near enough to whisper to Althea and ask her if we could leave early. We did and had a good laugh about it when we got to her place. I was thinking what you would have said about it. It was just like a funeral.

Wish tonight was the time for us to sit back and laugh about how impatient we've been. I love you so much, Darling, and want to be with you. Do you mind? I know though, I'll wait as long as it's necessary. It will be well worth it if I can have you for good. I know you're not the type to run around with Fräuleins, so I don't worry about people's remarks about what other Americans are doing. You're my Irwin, I know.

You know I won't make you wear pyjamas if you don't want to. I will wear them, of course. I always get so cold in bed, and what other way could I keep warm? All right, don't tell me. I remember. I don't think we'll get cold feet, ever. Do you? You make me tingle right down to my toes. You're wonderful. Wish there wasn't any need for pyjamas tonight.

Don't know how to start telling you about the way I felt when I read the part of your sister's letter you sent me, but I do know how glad I am that I love you so much and feel so sure I can make you happy. Things have to work out like we planned, Darling. Our love can't be wasted any other way. Your sister sounds like a wonderful person to me. After what she's been through, I expect she understands better than anyone else what it means to have the person you love with you for always. When she's my sister too, I'll thank her for helping, in a way, and understanding about us so our dreams can be realized. I hope she thinks I'm worthy of all you're doing for me. I'll do my very best to prove that it was worth it. We're going to be the two happiest people that ever lived, I know. It's good though to have somebody else approving of our plans, don't you think? When you told me that you'd written to your sister about us, I was a little scared in case she might try to talk you out of it. I'm so happy now that I could cry too. You know you're my everything, don't you, Darling?

This afternoon I went for a walk with my sister. We went to see my brother and stayed for tea. Then we all went to a political meeting, above all things, at the Albert Hall. It was quite interesting. People standing up and asking stupid questions spoil the whole thing, though. If these men will do half the things they say, Britain will be a wonderful place, but as soon as the election is over, they'll forget all their promises.

This is the first night since last Tuesday that I dream about you without being afraid in case I'll talk in my sleep. I'm really going to haunt you tonight. We're going to have lots of fun. Dream about me. I'm all yours,

All my love always,
Mary

Part Four

AUGUST 22, 1945–
AUGUST 27, 1945

Something very unpleasant happened
in our home about six weeks ago.

August 22, 1945

My Darling,

Yes, I know I'm a meanie, not writing for such a long time. I want you to know, though, that I haven't stopped loving or missing you for one minute. I'll go on loving you all my life, Irwin.

Something very unpleasant happened at home about six weeks ago. I went down to breakfast one morning, sensed the strained atmosphere, and wondered what was wrong. I soon found out. Mother told me she had something to say to me. Then all sorts of things ran through my mind, except the most obvious thing. She asked me how long I had known you were married. I was ready to die. Then I told her I had known all along. She wasn't nasty about it. Maybe it would have been easier if she had been. Instead, she told me how I'd hurt her, after all she's done for me. She didn't blame you either. Just explained how silly and cheap I'd been. When I told her of our plans, she laughed at me for being so dumb as to believe you. I prayed hard that I wouldn't get in a temper and say something I would be sorry for later. I still don't know how she found out about you. All I know is that within a couple of days, all my relations knew what a bad girl I was. Now I'm treated like a crazy person when they're around. I tried to figure some way of getting out of it all, but if I left Swansea, it would mean changing my job, and I can't do that unless I go to a factory to work. I wanted to write you and meant to every night since then, but I'm sure my mother would do something desperate if she thought I would do that. One night I went to bed and started writing when my mother came into my room, put the light out, and left my door open. She's done everything she can to stop me writing to you. Life has been more than miserable these last few weeks. I just couldn't stand it any longer. I had to write you tonight, and I don't care if she reads this letter. I'm scared in case you think I've forgotten you. I'll always be yours, Darling.

I'd love to be able to talk to you, so if you have the chance of a leave, please take it, Darling, soon if you can. They might send you home, now that the war's over. I don't want to think of you going that far away from me without me seeing you first. But whatever happens, please don't forget about me, Darling, 'cause I'll be waiting for you, no matter how long it may be.

Keep writing to the office, Irwin. My letters are safe there. I'm terribly sorry for the anxiety I caused you through not writing. I'll write every night now. I do love you very, very much, Darling, and want to be your wife as soon as I can, so we can have our house and kids and wonderful Sundays. I've had some super dreams lately. Remind me to tell you about them when I see you. You're wonderful, and I'm so glad that I love you. Keep loving me all you can.

All my love always,
Mary

PS: I saw Mrs. Humphreys last week. She wants to know why you haven't written. You bad boy. I love you. Mary

August 27, 1945

My Darling,

Excuse pencil please. This is all I have to write with. I'm in bed and wishing so very hard. Sorry I haven't written, but I don't think I need explain to you how difficult everything is. I want you to know, though, Irwin, that I'll always love you, so if you don't get many letters from me, please understand that it isn't because I'm not thinking of you. I am, always.

This morning I had a wonderful letter from you and the snaps you took when you were here. When I looked at them and thought how near you were to me then and how happy I was, I envied myself. They were very good, weren't they? I'm glad you didn't send the ones including me. I can imagine what they're like, and that's enough. Last week I saw Mrs. Humphreys. She said she hadn't heard from you and asked about the snaps. I told her I'd let her see them when and if they came. Having nothing better to do this afternoon, I thought I'd pay her a visit. I had quite a good reception, and when I showed her the snaps, she was thrilled. Frank made some nasty comments about her, and they laughed just as they used to. She asked if she could have them. I didn't like to refuse, but I managed to keep the one I took of you in the park. I wish I hadn't gone to see her now. I wanted the ones of you as I'll never see enough of my Irwin. They made me stay and have tea, and then her handsome son came in. Oh, Irwin, you don't know what you missed. He's funny, honestly. I was left alone in the room when he came in for something. He started to show me his books and read me a few chapters. I had to pretend I was interested and almost laughing the same time. Then he said I could borrow his books if I wanted to. Nice of him, wasn't it. He asked me about you and told me he danced quite a bit, then mentioned the fact that we got on well together after only knowing one another a few minutes. I was glad to see Frank coming in then, and I made an excuse to leave. When Mrs. Humphreys and I were alone this afternoon, she asked if you had said any more about getting married. That sort of question annoys me. I told her we hadn't decided when it would be yet, and she said she didn't think we'd ever get married. I wonder what made her say a thing like that. I asked her, and she couldn't give any reason. I certainly hope we can prove to her how wrong she is.

I've been wondering if the end of the war will make any difference to our plans, but when I read in your letter that you expected a leave sometime in September, all my fears were banished. I was scared in case you'd be sent back to the States right away. I don't know what I'd do if I had to try and forget you. I know though, even if you should go, we'd meet again somehow. Life couldn't be so cruel as to take you away from me forever. I'll pray hard every night that you'll get a leave very soon. I want to see you so very, very much.

You asked me in one letter if Elaine had anything to do with me not writing you. You needn't worry about that, Darling, she's very happily married. Her husband is stationed in England now but is expecting to go overseas very soon, and she's breaking her heart as he's her all. About three weeks ago we stayed at Langland, going to work every day and making the best of the evenings there. We had Elaine's trailer as our house. Most of the time the weather was wonderful, and we went swimming every evening, and we thought of staying there until September, until the Thursday night when we went to see what the dance at Langland looked like. We went in. It was crowded, so we decided to leave as there wasn't even a place to stand in comfort. Then an American colonel and a major came on to us and asked if we'd join their party. We both said no together, so they said we shouldn't mind dancing with them just once, but we did mind. We thought that was enough for them and left the place. We walked back to our trailer, which was quite near the hotel, and collected our things to go swimming. Neither of us wanted to go to the dance again, ever. After we'd had enough of the water, we made our way back to our little place again. It was getting dark by this time, and as we neared our trailer, we could see two men outside, and we were a little scared. When we got closer and saw it was the colonel and the major, we were terrified. I told Elaine to run to the next house and tell the man there what was happening, and I'd see what these things wanted. As Elaine started to run, the colonel chased her, and this dirty old major came towards me. I've never had such a feeling in my life before. I pretended to be brave and asked him what he was playing at. He said they'd seen us on the beach every evening and found out we were staying in the trailer. So they decided they'd like to visit us. I told him he had the wrong girls, but that didn't move him. He wanted to see the inside of the trailer. I told him Elaine had the key. He said he'd be patient. I was wondering what had happened to Elaine, when the colonel came along. He couldn't find her. I told them what I thought of them, but they weren't a bit concerned about that. Then Elaine came back with all the neighbors she could find, and as soon as they saw them, they made one dash. That was the last we saw of them. Elaine and I were too scared to stay on our own that night, so we slept at the house next door. We packed our belongings next morning, and that's the last of Langland for us. We've found out since that those old men were stationed at Bryn Road, and they are known as sex maniacs. We thought of reporting them but were afraid in case our names would be made public. I never want to stay in a trailer again, even though we had such a nice time until that happened. See, Darling, I need you with me always. Can't you do that? I don't want to wait much longer. All this love I have saved for you is getting too much for me.

Almost forgot to tell you. Nancy has a baby boy. It's a week old now. She's named him Barry as that's the name of the place where she met her husband. She's in hospital, and only her mother and husband are allowed to visit her. I'm longing to see this baby. It's a wonder according to Tom. I wish something like that could happen to me, and you, of course. Oh well, I can wait, I suppose. But I don't want to. I love you lots and lots and still dreaming crazy dreams.

All my love always,
Mary

Part Five

OCTOBER 10, 1945–
DECEMBER 4, 1945

Your letter to her was a masterpiece, Irwin.

October 10, 1945

My Darling,

Yes, I know I'm mean for not writing, but honestly, Irwin, everything has been against me. I'm sorry, but I do love and miss you so very, very much. You know that and I hope you understand how things have been. There's been no chance for me to write during working hours as we've taken over another firm, and I have to keep two sets of books, etc. Now we are moving to this other garage sometime next month, so everything has to be in apple-pie order before then. The only good thing about it is that I get double pay, as long as I manage all the work, and I think I can. The next blow was my sister, who usually sleeps at my grandmother's place, had to share my bed as my grandmother went away for a while. So that meant there was no chance of me writing in bed. You can imagine how thankful I was to have my bed to myself again tonight so I could write to my Irwin. I hope you'll excuse the pencil, Darling.

I've received six wonderful letters since you left me. You are worth years and years of waiting for, Darling, but I feel so happy when I think how soon you'll be mine for always, though we both know already how much we belong to one another. I miss you so much, and I want you to be there when I wake from my wonderful dreams. I have tons of love saved for you thinking these things. Otherwise I'll be terrible in our dreams tonight. You'll be disgusted with me. Now I'm kidding, aren't I?

Thank you for getting me the lighter, Darling. I'll be an independent little wife. I won't even want you to light my cigarettes. You make me mad when you say I am independent. I'm not a bit, really. I depend on you for everything now, Irwin. I don't dare to think what life would be without you, but I don't have to think of these things. You're mine for always, aren't you, Darling?

I haven't received the money you sent yet. Do you think it's safe to mail it that way? Perhaps it takes it some time to come different to ordinary letters, and there's no need to worry at all, but I'll let you know as soon as it arrives.

What I wouldn't give for one of those hours I wasted when I could have been with you. I could kick myself when I think of it. Remember that day when you were really mad at me? You were right, of course, but I wouldn't tell you then. It was difficult to get away from home most of the time though. I'll be so happy when you are the person who asks where I'm going, but you'll know most of the time as I want to be with you all I can. There'll be times, of course, when you'll be looking after the kids while I'm shopping or something, but you won't mind that, will you, Darling? I wish we could start our family now, don't you?

I'm going to dream now. You know what I dream better than I do. I think it's wonderful. I love you and love you so much, Irwin. Miss me and love me lots.

All my love always,
Mary

October 11, 1945

My Darling,

Love me tonight? Sure you do. Well, you should. You're my husband. Oh, Irwin, I miss you. It's awful. I'll never see enough of you. You're wonderful. I'm convinced there's nobody like you in the world or maybe it's just that I love you so very much that nobody else matters.

Since you left I've been to two shows, and that's the only times I've been out. Elaine phoned me and asked if I'd go to Langland last Saturday. I told her those nights out are finished with as far as I'm concerned. She seemed quite annoyed and told me that you wouldn't expect me to stay home every night. I explained to her that that's the way I feel about it. So she's finished with me, Darling. Completely ignores me when I see her. You can imagine how worried I am. We had fun at Langland, didn't we? I had everything then, and even now I have all those wonderful memories until I see you again.

I gave your message to Mr. Morgan, Darling. He sends his regards and thanks for what you did.

I think I could produce a phony driver's license tonight if you were here. Are you interested, Irwin? I'm in this little bed, thinking of you in your little bed when we could just as well be together. I'd better stop. I just wish that tonight was one of those hectic nights we had together, not the one when you were mean to me, and I felt so tired. What a husband I have. He's wonderful. I had the snaps of your brother and family. They look lovely. I could eat the little boy. He's sweet. Can I keep them, Irwin, please? I'd love to write to your sister and sister-in-law. They could write to my home. I do want them to like me, and your sister need have no doubts about my love for you. I'll always love you, Darling, as I'm all yours. But why should I tell you all this when you already know?

I'll answer all your letters tomorrow night. I got to go now to keep our date. I love you all I can, Darling. Love me lots and dream about me.

All my love always,
Mary

October 26, 1945

My Darling,

You can't imagine how I felt when I read your letter this morning, telling me of my mother's letter to you. That was the last thing I expected, but as you say, it may be all for the best.

This evening, when I came home from work, I was quite prepared for a showdown as she should have had your reply today. But instead, she greeted me at the door to take my wet clothes as there's been a storm raging here for the last few days and fussed with my slippers in case my feet were wet. She just couldn't do enough for me. All the time I didn't say a word and was determined to get everything straight as soon as my kid brother was out of the way. Then my brother, who was supposed to have returned to Italy last week, walked in. He's been held up in England owing to weather conditions and now has eight days leave again, so naturally that ended my plans. Your letter to her was a masterpiece, Irwin. She must have said some horribly insulting things to you. I'm sorry, Darling, for it all.

You know that I'll love you always no matter what may happen, but, Irwin, if you think that I'm not worth you taking the risk on the second attempt of happiness after some of the things my mother may have said, please tell me and I'll understand, Darling. All I know is that since I've met you, life has been wonderful. We haven't been together very much, but the thought is always in my mind, that a person like you wants me has made everything almost perfect. I know there'll never be anyone else, but unless you are sure that I could make you happy, I'm prepared to forget, or rather, try to forget, all those wonderful dreams of the future. I don't want to though, Darling.

I also received your money today. It will be quite safe, Irwin, and any time you decide you don't want me, I'll return all the things I have belonging to you. It seems awful just to think about it, and I don't know what I'll do if you make a decision like that, but it's up to you, Darling. I do love you with all my heart, and even if you don't want me, I'm all yours forever. Please want me a little bit. I love you so very, very much. I'll still keep on wishing that I'll be Mrs. Deems one day. You're wonderful. Good night, Darling.

All my love always,
Mary

October 30, 1945

My Darling,

Life's wonderful. Oh, I wish you were here right now. I don't think I've been so happy in my life before. You're wonderful, Darling, and I love you so very, very much.

My mother didn't get your letter until yesterday morning, and when I went home to lunch, she handed it to me. I pretended it was all news. I showed her my ring then. She thought it was lovely, and I was waiting for some sort of a scene, but all she said was that whatever I wanted to do, she would never stand in my way. I never thought she'd take it like that, Darling. My brother Walter came in, and we told him about it. He took it quite calmly and asked if he could be best man. You know the way brothers tease. Mother and I decided that we couldn't tell my other brother, the one that's on leave, as he has a terrible temper, but last night he was there with his wife, when my nice brother came in after being at his club, and told them all about it. They were surprised, but again, no scene. This all seems too good to be true. All I keep praying for now is that your divorce will be all right and that you'll keep loving me. I know Mother will accept you like a son, Darling, as soon as she meets you. I forgot to tell you what she said about your divorce. She said as long as there weren't children involved, it was all right. Do you think there's any need for me to enlighten her on that subject, Darling?

Wish we'd been married this morning and we were drinking that champagne now and wondering where the best place for my nightgown would be. We won't ever wonder, will we, Darling? You'll insist that I keep it on in case I catch cold. I can see your face if I did a thing like that. It's going to be heaven. I'd better stop thinking these things. I might be bad in our dreams tonight. Wouldn't that be lovely? I can hardly wait, Darling. Went to a show this evening, *Speaking Roughly*. It was very good, but I miss you so much, Darling, everywhere I go.

It's time to dream again. Be nice to me tonight and love me all you can. I love you and love you and love you.

Excuse pencil, please. I came to bed without ink. Love me, Irwin.

All my love always,
Mary

November 6, 1945

My Darling,

Happy anniversary, and thank you, Darling, for the flowers. They're lovely. Today I want you with me more than ever. It will always be an important date in my life, almost as important as our wedding date. We are so much nearer to complete happiness this November 6, aren't we? The night I met you, and I think we really did love one another right away, I didn't know if you'd turn up to our next date, and then last November things were pretty bad, and I didn't know if I'd see you again, even though I loved you a year more. This time, though, we don't have long to wait. Mother approves, and I love you with all my heart. I just pray that by this time next year, you'll be mine for always. It's going to be wonderful, Darling. You are wonderful, and when I think of you being all mine, I realise I'm the luckiest person in the world.

I hope you are more comfortable in your little tent now than when you first arrived there. When I think that if it wasn't for me you could be home instead of living in your present abode, I know you must love me an awful lot. One day soon, though, Darling, we'll have a home, and I'll try to do everything to make up for everything you've done for me. I'm not grumpy in the mornings, and I'm sure if you'll be there every morning to wake me, I won't be grumpy. Just you wait and don't be so inquisitive.

Have you made up your mind about staying in the Army or not? I'd like to have a home of our own, Darling, as soon as possible after we're married. So we can start our family, and I'll have you there all the time. I don't want you to leave me for a day, Irwin, but it's up to you to decide. Of course, if you could be stationed in one place for a long time, then we could still have a home, and being in the Army wouldn't be a lot different from any other job. I don't mind what you do as long as I can be with you. It's time our little family got together for a while. We've been separated long enough.

Mr. Clement noticed my ring today for the first time. He asked who the man was, at least he sked if it was you and said he hadn't met you but you looked very nice. That sounded strange coming from him, as he never comments on anyone's looks, but you are wonderful, Darling.

I showed Mother the snaps, and she's put one of you with the rest of her boys decorating the room. I'm so glad she took it the way she did.

Going to dream about us now. We're going to have extra fun tonight as it's our anniversary. Love me and miss me all you can.

All my love always,
Mary

November 8, 1945

My Darling,

How's my husband tonight? Love me? I do, lots. We have no time to fool around now, though. We're going to Langland tonight, so don't make a mess of me, well, not too much of a mess. We'll have plenty of time after the dance. I don't have to leave you at all. You're my husband now, unless, of course, you want me to sleep in my own room. I can just see you making me do a thing like that. Oh, Darling, I wish you were here, and we were married, so I could race you up the stairs and get into bed before you.

The postman handed me a parcel today. I opened it and found the cigarettes. I was thrilled. You're so wonderful to think of everything. I picked up one packet, and it felt heavy, and there was a lovely lighter. I noticed another packet that wasn't sealed. A lighter, again, and when I discovered the third, I thought my eyes were deceiving me, but there were three. Thank you lots, Darling. You're so good to me, that it seems mean just saying "Thank you." I just get over thinking how wonderful you are for sending flowers, when I get lighters and cigarettes. I wish I could see you to tell you how very much I love you, but you know, don't you, Darling? The silver Ronson is a lovely one, isn't it? The others are super too. No note came in your package, so I'm wondering if they're all for me. It seems incredible to have three lighters like that, at once.

Did you know that the florist sent anemones? They're my favorite and, for some reason, have been very scarce. I have them in my bedroom now. The other flowers were lovely too. Mother asked what anniversary it was. I tell her everything she should know about us. It's nice to be able to talk about you to her. She loves you already, Irwin, so you have a mother again. I'll always remember what you said about wishing your mother could have known me. That was the nicest thing you could have said to me, Darling. I wish I could have known her, Irwin. Instead, we'll have one mother between us.

We were supposed to move our office this week, but the roof of our new garage has suddenly collapsed after the storms. I'm in no hurry to get there anyway. It's a dismal place, worse than our present garage, so you can imagine. We also have a new boss. He was a lieutenant colonel and still thinks he can move people around like machines. You'd laugh if you saw how he dresses, typically English, only a little overdone. He's a horrible thing.

My brother's learning French now. I promised to help him with the little bit I know tonight, so I'll have to leave you for a little while until I get into my little bed again and put my arms around a pillow, a poor substitute for you, Darling, but it makes me dream some nice dreams. Keep loving me all you can, Irwin, and remember I'm all yours forever and ever.

All my love always,
Mary

November 9, 1945

My Darling,

You didn't show up in my dreams last night. What's wrong? You still love me, don't you, Darling? Of course you do. I wish I could hear you say it though, 'cause I miss you, honest, I do, and I want you to love me a little, Honey.

Elaine and the rest of the girls have gone to a dance in Llanelly tonight. RAF officers will be in thousands, so they told me. Of course, when I heard that, I couldn't wait until I got there. I don't want anyone but you, ever, so keep wanting me, Darling.

I'm glad you like your new job. It sounds interesting. You're forever telling me about good-looking men. I'm not interested, Darling. You look in the mirror and you'll see my good-looking man. You're everything I want, and I do want you so much, Irwin. I can't wait, but you know I will. Frank Sinatra is singing "Kiss Me, Kiss Me Again" on the radio now. He'll have me swooning too if he keeps singing that.

I worked from eight o'clock this morning until six thirty this evening. I'm not going to do it anymore. It's much too long to be in that miserable place. They can find somebody to help me, otherwise, I'll be a wreck when it's time for my honeymoon, and that can't happen until after. We're going to have a wonderful time making ourselves wrecks though, aren't we, Darling?

I'll think of you next Sunday morning when I fall out of bed and get into the car half-dressed when you are still snoring. How's the asthma, Darling? I'll never forget that night. I felt as though I was to blame for it, after running up that hill. I'm going to have something myself someday if I don't wear stockings. That's what my relations tell me. So you'd better be prepared. My chill came back again today. It's a funny thing. I can't see any spots. Just want to scratch at the most awkward times, when Mr. Clement is speaking to me or when I'm on a bus. But my brother brought me some tablets today. They'll cure me, so he said. And he knows everything.

Nancy was here with the baby this afternoon. Mother said the baby is wonderful. Nancy's husband has gone overseas, so she doesn't feel too good. My husband is overseas too, and I want him here with me so much. I love you lots and lots, Darling.

Bye now. Miss me terribly and love me all you can.

All my love always,
Mary

November 10, 1945

My Darling,

It's Saturday night again. What are you doing, Irwin? I'm all alone at home, and I don't feel a bit miserable about it. Elaine and the rest of them at the dance last night got themselves an invitation for a party at the RAF mess tonight. That RAF officer we saw at Langland that night gave Elaine an invitation for me too. She was mad because I wouldn't go. All the theatre people in town this week will be there. I'd like to have gone if it wasn't for that man. It's much nicer writing to you, though. I'm so glad you love me, Darling.

I'll give that lighter to Mr. Humphreys for you, Darling. I'll have to be in a very good mood before going there, though. I feel sick every time I see Mrs. Humphreys. Remember the things we said about her? If she only knew. Thanks for letting me have the nicest lighter. I suppose you still have that crazy lighter that you blow on before it will light.

You've put me on the spot when you asked me about your leaves. It would be wonderful to have you here for Christmas, even though we'd have to wait a few months before getting married. It would be nicer too for you to meet my people the next leave and then for us to get married the leave after that, don't you think? Maybe you won't get your divorce though for a few months again, and then we'd still be waiting. You decide though, Irwin. Sometimes, when I'm extra miserable, I don't think we'll ever be married, Irwin. Don't think I'm awful for even suggesting that, Darling. I know we love one another as much as any two people can and that you're doing everything you can to make us one for always, but, well, I don't know what it is. I think I'm scared in case I won't make you the wife you deserve, and yet I know I'll always love you, and there'll never be anyone else. I want to be your wife so much, Irwin, and I love you with all my heart. Maybe I'm crazy for thinking anything could come between us, so I won't think anymore. I'll just love you and miss you more every day.

Wish I could dance with you tonight, Darling. Life's awfully empty without you here, and there's no one in the whole world who could take your place. I was telling my brother about the dance at the RAF mess tonight. He told me not to even think of going. He's your friend, Irwin, and mine too. They're playing that "Blue Heaven" song, you know, the one you like, on the radio now, and I miss you terribly.

That little gangster driver keeps asking about you all the time. He's funny. Keeps me happy all day. He says some funny things. Even Mr. Clement laughs at him.

I'm going to bed very early tonight, Darling. Wish I could be with you tomorrow morning. You wouldn't sleep, Irwin. Love me all you can and miss me, sometimes, always.

All my love always,
Mary

November 13, 1945

My Darling,

You're wonderful, and I love you. Did you know? I miss you so very much, Irwin. Wish I could see you. Went to a show with Elaine tonight. *The Enchanted Cottage*. It wasn't bad. A bit depressing though, and I don't like Robert Young anyway. When I see people like him pitching woo, I wish you and I could show him how. It's a wonderful feeling when I just look at you, and I'm sure it will last all my life. I love you so much, Darling. I too have oceans of love saved up for you. We can use it all though, and I certainly am prepared for many sleepless nights. You just wait and see.

One of our neighbors' sons came to visit us tonight. He's just returned from a Japanese camp. We've been listening to his experiences. Their camp was liberated by Americans, the same Americans that were stationed on the hill here. He can't say enough about how good they were to him. He went to America before coming here and could have stayed there. Some boys did, but his mother is quite old, so he came back, but he'll never forget the way he was treated there.

My mother is quite resigned to the fact that I'm going to marry you, Irwin. I still can't realize she's taken it this way. It seems too good to be true. I wish we didn't have to wait any longer before getting married. Have you heard anything about your divorce? I go to sleep every night praying that it will work out the way we want it to. I discovered something today. People who have a divorce in this country have to wait six months before remarrying. I hope we don't have to wait that much longer, but if we do, we will, won't we, Darling? It's well worth waiting for, but I do so want to be your wife soon.

It's late, Darling, eleven thirty. I'm not used to these late nights, so I'd better hurry or else you'll think I'm not showing up at all tonight. Keep loving me, Irwin, all you can and miss me lots. You're my everything, Darling.

All my love always,
Mary

November 16, 1945

My Darling,

Don't you love me anymore? I haven't had a letter since Monday, but that's nothing to complain about after the way you've waited for my letters. I love you, Irwin, with all my heart, and right now I'm missing you extra. Wish I could have a few of those hours I wasted for us when you were here. When I think of it, I could kick myself. I'm all alone again tonight. There's been sentimental music on the radio the whole time until I could scream. Have you heard "My Heart Sings"? Everyone else thinks it's a terrible number. I think it's nice, though. Wish I could have you singing "Always" for me now. Remember that night, Darling? You told me so many wonderful things, and I believe I told you I loved you so many times that you were almost tired of hearing it. We had so much fun, Darling.

I've never been as happy as that in my life before. You're wonderful, Irwin, and I was so proud of you. I still am. You're everything anyone could ever want, but nobody could ever love you as much as I do. I'm sure they couldn't. I just ache to be in your arms again. I'll never look for a substitute, Darling. There's nobody else like you anywhere. When I wake in the morning, the first thing I think of is you, wishing I could wake you too. Then all day, I miss you, no matter where I am or what I'm doing. But what makes me miss you more than ever is when I go to bed at night and know that you are thinking of me and missing me a little too.

Nancy is going to live at London after Christmas. Her husband's work is there, so she's preparing his home before he leaves the forces. She seems quite thrilled about it too. I'm going to stay with her for a few days next week. She told me to be prepared for yelling during the night and not to expect too much sleep. That's married life, I guess.

I've got a million things to do before I go to bed tonight, so I'd better leave you now. Love me all you can, Darling. I'm all yours forever.

All my love always,
Mary

November 17, 1945

My Darling,

These Saturday nights alone are miserable, Irwin, when I think of dancing with you, instead, but this is the way I want it to be until we're together again. I wish that day would hurry. Elaine was annoyed again today when she asked me to go to Langland with her. I told her I didn't want to dance, so she asked if I'd just go there for a drink. She can't understand how I can be like this, but she couldn't possibly know how very much I love you and how worthless I think it is to go to a dance without you. I'd be twice as lonely there, thinking of the fun we had together and missing you so terribly the whole time.

I had a very lovely letter from you today, Darling. You put into words what I feel. We do love one another truly, and all this waiting is worthwhile. This letter was written on November 4. I'd get rid of those PWs who mess our mail up. I hope you've had a letter from me by this time. I want you to know how very much I love you. You do, don't you, Darling?

We must feel the same way about us, Darling. When I used to get into that room at Bryn, I wanted to be in your arms as soon as you'd have me. You're like a magnet to me, Irwin. Even when you're not here, I long to be in your arms. I do, Darling. You have no idea how much I do. I'm certainly all yours, so please want me lots, for always. I remember too the first time I saw you the last leave. I knew then there weren't any doubts about the way I love you, and I couldn't wait until I was in your arms, just to make sure you were here again, and you did love me like I wanted you to.

Our town won the football game again today. We're getting too good. You're not crazy for listening to the football scores. When I used to see keystones on soldiers' sleeves, I'd get weak in the knees, even though the soldier wasn't anything as wonderful as my Irwin could be. The announcers on the radio say "Swansea" as you do, Irwin. That's not the correct way. Only Welsh people can say it correctly.

You're taking a big job, Darling, fooling around with millions of dollars. I'm afraid I wouldn't be much help to you. I get nervous when I see too much money, you know. I get careless about the little coins. Don't get yourself in the jailhouse, Irwin. I want a husband to keep me warm these cold nights. It is awfully cold too. I've still got my chill. Don't laugh. That's what the doctor says it is. In addition to that, I couldn't pitch very much woo tonight. My nose has developed a chill too. It's inside though, so don't go imagining how funny I look.

How glad I am you are as you are. I know how most people act when they're away from their wives, etc., even though they love them. But I guess you feel the same way as I do about those things. It's not worth it, is it, Darling? Every minute I'd be with someone else, I'd be thinking that you'd be loving me less all those minutes, and I don't want to lose the tiniest particle of our love. I just want it to keep on growing the whole time, as I know it will. I just can't imagine kissing anyone else, and as long as we have sufficient faith in one another, we could be away from one another for years and still not be tempted. Irwin, they're playing "Always" on the radio right now. I feel so happy and yet sad when I hear that. It's our song, all right. I will be loving you always.

I'm going to wash my hair now. I told you I had it cut. Only a little though, didn't I? Dream about me and love me lots, Darling. I love you so terribly.

All my love always,
Mary

November 23, 1945

My Darling,

Today was nice. I had five wonderful letters from you. I was beginning to wonder if you were being mean to me, as you hadn't had any of my letters. I have written, Irwin, not every day, but a few times a week, and I'm just as worried as you are because you're not getting them.

You know as well as I do, Darling, that you need have no fears about me changing my mind about you. That will never happen. I love you for always and always, so don't ask if I like having your letters. You know better. I can imagine how you feel though and all the things that come to your mind when you don't get letters, but please, Darling, remember that you're the only person that matters in my life. Your sister is awfully nice, Irwin, for sending her love and wishes to me as well. I wish we were married already, honest, I do, but I belong to you now as far as you and I are concerned. I just hope that you'll always want me, like I'll always want you.

You must have been very miserable when you wrote on the twelfth. It wasn't a very nice letter, Irwin, but I understand. Don't you ever think that my letters may be delayed? You wrote something about someone at your camp having a letter from Cardiff in three days. That letter you wrote my mother and sent a copy to me at the same time was a week later getting to her than mine. See, you can't rely on their system. I do love you so very much.

I'm awfully glad about you meeting your brother. Has he changed any? I'd like to have met him, but I hope we'll meet him together one day soon when you're my husband. Don't be frightened, I'll never beat you. You know how very much I want to go home with you and meet Sue and Virginia, who are so nice about us.

Oh, Darling. I almost forgot to congratulate you. You're wonderful, and I'm awfully proud of you. I can wear my chief bars now without thinking I have the wrong ones on. I bet you had a surprise when they told you. Wish I could have been there to change the bars on your uniform, that's all, remember.

Imagine a thirty-day honeymoon, Darling. I wouldn't be able to work for a year after that, or rather, you wouldn't. You're a big sissy. I can take it, though. It would be heaven. Wish it started from tonight. I'd be terrible, would you?

My family will love you, Darling. Mother and the rest of them keep teasing me about America. I can't believe it's true it was accepted the way it was, but it makes me feel a lot happier. I know you feel better about it too. You'll have a mother again, Darling, and a few brothers and sisters too. My brother said last night that whatever you did to me, he didn't know, but I was awfully true to you, and funnily, Mother made the same remark tonight. There's no need to tell you how good I'm being, Darling. You know.

I hope you're getting my letters now, Irwin. I hate to think of you having any doubts at all about the way I love you. Dream about me and love me all you can.

All my love always,
Mary

November 24, 1945

My Darling,

Miss me tonight? I miss you so very much, Darling. Today has seemed endless. I haven't been to work. I was coming home in the bus yesterday, and I felt something prick my leg, but I didn't pay much attention to it at the time. It was just a little lump behind my knee, just where you like to fool around. I bathed it last night and thought no more, but when I tried to get out of bed this morning, I couldn't stretch my leg. I had some lotion from the doctor and thought it would go. I felt fine myself, so I phoned Mr. Clement and asked him to send a car for me. He told me I wasn't to go to work, so I've been sitting looking at the fire all day, bored to tears. It's nine o'clock now, and here I am in bed. My sister's boyfriend is on leave again, and he's been telling me all he knows about the navy all the evening, so you can imagine how I felt. I want to see you so much, Darling. You're so wonderful, and I love you so terribly. Let's go driving tonight, Irwin.

This morning a friend of Mother's came to the house. She lectures to GI brides every week as she lived in America for a number of years. She was telling us what kind of girls attend these meetings. It shocked her. She said she hoped they never got to the States as they'd be terrible representations of British girls. There was another neighbor in the house at that time. Her claws were nice and long, and she said that the Americans didn't marry the intelligent girls as they couldn't fool them so easily. They've got all the worst stories of Americans. I spend a good deal of my time having people tell me what can happen to me. You can imagine how I'm influenced by all this. All I'm concerned about is the fact that I'll love you forever as I want to do.

There's something I forgot to tell you. The cheque you sent on November 1 hasn't arrived yet. It should have by now. I told you that I opened a special account for it in the bank, didn't I? It's quite safe, Darling. You know all the formalities you have to go through before opening an account, signing your name a few times, etc.? Well, the man there looked at the check and looked at me and said, "Would you describe yourself as a spinster?" I don't know whether or not he was being sarcastic. Maybe I should have told him I was going to be your spouse, as it says on those forms, but he didn't worry me any.

Had some magazines today too. Thanks, Darling. Did you see in one *Yank* some drawings of girls from different countries and their opinions of the Americans? My brother was really tickled about them. They were funny though. Do I look like the idea of an English girl, Darling? I hope not.

My brother Ken, the one in the RAF, is arriving here next week some time for leave, so we're all excited again. Harry, my brother who just returned to Italy, is leaving there on the twenty-first of December. I mean leaving the Army for good. He's coming by boat this time, so I don't think he'll make it for Christmas. Mother said if you come home after Christmas, she'll have all her family together. She's looking forward to meeting you, Irwin. Not half as much as I'm looking forward to seeing you again, though. It seems such a long time since I was there in your arms, and yet when I'm with you again, it will seems as though you've never been away from me. You're always in my thoughts though, Darling. Am I in yours? Even when you're trying to balance millions of dollars? You're going to have a mental strain if you keep on with that job, and you'll be too tired for a honeymoon. I'm kidding. I'm really awfully proud of my husband.

Remember that girl you met at Langland? The one who came to our table and introduced herself? She travels on the same bus as me, and the other day she showed me some snaps. One was herself with an officer who was at Penclawdd with you. She did tell me his name, but I can't remember it. He's a big blond fellow, she said. Something about him being a trifle boring as he didn't drink, but she went to see him at Bridgend a few times. Then she asked me if I knew Hap Reynolds. She knew him quite well and all the details of his life. I was quite surprised when she said about him getting engaged to a lovely girl like Betty, when he was already married. Is that right, Irwin? I didn't know he'd been married. I was wondering how much she may know about us, as she seems to delight in other people's misfortunes. But she didn't know you before. At least she said she didn't. She has quite a nerve to talk about anyone though, as her life isn't exactly a dull one.

I had a crazy dream last night. We were married, but I couldn't remember the ceremony, and I didn't have a wedding ring. We were staying at a house full of people. There was no room for me to sleep there, so every night you'd send me home. One night, though, I got really annoyed, and we were just deciding that we couldn't share a bed, when my mother's voice came to wake me from my dreams. I woke up mad and tried to sleep again so I could finish the dream properly, but it was no good. Would you have been bad, Irwin? I would have been. I'm going to see if I can do better tonight. I love you with all my heart, Darling. Keep loving lots for always, and miss me lots.

All my love always,
Mary

November 26, 1945

My Darling,

I love you and love you so much, Irwin, and time seems to go so slowly now, but as long as you love me and want me, I could wait for a long, long time yet. I don't want to, though, and besides, I already have more than enough love saved to last us a lifetime. Could you use some right now? Wish you could and I'd be there, seeing you loved me too.

The cheque came all right this morning, and it's safe in the bank for our wedding. You should have seen me limping to work this morning. The drivers asked me what was wrong, and not thinking, I said I'd been bitten. You should have heard the things they said. The little man wanted to know if you were here again. I was sorry I opened my mouth.

My brother Harry, the one who just returned to Italy, wrote a letter we had today, asking if I was still blinded by Yank Stardust and said he wished I'd recover from it, but it was my affair anyway. What he thinks doesn't worry me a bit, and after the mess he made of choosing a wife, he shouldn't have the nerve to interfere with me at all. We do love one another truly, and I know you've been as true to me as I've been to you during the period we were separated. There can never be anybody but you for me, so love me lots, Darling.

They've started running a daily service from here to any part of the continent. Anyone can travel. That's something, isn't it? Maybe I'll surprise you one day. Just hide in your tent until you finish work. That plan of your tent was very good, Darling. We wouldn't need two beds, silly. You could sleep on the floor.

I feel extra tired tonight, don't know why, but I do. Do you mind if I leave you now? I'll see you in my dreams, Darling. Wish I could be with you though, to tell you how much I miss and love you every minute of the day. Miss me all you can and love me too.

All my love always,
Mary

November 28, 1945

My Darling,

I'm more than happy about your receiving a few letters from me at last, just to let you know that you are the dearest person to me in the whole world. You are, Darling. I love you so very, very much, as you know.

My mother did write you then? She does rave when she's angry, but it doesn't last very long. She starts to laugh and spoils the whole thing. She doesn't know you. Otherwise, she wouldn't be angry with you. Naturally, she doesn't entirely approve, but I'm sure she will. I don't worry too much about that anyway. As long as you love me and want me, I'm the happiest person in the whole world.

Virginia is nice to plan things in case I should get there before you, but I'd like to go with you, Darling. She's awfully good to me considering how little she knows about me. I hope they'll like me, though, when they do know me. I think it would be nicer for us to get married in Swansea now, Darling, and go on our honeymoon right away. I certainly hope you can be here for New Year's Eve if you can't make it for Christmas. With those few days, we'll be able to straighten a few little things out. You'll meet my family, and we can make definite arrangements for our wedding.

This evening my mother asked me to visit my aunt with her, as it's a lonely walk to where she lives. My leg is still sore, but I went. I thought I'd never get there, but I did. My aunt was more than surprised to see me. She knew about my ring, congratulated me, and gave Mother a good lecture about acting the way she did. It seems that my mother's marriage wasn't approved of by her people, and it led to a lot of unpleasantness in the family, but she married the man she wanted. I didn't know about this until tonight. My aunt asked when your next leave was. I said you may be here in January, and naturally, she asked if we were getting married then. I was about to say "not quite as soon as that" when Mother said, "Of course not." Then my aunt started again. I didn't know I had so many relations on my side before. They're all putting their bit in for me and all willing to prepare a wonderful wedding. I'm afraid I'll have to disappoint them there though. I couldn't stand much fuss, and I know you couldn't. As long as we have our driver's licenses, we don't worry about the rest, do we, Darling?

I forgive you for drinking after dinner Thanksgiving Day, as long as you had a good dinner. I still haven't had a drink, though. Don't want one, either. There's no fun in it without you there to put up with me. There's no fun doing anything without you by my side. You're wonderful.

I promise to stay on my own side tonight, for five minutes anyway. I love you more all the time, Darling, and miss you so much. Dream about me, a good bad dream.

All my love always,
Mary

November 29, 1945

My Darling,

I've been working hard today. Didn't finish until seven o'clock, and I don't know why, but I don't feel a bit tired. I'm in the mood for love. Lots of it. Wish you were here, Darling, so you could know how very much I miss you. These cold winter evenings are lonely, and I need someone to keep me warm. When I think how warm we get together, I realize what a help you're going to be, only in the winter, though. I can take care of myself in the summer, and you can sleep in your own bed. I can see your face now, when I tell you that, and if you were here, you'd tickle me until I told you I didn't mean what I'd said. See how scared I am of you? Oh, I love you so much, Darling, and the more I think of you, the more I love you all the time.

Before I started this letter, I felt extra lonely, so I took all your snaps out, and looking at you made me feel as if you were here with me, telling me how much you loved me. Then I didn't feel lonely anymore. You're so wonderful, Darling.

We had a letter from my brother Ken today. He's at Milan waiting for transport home. He hopes to arrive here Monday. Mother's all thrilled. He gave us strict instructions not to have any fuss when he arrives. I don't know what he thought would happen. All I know is that I have to move out of my bedroom while he's here, and I don't like that. He could easily sleep with my other brother, and besides, my little bed won't stand his weight for long. If it was you, it would be all right. You're only a shrimp. I'm sorry, Darling, I know you're too big for me, so don't remind me of what I said when you see me. You know how very, very wonderful I think you are. Don't know how I'm so lucky to have you to love. I do love you with all my heart.

Hazel came into the office this afternoon. She was all excited. They'd had a telegram from her American brother-in-law. He's just landed in the States, so now, she said, her sister will be going here too. Then she and Eddie can get married and live with her people. You should see the people who already live at her home. They only have four rooms, and there's her mother and father, two brothers, one married sister with a daughter, and now she wants Eddie there as well. You know that little driver we have? He was in the office when she was telling us her plans, and he wanted to know if they slept in hammocks at her house. She just laughed, but I often wonder myself. Then that little man gave his views on marriage, and a few other drivers gave their opinions as well. I said that whatever they said about their wives, they wouldn't leave then if they had the chance. The little man gave a little whistle and said that was him as a skylark if he'd have half a chance. If their wives could only hear how these men talk about them, they'd never work again. One of them said if his wife sat on his knee, she'd want to get engaged. I have to listen to some terrible discussions. They call their wives their old girls. You won't call me that, Darling, will you, even when I'm not around? I'd hate to think of us ever thinking the way they do about one another. I want us to be sweethearts all our lives. We will be, won't we, Darling? You'll always be wonderful to me, and I know I'll always love you this way.

I'll see you in my dreams in a few minutes, Darling. Then I'll know how much you love me. Love me all you can and miss me as I miss you.

All my love always,
Mary

December 4, 1945

My Darling,

Haven't had a letter this week yet. Are you making me realize what it's like to be without hearing from you? I quit, Darling. It's awful wondering if you still love me and hoping everything's all right. You do love me, don't you?

Last night I went to see *Weekend at the Waldorf*. It's wonderful. Elaine said that when she sees things like that, she doesn't believe she's living. It didn't make me feel that way, though. I'd settle for you and me together anywhere. Van Johnson was in the show too. I like him. He's even nicer than Tyrone. I went home and told Mother about it, so she's gone there this evening. My brother hasn't arrived yet. We waited until one o'clock this morning, thinking he'd come home on the last train.

Went to work this morning. Mr. Clement is still away. The auditors are here again, and the colonel paid us his daily visit. He asked when Mr. Clement was returning, though he said it didn't make much difference, and in a very pucker voice, he said, "Force on, regardless." I don't know how I didn't laugh. I came home to lunch and forgot to return. They're slowly getting on my nerves. When I don't hear from you, I can't feel pleased about anything. Nothing else but the knowledge that you love me interests me.

My brother has a cold. You'd think he was dying. I wish someone would marry him out of the way. I have to get his supper in a few minutes, and right now he's nagging me like an old woman. All I have to say to him is, "Your hair is awfully thin," and he gets really mad, and I get called a few things.

Well, Darling, I have to leave you know. I hope I get a letter tomorrow. Please love me all you can and miss me lots. I love you with all my heart, Darling, and you know how I miss you.

All my love always,
Mary

Walter, Mary, Irwin, Mam, and Mair

Dot   Ken, Con, and Walter

Part Six

January 10, 1946– April 8, 1946

Mother said there isn't any difference where you get married. It means the same thing.

January 10, 1946

My Darling,

How I miss you. Oh, Irwin, I don't know what I'll do the next few months when already I feel like this. As soon as you left the station this afternoon, everything seemed empty and flat. You're so wonderful, and I love you so very much. On my way back to the office this afternoon, I met that girl who knew Hap Reynolds. She told me I looked as though I were in a dream. But she understood when I explained my reason for looking lost. She was going to have coffee, so I went with her, and when I did get back to work, it was three thirty, and I had promised to have tea with Elaine at four o'clock. So that just gave me time to get to her office. We had our tea, and then we went back to work, and I thought I'd feel a lot better if I went back too. I just couldn't go home alone at that time. I worked until eight o'clock. All the time I was thinking about you and wondering exactly where you were and hoping you were missing me lots. When I got home, Mother asked where you were. She's heard the gale warnings again. She likes you a lot more than you and I think. She's been saying lovely things all the time and said how empty the house seemed without you, and of course, she's still asking when you'll come here again. I came to bed at ten o'clock, and I feel pretty sleepy, so you don't mind if this is a short letter, do you, Darling? I'm dreading working tomorrow morning. It's been so wonderful these last eleven mornings, to wake and know that I'll see you that day. You're my whole life, Darling, and it will always be that way, so keep loving me and miss me terribly. Wish I could be in your arms right now. Oh, I love you, Irwin. And right now I have a suspicion that I'm going to have wonderful dreams tonight. I'm hoping, anyway. You should see those sucker bites. They're the best yet. You aren't slipping, Darling. You just get more wonderful all the time.

I'll see you in my dreams. Don't be good, Darling, I don't want to be. You're perfect, whatever you do, and I want you to know that these days I've spent with you are the most wonderful days of my life. I certainly hope that there will be thousands more. Good night, Darling, and bless you. I love you with all my heart forever.

All my love always and always,
Mary

PS: Hope you're in a nice bed tonight too, then I won't have to stay on my own side.

January 11, 1945

My wonderful Darling,

If you only knew how I'm missing you right now. It's only ten o'clock, and I'm in bed, wishing that you could be here too. I do, Irwin, I love you more and more every minute, and I'll just save all this love until I'm with you again.

Went to the office early this morning. It was an awful feeling, though, knowing I wouldn't see you in a couple of hours. I was waiting for eleven o'clock to come so I could hear you again. At ten thirty our phones were out of order. I prayed hard that they'd do something about it. I went around to the exchange to tell them, and they fixed it. You know, Darling, just to hear your voice makes me feel weak. You certainly do things to me, but I love you so awfully much, and that's how you should affect me. When I think of you there in London, I feel cheated. The days you were here simply flew, and every second I'm with you is so wonderful. There were more gale warnings on the radio tonight. I want to see you so much, Irwin. I hope they'll let you come to me.

Went to a show with Elaine tonight, *Her Highness and the Bell Boy*. I liked it, but all the way through they played "I'm in Love with You, Honey." I could have cried. I was missing you so extra much. I heard the last two lines of it too. It's a nice number, Darling, and has such wonderful memories for me. Con and Mair were here when I got home. They were asking about you. They liked you a lot, Irwin, but who wouldn't? Remember me telling you that my mother, who was always telling me about staying in so much? Well, tonight she asked me who I went to the show with, and when I told her, she said that as Elaine didn't run around anymore, she'd be good company for me. That made me feel good, Irwin, just to have her think the same way as I do about staying in, and I won't feel a bit miserable now. I never cared about staying home Saturday nights, as well as the other nights. It was just the things my mother said about it that made things unpleasant. I want to spend all the time I can alone, thinking about you, until we can be together again.

Good night, my Darling, and keep remembering that I love you and miss you more all the time.

All my love always,
Mary

January 17, 1946

My Darling,

Love me? Wish I could hear you say it. Oh, I love you so much, all day long my heart and mind are with you. Nothing else seems important. I'm all yours, Darling, and it's a wonderful feeling, so please keep loving me always.

I worked until nine o'clock this evening. I didn't mind, though. It took away some of my lonely mood. I did feel extra lonely this afternoon. Maybe because a week ago today was the last time I kissed you, that hurried one as you got on the train but nevertheless wonderful. I miss you, Irwin, more than you could ever realize, and I want to be in your arms as I was just eight days ago.

I'm terribly tired, Darling. I've been writing steadily for ten hours today, so will you please excuse this very short note? Love me all you can and miss me all the time.

All my love always,
Mary

January 19, 1945

My Darling,

It's Saturday night again, and how I miss you. Are you at the Folies tonight, Irwin? I know you're not, and I like to think of you in your bed at ten o'clock, dreaming about me and missing me almost as much as I'm missing you. I'm very impatient, Darling, when I think of being with you for always. Just can't wait until that wonderful day comes, but I will, as you know.

Went to a show with Elaine tonight, *Over 21*. It was all right, and that's all. I was home at nine o'clock and in bed by ten o'clock. Wish you were here, though. It's so cold I wouldn't stay on my own side at all. You wouldn't mind, would you, Darling? What thoughts! And that's just the start of them. When we're married and you tell me about the Folies, I'll tell you all that I think these lonely nights, as though you didn't already know.

I'm going to visit Con and Mair tomorrow evening. I'll have to walk all that way alone. It's the first time I'll be going there since you were with me, so you can imagine how I'm going to miss you. You're so wonderful, and I want you with me everywhere I go.

Dorothy's Sid came home again today. Unexpectantly this time. John doesn't fight with her when he's here, so it's a bit more peaceful than usual. I could scream when they start to perform sometimes. What you heard was quite mild compared with what they usually are. I only have to say something to them, and all I get is "Keep quiet, Yankee," so I do.

I have to be at work by eight o'clock every morning now. There's another boss. He's in at six thirty, and this morning I walked in at ten o'clock as usual. He didn't exactly say I was late. Just asked if I had lunch before getting there. I'm in his bad books, I know. Yesterday the colonel was looking at me having tea with an impatient stare. I just don't know who I'm going to annoy next.

Tomorrow is Sunday, Darling. You don't have to work, so what should we do? Yes, that will be wonderful, but it's your turn to get my breakfast. Oh, Darling. I wish all those dreams would hurry and come true, don't you? Dream about me, nice bad dreams, and remember that you have all my love forever. Love me lots, Darling.

All my love always and always,
Mary

January 21, 1946

My Darling,

No letter from you yet. Should I start to worry? I was expecting one today, but it isn't giving it much time when I come to think about it. Anyway, I love and miss you more with every minute that passes.

I didn't write last night, Darling. Went up to Con's and meant to get the nine thirty bus home. Just as I was ready to leave there, we heard the bus flying past, so I sat by the fore a little longer before I started my walk. It was awful going home alone, and it was cold. Why can't you always be with me? I didn't get home until eleven o'clock, and then I was too tired and cold to do anything except crawl into bed. Con and Mair send their regards and want to know, so soon they'll see you again.

Was in work at eight o'clock this morning. It's been a long day. Brookman is working days this week. I haven't spoken to him for a long time. He asked in a very sarcastic voice when was I going to America. I told him I couldn't give him an answer. To that he said he'd bet any money that I'd never marry you because you weren't serious about me and made other dirty cracks which could have made me mad if I'd taken any notice of them. Instead I told him I didn't want to discuss my affairs with his type. He apologized in his own way and said he just expected something better of me. I could cheerfully murder him on times. He's so horribly sarcastic sometimes it does hurt, and whenever anyone says we'll never get married, I feel miserable and want you there to reassure me. I don't know what I'd do if we couldn't be together finally. You have all my love, and I never want it back. I just can't imagine life without you, never having your letters and never being able to hope and dream of our life together eventually. I know all these dreams will come true. They have to, Darling. I love you so very much, and as long as you love me too, nothing can keep us apart. You don't know how I long to be with you again. It's like living in a different world when you're with me, and I know I'll always feel that way.

Went with Elaine to see Deanna Durbin in *Lady on the Train* tonight. She was awful. Quite the worst film she's made. I wish I'd stayed home now. Elaine bought all her sweet ration. John had used mine before I had a chance, so she kept giving me chocolate all through the show. I honestly didn't want it, but she thought I was being nice not eating her rations so insisted I did. I felt sick in the end, and Deanna's face just made me feel worse.

I came to bed at ten o'clock tonight. I still don't know where you are, so I can't picture exactly where you are in bed. I only close my eyes, though, and you are right beside me. I still turn towards you every night. It's strange how we both thought about that. Hope you're missing me lots wherever you are. Love me all you can, Darling, and be good for me. You're wonderful.

All my love always, always,
Mary

My Darling,

It's been raining all day, so I spent my day off in the house. The rest of the family are at the local show tonight. I'm all alone, and it's only seven thirty. I wonder what you are doing right now. Maybe you're writing to me. That's what I want to think you are doing. Hope you don't have to work late every night.

Walter wasn't working this afternoon, so there was my mother, Walter, and I sitting around the fire. We started talking about clothing coupons, and I said I wasn't going to use the new ones until later on. Naturally, they jumped to one conclusion. Walter said I wasn't having any of his coupons as if I married you it wouldn't be in a church, and he didn't like that. Mother said there isn't any difference where you get married. It means the same thing. I didn't think she'd feel that way about it, but I'm glad she does. It's definitely a law in this country, Irwin, about us not being married in church. I've seen it written since I told you about it. No preacher is allowed to marry divorced people. I don't mind a bit, though, do you? Connie didn't get married in church, and she had a nice wedding. All I hope is that you can be my husband for everyone to know. I love you so much, Darling.

I know how you felt writing to me and not having any letters to answer. It's like writing to myself all the time. I know I shouldn't be expecting a letter yet, but I wonder if you still love me and miss me? Say you do, Darling. That's all I want to know. I'm wondering too if you've heard anything from the States. It's time now, isn't it? Wish I could be with you, wherever you are. I miss you lots, Darling. More when I'm sitting by the fire alone, remembering all those nights we spent together, saying how early it was when the clock struck one.

Bye now, Darling. Dream about me, and please keep loving and missing me.

All my love always and always,
Mary

January 24, 1946

My Darling,

You're wonderful. I had two super letters today, written on the thirteenth and fourteenth. I love you, Irwin, how I love you. It's a wonderful feeling to know you love me and miss me, so don't ever stop telling me, will you? You'd laugh if you could see my mother when I'm reading your letters. She asks how you are, where you are, and naturally, when are you coming again. I tell her all she should know.

My brother Harry came home yesterday, finished with the army for good. I'm not kidding, but I think he's a little sorry. He and his wife were here until two o'clock this morning, so I didn't get around to writing you, Darling. I'm sorry.

Gwenda came to see me this morning. She asked me if I could go out and buy a hat with her. I asked her what she wanted that for, and she calmly said she was getting married next Thursday. That's if her intended husband doesn't have to go to a cattle sale. She's getting married in a Registry Office in Carmarthen and no honeymoon as they're pretty busy of the farm right now. They're having a small reception at a hotel in Carmarthen though. It's all very hush-hushy. She was telling me all this, and I was wondering how I'd get to Carmarthen and back as well as having the day off to go, as naturally I thought she was building me up for an invitation. You could have knocked me down when she was leaving me and just said, "Wish me all the best." It wasn't that I wanted to go so much, but it was expected. I believe I'm the only friend she ever had. People are funny, though.

My aunt phoned this morning wanting to know why we didn't go to see Nancy while you were here. I made some excuse and promised her I'd go there this evening, which I did. I nursed the baby all night. It didn't cry once. I was a bit of a wreck after he finished pulling my hair and pinching my face, but it was fun, though, and I think he liked me. He's a lovely kid. I walked all the way home from there. It's eleven o'clock now, and I just got to bed. They wanted me to stay the night, but I pictured myself pacing the floor with the baby instead of sleeping if I did that, and I wanted to write to my husband.

I'm awfully glad you didn't have much trouble getting back. I was with you all the way, though. We didn't get seasick. You ask me if I remember that Wednesday night, the last night we had together. It was wonderful, Darling. Just thinking about it makes me glow all over. I remember every minute though, and they were all perfect, just as you are. Your sucker bites have disappeared now, but they lasted a few days. Wish you could renew them right now, I do.

It's strange how I haven't had any letter from Sue. I would love to hear from her, and you know I wouldn't find her letters dull; nothing reminding me of you could be dull. And I liked her in that snap too. So tell her to write me, please. That's wonderful news you had from your lawyer, Darling. I didn't want you to go to the States, even for only thirty days. I know I shouldn't feel that way, because I trust you with all my heart. It's something that I can't figure out myself. All I know is that I want to be with you all the time—forever.

Darling, what did you say when I asked you where we were going to stay when we got to London? All right, I'll wait until it's my turn. There are a number of questions you have to answer on our wedding night. Firstly, about the "folies," of course. I wonder how much talking we'll do. We'll be so tired after the train journey that all we'll do is sleep. I laugh when I think of us doing that, don't you?

Good night, Darling. You're a real honey, and I love you, my little husband. Bless you. Be good and love me lots.

All my love always,
Mary

January 25, 1946

My Darling,

Are you cold too? It's freezing here. I know of a good way to get warm, though. Shall I tell you about it? First of all, you take Irwin and then Mary near him, and well, that's all there is to it. It doesn't take very long either. H I wish you were here, or I was there, not only because I'm cold, but just because I love you so much.

Nothing important happened today. No letters. I moved over to my own office, though. It's nice now. I'd prefer it to the other garage. At least we are able to see people passing. That breaks the monotony. The driver's faces aren't very pleasant things to gaze at each day. I'm extra good tonight. It's only nine o'clock, and I'm in bed.

You know what? That song "I'm in Love with You, Honey" is on my mind all day, and what's more, I know that last line. "Every day will be so sunny, Honey, with you." Aren't I clever? I'd give anything to hear you sing it now. Our voices are so sweet, aren't they? You love me, and I love you lots, so who cares about singing anyway? You're wonderful. Wish those thirty days would hurry.

We're getting rich, aren't we, Darling? We have more money than I thought, and we have all this love too, so I guess we're almost millionaires. I explained it to my mother about me saving your money, and she thought it was a good idea. So, Darling, you can send the next one home. I haven't received the last one, but it does take quite a time to come, so I'm not worrying.

I'm glad you didn't go to Switzerland for six months. It's a long time to go without seeing you. My brother came through there on his way home this time. He said it looked like Fairy Land, but I wouldn't want you to go there anyway.

Did I tell you I found another snap in my drawer of Mr. Humphries and Mary? I think I'd better take it to them when I'm passing that way. I've kept all your letters. I was just looking at them this evening. Can I take them with me wherever we go? I'll carry them; it's all right. I burn my other letters, but yours are so wonderful that every time I read them, I glory in the fact that you love me. I get the biggest kick out of reading your first letter though. It was so polite and matter-of-fact. Isn't it marvelous when you think of how our love has grown? I'm sure it will keep on growing too. Our love is for always.

We had a letter from my brother Ken in Greece today. He's kicking his heels waiting for the boat to come home. My mother was thrilled when she read it. She didn't think he'd be coming home so soon. Dorothy upset her though. She said, "That's good. Now we'll have some more presents." She always manages to say the wrong thing. When my brother came to the house with his wife the other night, they were talking about having a party, and Mother said that all we wanted now was to have Irwin home. Dorothy wanted to know if Sid came into her mind at all. She's a real spitfire on times.

It's getting colder all the time, so I'd better move over to your side tonight. We're going to have lots of fun. I love you with all my heart, Darling, and miss you so very much. Keep loving me lots.

All my love always and always,
Mary

January 26, 1946

My Darling,

Saturday, there you are, and here I am all alone. It's silly, isn't it, Darling? I had a letter today, though, a lovely one, so I'm happy. Elaine asked if I'd go to a show tonight, but I've seen all there is to see in town, and somehow I wanted to stay home, so here I am.

I feel mad too when I think you could have stayed longer. It does seem an awful long time since you were here, but when I think of the next time, I don't care if I spend these days and nights all alone without ever anyone to speak to. It's worth all the waiting and wishing I've done. I just wish that time would go faster. I love you so much, Irwin. You know that. And do I miss you? I'm really convinced, Darling, that everything's going to be just as we want it.

I'm glad too that you've stayed at Bryn for the last time. That day I went there with you, I was sitting in the chair wondering if something was crawling over me, so I wouldn't want you to stay there again. Of course you can stay in my little bed when we return from Scotland, where did you think we were going? That's going to be wonderful. After all those dreams I've dreamed in that little bed. We'll have to have a bigger bed, though. I think your feet would stick pout of the bottom of mine, and I wouldn't want you to have cold feet. Who wants you to behave, Darling? You talk as though I did. Well, I don't. So don't have any ideas. They're playing "Symphony" on the radio right now, in French too. It's nice, and do you remember how many times we heard it played together? This is a nice programme. "Embraceable You" is on now. Oh, Darling, I miss you and love you so very much. It's been a long, long time, all right. I'll never see enough of you, so I guess you'll have to take me to work with you. Do you know what I wonder, Irwin? Can all these people who are supposed to be in love are as much in love as we are? When I see other people together, they don't look anything as happy as we feel when we're together. Everybody tells us how happy we look. I think our love is perfect though, just as you are.

Almost forgot to thank you for the magazines that came today. My mother was tickled pink with the last edition of *Yank*. I'll keep that one. It's a good souvenir. Van Johnson was the cover boy on the *Look*. I don't like him anymore. He has too much glamour.

A good many girls from Swansea left on that GI bride boat today. Hazel's sister didn't though. Everybody is saying how sorry they feel for those girls going, not knowing what they're going to. You'd think they were going into battle, the way some of them talk. Nobody seems to envy them.

I wear my watch to bed every night now. It keeps good time. Gwenda thought it was super. Everybody does. Durk, our little driver, keeps asking me the time all day. He's funny. He calls me GI bride now and tells me all the dirt about Americans. He has a vivid imagination.

Time to wash my face and brush my hair before I start to dream, extra special dreams tonight as it's Saturday. So don't be late. Love me lots and miss me, Darling.

All my love always,
Mary

January 28, 1946

My Darling,

Are you missing me lots? I went to see Nancy again yesterday and stayed the night. I didn't want to walk home, so you see, Irwin, that's another black mark I have for not writing you. Babies are fun, all right, to look at. It may be different when it's your own. But last night, well, I've never heard a baby cry so much. I was wondering to myself if I could be the sort of mother I'd want to be if I had a yelling one like that. I guess I'll have to wait and see.

I had a nice letter from you today. You loved me and missed me just as I wanted you to. You're wonderful, Irwin. Almost as soon as I got into work this morning, I was wanted on the phone. Guess who it was? Eva. She asked for Doc's address. I told her that I had a letter from you this morning saying your letter to Doc had been returned, so you thought he'd been discharged. She'd been writing to Doc all the time but hasn't heard from him since last August, and all her letters had been returned, so she wrote to his brother. Had no reply. Then wrote to his sister and still no reply. So she's beginning to panic. What she said was she couldn't hang around indefinitely. I told her I didn't have any information for her and that I was busy. So she said she'd call at the office one day. I don't want to see her. Wish she wouldn't bother me. If she had any sense, she'd know by now that Doc doesn't want to hear from her anymore, but maybe she does love him. Went to a show with Elaine this evening. *Dead of Night.* It was thrilling even though it was British. Elaine's husband is in Austria now. She's awfully upset about it. I've never seen anyone change their ideas of life as much as she did.

I didn't know Johnny Monson was married. I'm glad he's happy though. I'd like to meet him after hearing so much about him. It was nice of him to send his best wishes to me. I want everyone to know that I belong to you. He's one of millions, I suppose, that doesn't have any work to go to. It's terrible here. Listen, Darling, if you think it's better for us if you stay in the Army, I have no objection as long as I can be near you. That's all I worry about. Maybe things will be better in civilian life in a few years' time. Then you could do something you wanted to do. I wouldn't want you to take a job and not be interested in it. Just working for the sake of money and not getting anywhere. Well, you know what you want better than I do, so that's what I want too. I'm happy as long as you are.

Well, Darling, it's dream time again. I'll see you. Love me and miss me half as much as I do you, and I'll be happy. Wish you were near for a few super good night kisses, then turn out the lights, and then—Oh, I love you so very much, Irwin.

All my love always,
Mary

January 29, 1946

My Darling,

No letter today, so I stayed in bed until twelve o'clock, my day off again. It's been raining and blowing a gale, so I didn't go out at all. My brother and his wife came to see us this afternoon. They're having a big party next Saturday night. I've already booked seats to go to a symphony concert at the Brangwyn, with Elaine, so that's a good excuse not to go to their party. I didn't tell you before about going to this symphony thing, did I? One day I went to Elaine's office, all the girls were there, and they suggested going, just for somewhere to go. We didn't realize it was on a Saturday night before buying the tickets, and we arranged to go straight from the office to have dinner at the Grand and be really respectable. You should have heard them when they discovered how they'd ruined their Saturday night, but we're all going anyway. I'm going to sit near the door so I can take a walk through the corridor if things get too boring. It's going to be funny. We're going to laugh and spoil the whole thing. I'm sure something will happen.

My mother and John have gone to the local cinema tonight. They wanted me to go, but I've seen the show about two years ago. So I've listened to the radio in peace all the evening. Anne Shelton singing "I'll Be Seeing You" did things to me. Oh, Darling, it's awfully lonely without you. But I know you're missing me too, so I don't mind.

I haven't had a drink since you left, and there you are drinking champagne. I envy you. Our new garage is next door to the nicest hotel in town. You can only drink there, though. Taxi drivers aren't allowed to go there. It's our colonel's visiting place. He spends most of his time there, even had a secret entrance into the place, but Mr. Clement had it blocked. You know that I won't drink unless you're with me, though I don't care if I ever drink again. I like the taste of champagne. Wish it was New Year's Eve again, not for the champagne particularly though. I want to see you again. I love you so much, Darling. That certainly was the best New Year's of my life. That's the first one we've been together. You're the only person I'll kiss all the year. You're my husband though, and the person that exists for me in the whole world.

I played cribbage this afternoon. I'm learning slowly. Maybe I'll get 250 before you next time. That's if you don't take my mind off it with the usual interruptions. Do you think of me when you play it now? This afternoon you were with me telling me how to count. I'll never forget how annoyed you looked every time I forgot a few cards. I was dumb, wasn't I? Remember the look of surprise on my mother's face when she saw the cards on the table that night? She didn't expect that.

Harry, the brother you haven't met, said something this afternoon about me being crazy for thinking of marrying an American, and Walter, of all people, told him he had no right to interfere with our affairs. I'm sorry you didn't like Walter. He's not the person you think he is. Normally he's happy-go-lucky. Nobody bothers him. Actually he annoys me on times because he says things that he means to be witty, and seem sarcastic to other people, but he's all right.

Good night, Darling. Don't go to sleep right away, though. I want to talk to you. Be good and love me all you can. I love you more and more every minute and miss you so very much.

All my love always and always,
Mary

January 31, 1946

My Darling,

Two wonderful letters from you today. I love you more again after reading them. You certainly missed me. That's good. I hope you think so too because I don't mind how much I miss you. You're on my mind every second though, and you're wonderful.

Went to see *Duffy's Tavern* with Elaine this evening. It wasn't so good, and I don't know why, but nothing seemed funny to me. It's only eight thirty now. Dorothy's writing a letter to Sid. There's no one else at home. Wish you were here, Irwin, I could pitch lots of woo. But of course, you'd rather go to the pub and leave me alone at home. Well, tomorrow night, you won't have the chance. I'll go out, and then you'll be sorry. I won't leave you any money, either, so you'll know who the boss is in our family. Did I say we were alone at home? Walter's just arrived. He's standing behind Dorothy, reading as she's writing, and she's concentrating so hard she doesn't realize what he's doing. She'll get mad when she does.

When you look at my arms in those pictures, Darling, remember that in my mind they are around you tight, never wanting to let you go. You're my everything, and you know I'm all yours, forever. I want to be as near as it's possible to be to you, Darling. Then I'll have all I want. How I love you! I'm the luckiest person in the world, being able to love you and know that you want my love because you love me too. It's a wonderful world, all right.

We haven't had any snow yet. It just rains and blows, the depressing season. Everybody looks as if they're too tired to walk. All the people at work have colds, but my office is nice now, and the biggest part of the day, I'm all alone. You'd be surprised if you knew how many times a day I just put down my pen and think hard about you. Lovely thoughts. I go over every minute I was with you and everything you said. Then somebody barges into the office and I come back to Glamtax once more. We have another colonel with us for a few days. He's one of our directors. Very nice, though. Sensible compared with the rest of them. He even had a cup of our tea this morning, and then we smoked his cigarettes.

I didn't know you really stayed at the reindeer club. You know the morning you phoned me. I thought you said, "I'm in the rain, dear." Crazy, that's what I am.

I'm going to bed now, Darling. Will you be very long before you come up? I love you with all my heart, Irwin, and miss you all the time. Keep loving me and be good. I know there's no need to say that. You're mine, just as I'm yours, until we die.

All my love always,
Mary

February 1, 1946

My Darling,

It's been a long time since I kissed you good night, and right now I could use a few super ones, even those hurried kisses when you were leaving late at night would make me feel good. When I think of us not having to say "good night" at all, just going to bed early instead, I want time to go so much faster. Please don't dream about me sleeping on my right side. I've told you before, I don't do that anymore. I sleep on my stomach. What are you going to do about that? All right, don't tell me.

I worked hard all day, and I've got a cold, so when I came home this evening, I felt awful, and everybody was annoying me. Harry and Walter were biting my ears and pinching me until I got really mad. They don't realize how strong they are. My mother was yelling at them to leave me alone, but every move I made, I had it. In the end I came to bed. It's only seven thirty now. I don't know what I'm going to do when they're all home. I'll have to get someone to protect me. Walter said he was making up for lost time this evening, as he didn't touch me when you were here. See how I need you beside me always? I do. I have so much love saved for you, and I want to see you more than you'll ever know.

Before coming to bed, I took tablets for this cold, and they seem to be making me sleepy. As I'm writing, I start to dream you're there, wonderful as ever. Do you mind very much if this is a very short letter? Maybe I'll feel a lot better in the morning if I go to sleep now. Even when I feel like this, I want you here to pester me, as you call it, but it really is a pleasure, Darling. Bye now. I love you twice as much as yesterday and miss you more all the time. Keep loving and missing me all you can.

All my love always,
Mary

February 2, 1946

My Darling,

I've just returned from the symphony concert. It was terrible. Elaine was bored to tears as well. The orchestra had only played about three bars of music when she said, "It's awful. I'll never come here again." We came about before it was over, and the rest of the people were tittering when we disturbed them. There was a man sitting in front of us, and he kept twitching his shoulder all the time. Everything was so quiet, and every time this man's shoulder moved, his chair creaked. I felt sorry for him, but at the same time, it tickled Elaine and I. I was certainly glad to get out of that.

The rest of the family are at my brother's party tonight, so I came to bed as soon as I came home. Why don't you use my window tonight? I'm waiting with lots and lots of love for you as usual. Of course, there is the possibility of you catching my cold. I still have it. But we'd have colds together, and there's only one way to cure them. We'd have to stay in bed. Wouldn't that be nice?

As I was tidying up the office today, I came across a railway timetable. It's the one that stands now. Naturally, I looked up the trains to Scotland. They only run three a day, 8:30 a.m. That's too early. The next is 12:30, and then 7:00 p.m. We'll either have to get married early in the morning or travel overnight, Darling. Even as I'm writing this, I'm thinking how I'm taking everything for granted. I do hope, though, that things will be so we can make plans like this. I love you so very, very much, Darling, and want you with me all the time.

Good night, Irwin. I'll see you in a few minutes. Wish you were really here, though. Love me all you can and miss me lots.

All my love always,
Mary

February 3, 1946

My Darling,

It's done nothing but rain all day, so I worked until four o'clock. We are opening our garage at Mumbles next week. That means a little extra work. Sunday could be the most wonderful day in the week if we were together. You wouldn't have to go to work, so you wouldn't have an excuse for staying out late. I'd have you all to myself. We'd be a pair of wrecks by Monday morning. Oh, it would be wonderful.

You were terrible in my dreams last night, lovely terrible, I mean. When I woke this morning I found myself on your side of the bed. I wonder why that was? I like it better that side though.

Everyone in the house has a cold now. Of course, I'm to blame. I had it first. It's the weather, though. I wish spring would hurry and come for lots of reasons. I want to be your wife, but if that isn't possible, I want to see you just as much as I always will. Every day I'm without you makes me want to be with you more and more. I love you, Darling, and I'll never stop. I'll just keep praying that things will be as we want them.

I'm glad I didn't go to that party last night. Everyone was bored and didn't know what excuse to make for leaving early, so they stayed until one o'clock. Walter thought he'd have beer there. Otherwise he wouldn't have gone. He took a few of his drinking friends with him, and all he had was a cup of tea. That's all he's talked about today, until I could throw something at him.

Hope I get a letter in the morning. It's a lonely day when I don't hear from darling. Love me and miss me as you know I want you to, and remember that I'm loving you and missing you every minute.

All of my love always,
Mary

February 4, 1946

My Darling,

I was disappointed today. I expected a letter from you, but I wasn't lucky. There's always tomorrow though. I hope you're getting my letters all right, just to keep reminding you that I love you and miss you as always.

Went to see *The Glass Key* this evening with Elaine. It wasn't a new show, but we liked it a lot. Vey soon Elaine and I will know the names of all the producers and directors. I'm getting just a little tired of seeing all these shows. I think I'll become a critic.

I have a day off tomorrow, so I told my mother she could stay in bed for the day as she has a cold, and I'd take care of everything, but I know she won't do that. She thinks we couldn't get along if she wasn't there. I'll surprise her though. I'll get up before her, I hope. You'd better behave yourself in my dreams tonight. Otherwise I'll be in bed until twelve o'clock again.

You don't know how lonely I feel without you. When I walk down the street, it doesn't seem right without you. It's just as though part of me was missing. I hope you feel that way too, Darling. Whatever I'm doing and wherever I am, you're always on my mind. The more I think of you, the more I love you and want you. Wish I could be with you now. There's tons of love saved for you. I'd like you to make a big withdrawal as soon as you can. Can you arrange that? I look for you every night when I get into bed, but I have to sleep before I see you, and then you disappear when I want you to stay most. I'm longing to be close to you, with my arms around you as far as they can go, and then, well, you know. Miss me lots and love me all the time, Darling.

All my love always,
Mary

February 5, 1946

My Darling,

I've been housekeeper all today. I was starting my duties at seven o'clock this morning. Did all the cleaning and cooking. Wish you could have tasted my dinner. Even Walter said it was good. I kept thinking all day how wonderful it would be if it was our nice house, the one we want, with everything new, and I was cooking for you. Then you come home after work and tell me all that happened during the day. Maybe we'd get ready to go somewhere after you had a little rest, or maybe we'd just sit around. You reading the paper and me darning your socks, or maybe just reading the paper with you, like we did one night. Only somehow, the paper gets neglected. What an imagination I have. It's certainly been running riot today.

In the middle of washing the dishes after dinner, a knock came at the door. It was Glamtax, a special message from Mr. Clement. Would I come to work early tomorrow morning. The auditors will be there. That wasn't good. The driver asked if I had a cup of tea for him. So I couldn't refuse. I had his gay chatter for twenty minutes. It spoiled my dreams a little. I don't want any men calling at our house when we're married.

I haven't told you the most important thing that happened to me today. I had two lovely letters from my darling. Maybe that's what started me thinking so much about our home. I read them about five times, just to see how much you loved me. You do love me lots, don't you, Darling?

Yes, I could use a couple of sucker bites right now, even though they do hurt. Guess I'll have to find something to do to you. That'll make you scream. Just wait. You'll be sorry. You won't have any sympathy from me. I just remembered what you told me about not being able to stand anybody fooling around one certain spot. Do you remember? You will.

The *New York Times* as good as said the Americans were crazy. There's an article published on our paper tonight about them saying that the English girls arriving in America are starting a pilgrimage of women with common sense who will do a lot to increase the stability of the minds of American people, and that's what they need, Darling. Do I do that to you? I think we're both crazy about one another, and that's all I worry about.

I've had a hard day, so don't you try keeping me awake tonight. I'm not playing. Don't you ever get tired? Love me and miss me, like you've never missed anyone before and dream bad dreams about me, being bad, I mean. I love you and miss you all I can.

All my love always,
Mary

February 6, 1946

My Darling,

Happy Anniversary. It's been a long time, twenty-seven months, and I've loved you and missed you. I've been happy and sometimes a little sad during that time, but every minute waiting for you has been well worth it, and I'm so lucky to have your love. Oh, Darling, I wish we were together now.

There's been a bus strike here today, so you can imagine how busy we've been. I worked from eight o'clock this morning to eight o'clock this evening, and when I got home, I had a wonderful surprise, four letters from my darling. I love you.

What do you mean when you say you hope we have time for lunch after we're married? I promise not to disturb you, Darling. I'll eat too, then just a kiss until I see you after you finish work, and then, I suppose, you'll want more to eat. It is hard waiting for those days to come, Darling, but you know I'll wait. It's going to be so wonderful, and I really don't think our marriage is going to be one of those affairs that just become a daily routine. Every minute will be as precious as if it was a lifetime. I know we'll be happy forever.

Hazel's sister is going to Hazleton. She had her papers to go to Tidworth today. That's all we read and hear about now. The GI brides and the divorce papers they are sent, before they know there's anything wrong. The country is quite disturbed about it.

We had our rations cut again. We only get an ounce of fat a week now, so if you see a door opening and nobody coming in, it's me. People won't be able to exist on this food before long. There's no variety, so you can't really look forward to a meal. Walter says that as soon as all the GI brides and children go, there'll be lots of food.

I envy all the people who don't have to say good night. Not only Nancy and Tom. Anyway, they had a baby disturbing their sleep, and they haven't had so very much time together. I'm just making excuses now, not to seem jealous. It's going to be heavenly when I can have my arms around you and not worry about the time. Oh, and I musn't think those things now, otherwise, heaven knows what I'll dream about. You're a bad man in my dreams, and I love you because you're so perfect.

Thanks for all the notes to add to our collection. My drawer is beginning to look like the Foreign Exchange. We're worth quite a lot of money, aren't we, Darling?

You better tell Rankin for me that you're the most perfect person in the world, and I wouldn't want any part of you different. Let me tell you something, Darling. When I read the two letters from you yesterday, something seemed wrong in them, and I thought maybe it was the beginning of the end. They don't sound like your usual letters do, and I was more than relieved to have these letters today. I was beginning to worry. Maybe you were tired or something when you wrote, and I was just looking for trouble. I'll be glad when I don't have to read between the lines to see how much you love me. I want to hear it, and I'll be in your arms. Though after reading those four letters, all my fears have vanished. I love you for always.

We had a letter from my brother today. My mother must have written to him about meeting you, as in this letter he said that if Irwin was as nice as she said he was, things will be fine at home. That's good, isn't it, Darling? But I know the way she likes to talk about you, how much she likes you.

I'm tired, sweet. Please unfasten something for me, and let's get to bed. Love me and miss me lots.

All my love always,
Mary

February 2, 1946

My Darling,

How's your bed tonight? I'm sure mine would be much more comfortable for you, and as it is, I'm cold, so why not share it with me? It's a lovely thought, anyway, and from it I think of all sorts of things. I'm in the mood for pitching lots of woo. I'd like to start right now and still have you with me in the morning. Maybe we could have some sleep as well. That would be nice. I'd be in your arms or you in mine, and I'd open my eyes to find my darling. Then I'd wake you to tell you how very much I love you, and we'd have to eat breakfast, but who knows what we'd do. I'm going to love you to death, Darling. Just wait.

Went to see *Ten Little N——* tonight. It was thrilling. Elaine kept pinching me all the time. I had read the book, so I knew what was coming. There was a big man in front of me. He kept leaning forward, so I couldn't see very much, and when he put his arms up to stroke his silly moustache, that was the end. I told him about it eventually, so he sat back like he should, then he dropped something on the floor and started searching for it. Elaine got so mad she told him in a nasty voice that she's never seen such a disgusting exhibition. After that he walked out. He was annoying, though.

That captain I told you about who sent me that letter phoned me this morning. Wanted to know if I'd make up the number for a party at Langland tonight. I told him I wouldn't, so he just asked what I did with myself when I wasn't working as he hasn't seen me at Langland for a long time. He wouldn't believe me when I told him but apologized very nicely for bothering me. Elaine had an invitation from him afterwards, but she wasn't playing either. I think I should introduce him to Eva.

Mr. Clement and I were talking about the colonel this afternoon. He has a terrible reputation, by the way, and I was just saying that I wished he'd join the Army again when I saw him standing at the door. I didn't know where to look, and Mr. Clement looked like a ghost, but the colonel didn't say anything about it, so I left the room as soon as I could.

You know Peter, the boy who helps our mechanic? I remember who he looks like. That boy with the photographic mind. It's been worrying me ever since you mentioned that he reminded you of somebody.

I was looking at the map of the world tonight. You seem awfully near to me on that. It looks as though I could just step across the water and I'd be with you. Then I looked to see how far you were from home. That really looks a long way. You've traveled some miles. I was thinking how strange things are. You from that big place all the way over there. Me from the small little island, and us meeting and loving one another as much as we do. I don't want an inch between us, though.

Had the cheque for January today. Darling, it's in the bank now. Want to know how much you've got? 99.3.2. There's 6 interest so far. That's a lot of money, isn't it?

You were bad in my dreams last night. Will you be the same tonight, please? I love you with all my heart, Darling. Love me.

All my love always and always,
Mary

February 8, 1946

Hello, Honey,

Miss me? Or are you at the Folies? I read on the paper today about there being a shortage of girls for the Folies. I was wondering what you thought of the situation. Don't tell me. I know. You haven't been there since, since last Saturday night, of course. That's as bad as me going to Langland, you know. Same thing happens, but I do trust you, Darling. It's the girls I don't trust. I don't like the thought of you wandering around France at all. Lots of girls may think the same as I thought when I saw you. They can't have you, though. You're all mine. Aren't you, Darling?

Hard day today. Didn't get to work until ten o'clock. Tea at ten thirty. Then to the bank. Went to see Elaine, and lunch at twelve thirty, by the way. Elaine and I had one beer each with our lunch. We did a little shopping afterwards, and I got back to the office at three o'clock. Captain Evans was there. He told me about his wife, how charming she was and how charming she said I was, until it was four o'clock, and I left for home. Now, isn't that what you call work?

My brother and his wife were here this evening. She has toothache, headache, and all the rest of the aches. I was glad to see them leave. Mair phoned me today. The doctor told her to take it easy. She has bad nerves and a few more ailments. I don't know what's wrong with all these people. Must be married life. What am I going to suffer with, Darling, after we're married?

It's awfully late, one thirty, so I'll have to leave you for a while. Be good, Darling, 'cause I love you and love you and love you. Love me lots too.

All my love always and always,
Mary

February 9, 1946

My Darling,

These Saturday nights are terrible. Elaine and I went to another show. A British effort too. We were bored to tears. When I met Elaine this afternoon, she rambled on about there being nothing to do. I knew what was coming. "What about Langland?" But I pretended to be slow on the uptake, and that put an end to her suggestions. Oh,

Darling, I really want to go to a dance, but it must be with you. I hate to see Saturday nights come around as it is.

Today I received three letters from you. Wonderful ones as usual. I've been extra lucky this week. They were written on the twenty-eighth, twenty-ninth, and thirtieth. You love and miss me in all of them, and that's what I want to hear most of all.

You know as well as I do that frightened is the last thing I am at the prospect of having you around all the time. I'm going to love every minute of it. I want to be with you for always and always. Maybe you're the one who should be frightened. We'll both be crazy though, but it's going to be wonderful.

You must love me, when you write early in the morning before most people are out of bed. I hope you find the missing $1,500. That's a lot of money. Surely it's a mistake in the records or something. I didn't envy you counting 165,000,000 francs. That would have driven me crazy, all right. I bet you dreamed of them all night afterwards. I could have helped you with them, though. Maybe you'd be another few hundred out, but that wouldn't make much difference, would it? I go crazy when there's a shilling missing, so your lieutenant must be in a bad way. I don't think I'd like his responsibilities at all.

We didn't have any coal today, and we all have colds. So when I came home from the show tonight, I suggested we all go to bed right away. I was just washing my face when my brother Harry and his wife came in. Well, I could have screamed. He was in his old uniform and a sack of coal on his shoulder. We were never more glad to see him. So we had a big fire and didn't come to bed until twelve o'clock. After we lit the fire, Mother said, "Now, Irwin should be here to see this."

John has gone to stay with his friend in Cardiff for the weekend, and it's awfully quiet without him, and Dorothy's miserable. She said tonight she misses John more than she does Sid, after all the fighting they do.

I'm just feeling exactly right to snuggle up to you and make myself comfortable to sleep for a couple of hours. Certainly wish I could do that. I wonder if a substitute would be any use. I'm only kidding. There'll never be a substitute for my Irwin. I'm all yours for always, so you'd better want me, Darling. You have my heart over there, so how could I have any love to spare? Miss me, Irwin, and dream about us as I do.

All my love always and always,
Mary

February 11, 1946

My Darling,

I'm sorry, but I didn't write last night. I went to Hazel's home. Her sister was giving a party as she's leaving for the States tomorrow. I had a nice time too. They're friendly people. I met that woman with the wonderful ring. She's still waiting for her husband to come and get her. She's not very nice, though. Her husband one minute was a playboy, then she said he was a gentleman farmer, the manager of the biggest milk factory in the States, a teacher of navigation, as he's a captain in the Navy, and that's his career. I got so mixed up that I didn't get around to asking what he really did. Hazel was standing near me all the time, telling me not to believe a word she said, as if I would. I didn't get home until twelve o'clock, and then my mother said that I was expected home earlier, as I'd never get up in the morning. Maybe she didn't know what time you used to leave after all.

I had a wonderful letter from my darling today and also a letter to myself. I wrote it to you on November 2, when you were at Mailly, and on the envelope it says there's no such place, and it looks as though it's been to a few other camps. So you see, Darling, that may happen to a few more of my letters. It was a long letter too. It seemed awfully silly to have it back like that.

Went to show with Elaine tonight. *The Seventh Veil*. It was super. You would have liked it too. I don't suppose you'll see it though, as it's British. I want to see *The Dolly Sisters*. I don't mind you having June Haver as your pin-up girl. I think she's lovely too.

You don't know how long it seems to me since I was in your arms hearing you say you loved me and having you near so I could kiss you without wasting any time. Oh, Darling, it seems an eternity, and the days are so long, but I know it's going to be worth more, waiting like this. Those thirty days, Irwin. Who wants to spend time talking and being nice to people. I want to be alone with you just as much as you do, maybe more.

No, Darling. I've never had a letter from your sister or Sue. Maybe they changed their minds about writing, and you can't blame them for that.

No work tomorrow. Let's stay in bed for a couple of hours extra, shall we? I forgot you have to go to work. I don't want you to though, Darling. We could have lots of fun. All right, you can tell me in the morning how you feel about getting up. Dream nice dreams and love me lots. You know I love you so very, very much and miss you every minute.

All my love always,
Mary

February 13, 1946

My wonderful Darling,

I'm missing you terribly and loving you so much more all the time. How can I ever thank you for the lovely flowers, Irwin? They were really lovely. You know I'm your Valentine for always, and you're my only Valentine. You were wonderful to send me the flowers. I just wished when I saw them that you could have been with me. That's what I'm wishing all the time. But I've been missing you extra today, and when I saw them, it made me miss you more. I have millions of super kisses waiting for you too. It seems such a long time since we were two sleepy people who'd have given anything to be able to just fall asleep in one another's arms. We don't have long to wait now though, do we, Darling? Life's pretty wonderful right now, having your love and being able to love you. But soon life is going to be more than wonderful, no good nights. And having you with me day and night for at least thirty days to start with. I wish time would go faster. I want to see you so very, very much.

Went to see *The Green-Eyed Women* with Elaine tonight. It was good. As we were going into the show, I almost fell down the stairs, and I thought there must have been something wrong with the floor. It seemed uneven. I soon discovered what was wrong. The heel had come off my shoe. I didn't know what to do. I couldn't find it in the dark, so I just sat down. Elaine was laughing too much to help me. It was all right until it was time to leave, then I did feel silly. There were a crowd of people outside, and I had to walk to my bus, so I phoned for a car to take me home. Everything that could happen to anybody happens to me. It was a funny experience though. My mother couldn't stop laughing when I told her what happened. Maybe it's a good thing you weren't with me. You'd have had a good laugh at my expense.

I had the awful task today of asking all the staff their ages. We're starting a pension scheme. I asked Miss Baldwin hers, and she said thirty-eight. Then I explained to her what it was for, and she said her correct age was fifty-one. I don't know which of us felt the most embarrassed. I didn't like that a bit.

I didn't have a letter today. I had so many last week, though, that I can't expect any for a few days. I hope you're getting all my letters so you know how much more I love you every day and how important you are to me, the only person that exists for me. You're wonderful, Darling, so love me all you can and think of me sometimes. I know you do, Irwin, just as I think of you all day long. I'm coming over on your side tonight. Want me?

All my love always and always,
Mary

February 15, 1946

My Darling,

Oh, I love you. Wish I could see you. I miss you so very, very much. Yesterday I had three wonderful letters from you and a very pretty Valentine from Virginia. Isn't she nice to me, Irwin? I'm sorry I didn't write last night. I went to see Con and Mair, and just as I was leaving to get the bus, Con decided to come home with me as it was so dark. By the time he put his coat on, the bus had gone. So we walked all the way, and I was tired when we finally turned the last corner, so I went to bed right away and dreamed wonderful dreams. Am I excused, Darling? This morning I had another wonderful letter from you and also a lovely letter from Virginia. I was thrilled when I read it. She's had a bad time with all that illness, hasn't she? She made me feel that I was already one of the family, and you can't imagine how good that is to me. I wrote to her this evening. I hope she'll like my letter. I really want her to like me, Irwin. I love her brother so very much.

You said you had a grin on your face when you wrote that I make a pretty good Daddy. Well, it's nothing to the grin I had on my face when I read it. You're awful. I'll show you though. Just wait. Wish we could play house right now. I'm in the mood to play Daddy and Mother, aren't you? It's been a long, long time.

Oh, Darling, it would be more than wonderful if you could be transferred to England. I'm certainly keeping my fingers crossed for us. It seems a lot more lonely without you here since your last leave. Honestly it does. And when the weekend comes around, I could scream. But seeing you often would help such a lot until the day I can be with you for always.

Good night, Darling. I'll answer all your letters tomorrow night. Bless you and love me all you can. I'm yours for always and always. Miss me.

All my love always,
Mary

February 16, 1946

My Darling,

Are you missing me extra tonight? This is the night we should be out dancing. That's if I ever managed to get dressed with you around. It would be heavenly if I couldn't though, and we just stayed home, Irwin. I love you and miss you so very much.

This morning I had another one of my letters returned. I wrote it on January 16. I wonder what's going on. That's two this week. Maybe all this explains why you don't get my letters. I've never had a letter returned before. That I suppose was too much trouble for them. It's got me worried.

As I was going down the stairs of the bus this morning, the bus jerked forward, and I fell right to the bottom. I was scared. I put my arm out to save myself, and I must have twisted it or something. It's sore, anyway. Apart from that and a couple of bruises, I'm all right. The people in the bus were scared too. I felt awfully silly picking myself up.

Went to a show again this evening with Elaine. *That Night with You*. It was boring. Elaine went to Langland last night. She kept telling me what a wonderful time she had. It didn't bother me any. I know my Irwin is waiting as patiently as I am until we can have all our fun together. Wish we could start right now. I could use lots and lots of love. Could you? You know you have tons in your account now.

You know, Darling, that I don't care where we live after we're married, as long as I could be with you. You say where it shall be. You know more about these places than I do. It will be wonderful though if I can be wherever you are.

I'm glad the hairbrush is doing a good job, but you know I didn't buy it because I was scared of my husband being bald. I love you for always, Darling. You'll always be the most handsome man in the world to me.

So you bought clothes after all. I'm glad they were nice. (What did you expect me to say? I fooled you.) It's a shame they didn't have a shirt small enough for my little husband though. You'll have to wait until you're big, Darling. Don't bite me. You know I'm only kidding.

What do you mean by asking me how many times does someone have to awaken me before I get scared. Do you want me to find out for you before you marry me? You know that neither of us would have a very good chance of sleeping. It's going to be wonderful. Let's go on our honeymoon right now.

Bye now. It's time for those lovely bad dreams. Life's wonderful. I love you, my darling husband. Keep loving me.

All my love always,
Mary

February 16, 1946

My Darling,

Did you think of me when you were in bed this morning? I woke at seven thirty, and the sun was streaming in through my window. Yes, honestly, it was real sun. I looked at my watch and thought of you snoring away for another few hours and wishing hard, of course, that I could awaken you, and then we could decide what to do on a sunny Sunday morning. But I had to leave my bed and wait for the car instead. Didn't have to wait long though. It was a wonderful morning, and I kept thinking how perfect everything would be if it was our car with just you and I going out into the country. I had to go to a dismal office instead though. How I wish I could be with you very soon. I miss you so much, Darling.

The colonel and his brother called in the office this morning. They were all dressed up to go riding. I don't know where the horses were, though. All I could see parked outside was their MG. The colonel's brother is like Charlie Chan's honourable son. He's all right, though. He thought it was terrible that we had to work on such a lovely morning. He asked if I went riding. I told him my horse was in the next office waiting for me. I don't think he liked that as he didn't say any more.

I went for a long walk this afternoon, all alone. It was nice, though. Just thinking of us and wondering if you were missing me as much as I was missing you.

Now tonight, there's a wonderful moon. It certainly does things to me. How I wish we were both looking at it from this position. Yes, Darling. I'm in bed. Oh, Irwin. I love you and love you and love you. I'm going to dream about us now. You can be Daddy tonight. Love me and miss me lots.

All my love always,
Mary

February 18, 1946

My Darling,

No letter today, but I know you love me anyway. You'd better, or you'll be sorry in your dreams tonight; I'll love you to death. Right now I'd like to be with you. That's what I always want, of course, but I'm missing you extra much again, as it's ten thirty. I'm in bed, and there's lots of room for you. If you were here, I'd have my arms so tight around you that you couldn't move, and it would be just one long kiss. Then we'd forget that we were ever apart from one another, and time wouldn't bother us. We wouldn't have to say good night. Oh, Irwin, I love you so very, very much.

I've had a hard day. Mr. Clement has flu, and the captain visited us. He kept me busy the whole time. I have to work tomorrow again, so don't imagine that I'm sleeping tomorrow morning, Darling.

Went to meet Elaine at her office. When I got there, she was crying. I thought something had happened to her husband. She showed me this evening's paper. Apparently six months ago she met a wing commander at the RAF Officers' Mess, and he'd bothered her a lot since, but she never went out with him. Last Friday though, she went to Langland, and he was there, so he stuck to her all the evening. Elaine was telling me Saturday how nice he was. Then this afternoon she read that he'd been killed Saturday morning in a plane crash. It must have been a shock to her, remembering that she spent his last few hours with her. Life's funny, though.

We went to see *Valley of Decision*. It's very good. Have you seen it? It's all about Pittsburgh, seventy years ago, though. It looked awfully dirty then. Almost as dirty as Swansea looks now.

Well, Darling, I can't even start telling you how much I love and miss you. You know though, Darling, how I'm longing to be in your arms again, hearing you tell me that you love me. Wish I could see you if only for a couple of minutes. You're wonderful, and I love you, my darling husband, for always and always. You'll never get rid of me. Love me all you can and miss me lots all the time. I'll see you in my dreams in a few minutes. I know you'll be waiting for me too. You looked so wonderful last night.

All my love always and always,
Mary

February 19, 1946

My Darling,

You'll be as mad as I was when I tell you that I had three more letters returned today, the ones I wrote on the twelfth, fourteenth, and fifteenth. I don't quite know what to do, Darling. It seems silly writing to myself, and the postal authorities must think I'm a terrible nuisance, but, Irwin, you must have come to the conclusion that I'm just not writing to you, and maybe you won't love me so much. I don't want that to happen. I've only missed writing about four times since you left. I know you want my letters, so you can imagine how I feel when they're handed to me.

I had a wonderful letter from you this morning, though that's another thing. I don't see why the people who sort the mail out aren't observant enough to see that the same day I have letters returned with a "Not To Be Found" notice written all over them, there's also a letter for me from the same person. It just doesn't make sense. I hope you get some of my letters though. I want you to know how very much I love you.

I hope everything was all right for those people from the Inspector General's Office. I don't want you to be working until ten fifteen every evening. You know, Darling, you need someone there to take care of you. Can I have the job, please? I'll see you don't work late and that you get plenty of rest—in my arms.

It's strange how Virginia had her Christmas box returned to her. There's something funny going on there. It must be awfully annoying for you, Darling, but maybe it was something to do with your changing your APO number. I feel so miserable when I think of you thinking that I can't find time to write. I really don't think I'll have to pay duty on hosiery, but if I do, I'll be so grateful for them that you'll never know about it, Darling. Don't get mad. You said I was boss in our family. Virginia didn't say anything about not hearing from you in her letter, so I thought she knew you'd been with me for New Year's; otherwise, I'd have made a big point of telling her.

I don't know if Webb's wife has gone to the States yet, but she was expecting to go this month. Did you ever hear from Webb? When you talk about the mud in France, I still feel responsible for your having to put up with everything, when you could be in the States. I owe you a lot, Darling, and I hope I can repay you by making you so very happy. I'll do everything I can so you'll never regret what you've done for me. You have been wonderful, and I love you so very, very much.

Wish your cold feet were on my back right now. I'd love it. I know they wouldn't be there for long. You'd at least want to kiss me good night. I'm very impatient to have you in my little bed, Darling. It needs you. Dream about me, and remember that every minute, I'm loving and missing you more. Love me all you can, my wonderful husband. Wish you were here.

All my love always and always,
Mary

February 20, 1946

Darling,

This morning I had three very lovely letters from you. I love you, Irwin. You're as wonderful as your letters. More wonderful, of course, but you know what I mean. They're the best substitute of you that I can have. You seem so very near when I read them.

We've had snow today. Not very much, but it made me want you with me extra this evening when I was sitting alone by the fire just dreaming of you and remembering how you look and how you say things. I miss you, Darling, more than you'll ever know.

This afternoon I had magazines from you. Thank you, my darling. They were all nice ones. John was especially thrilled with *Flying*. He said you must have meant him to have it, so I didn't get a look in there.

That was a very special letter you wrote on the sixth. You know I'll always love you, but don't tell yourself that you'll be fat one day. I'm sure you won't be. It doesn't make any difference, though, you'll always be wonderful to me. But I'd like to start counting the years of our married life right now.

I'm awfully glad the inspectors were satisfied with everything. Maybe they'll send you to England now. Wouldn't that be wonderful? You're forgiven for playing cards instead of writing, especially as you won.

Thank you, Darling, for getting the watch bracelets. I'll look out for those magazines. They don't usually take as long as the letters.

Thank the lieutenant for loving me. When you beat me, I can have him to tell my troubles to, but I'm afraid I haven't the slightest scrap of love to spare him. My husband has it all. It would be nice if he could come to our wedding, though. You should have one of your friends as best man. And you know what they say. "Best man—first night." I wouldn't want that, though. Would you?

Mr. Clement left his little girl, Pauline, with me this afternoon. She's five years old, and she's really sweet and well-mannered. She told me all the fairy stories she knows and sang for me. In the end she asked me if I could go and live with her. I hope our little girl will be as sweet as she is. She'll be the sweetest girl in the world, though. I hope she won't have red hair and an Irish temper like her father. I'm only kidding. I hope she'll be like her father in every respect. Except that she's a girl, of course.

One of our drivers was very annoyed this morning. A Yank he was driving asked him when he passed the Civic Centre if that was the post office. You should have heard what the driver said he told him. I couldn't stop laughing.

Good night, Darling. Wish you were here to say your good night personally. I love you and miss you so very, very much. Love me and dream about us.

All my love always and always,
Mary

February 22, 1946

My Darling,

I'm cold. Wish you were here in this bed to keep me warm, and of course, I'm ready to pitch lots of woo. Are you, Darling? I miss you so very, very much, especially in the evenings, when I have nothing but you on my mind and nobody to disturb my dreaming. I have a wonderful imagination, Darling, and yet all the things I dream about can be realized when we're married. I just want to be there waiting for you to come home in the evenings and hear you criticize my cooking, telling me you love me if you like it. Then we'd have from that time until I kiss you at the door in the morning, when you go to work again, all to ourselves. Oh, Darling, it's going to be wonderful.

I had a lovely letter today. The one you wrote on the twelfth at 5:30. You know, the day after you slept while listening to the radio. It has happened to me. You must have been tired after working late for a few nights. You'd better kept plenty of sleep in store, Darling.

I told you about the letters that have been returned to me. They opened the letters to get my address. That made me mad too. I don't know what to say about your not getting my letters now, though I'm scared in case you think I'm not writing. It must be awful for you, not having them. I'd begin to panic myself. I hope you get loads soon. Then you'll love me lots, won't you, Darling?

Haven't seen *The Spanish Main* yet. In another four years, they'll show it at the Manor. Eddie Cantor's there this week in *The Kid from Spain*. There's nothing like being up-to-date with the world. I haven't been there since you were with me. You need a bodyguard there. My honey isn't there, so what am I to do?

It will be wonderful if I can be with you after we're married, as long as you promise not to tease me about being seasick. I can just see you laughing at me now. I won't mind though. I'll be happy every second I'm with you. You know I will. So, Darling, don't ever ask me if I'll be happy. Only you can make me that way.

I didn't finish work until six thirty this evening. We were all caught this morning. Ms. Baldwin is supposed to be in at eight. She strolls in at nine to find Captain Evans acting telephonist. He wanted to know where everyone was. Mr. Clement arrived at ten, and of course, I had to be there five minutes later. Captain Evans is getting another telephonist now, to make sure it's always a female who answers the phone. He told me he didn't mind what time I arrived as long as I got the work done. So I like him now.

Time all good people were being bad in their dreams now. So good night, Darling. I love you with all my heart. Keep loving and missing me more all the time.

All my love always and always,
Mary

February 23, 1946

My Darling,

Didn't even go to a show this evening. Stayed home and listened to the radio. I wanted you with me, as I always do, but otherwise, it didn't bother me, staying home on a Saturday night. Mother didn't go to the Manor, either. She's seen the show before. We were listening to some programme, and she said, "I wonder if Irwin is hearing this too." She talks about you more than she does about Ken, and he was her chief topic. It's nice though. You're my everything, and I love you with all my heart, and when you're included in family talks, I feel so good. Did I tell you that Mother said the first time she saw you, she felt she'd known you for years. You didn't seem a stranger to her. She liked you right away, Darling, but I loved you when I first saw you. I like to go over the memories of the night we met and the way I felt when you asked me to dance and how much I wanted you to ask me again. My world began that night, all right. I haven't told you this before, but you were in my dreams that night too. You were my ideal darling, though I confess I never thought you'd be mine. You are mine, though, aren't you, Darling? I'm yours completely for always, and I want you so much, Irwin. You're the most wonderful person in the whole world, and I feel so conceited when I think that one day soon all the world can know you're mine. Right now I envy all those people who just talk to you. I wish I could change places with your lieutenant. Do you think he'd agree? Tell him there are lots of lonely girls who need comforting in Swansea. Maybe he would then.

Elaine and the rest of the girls went to Langland today. I was invited too, but I had no inclination to dance without my honey. They were celebrating tonight, though. One of the girls is leaving the office. She's going to join her husband in Austria. I suppose they'll get nice and merry, then dance with drunks who don't know they're even dancing, and then think they're having a wonderful time. They can have it all.

I wrote to Virginia, as I told you, and posted the letter last Saturday. They announced on the radio this morning that all mail posted to the USA last Saturday was lost in the Liberator that crashed Wednesday, so I'll write tomorrow again. Otherwise, she'll think I'm awfully rude, and I want her to like me.

Saturday night dreams are usually extraspecial. I hope you're bad tonight. Don't be late, Darling. I'm always waiting for you. I love you and love you and love you and miss you just as much. Keep loving and missing me all you can.

All my love always and always,
Mary

February 24, 1946

My Darling,

Did you have a nice long sleep this morning? I was with you, wasn't I. You had your back to me all the time, though. But even that was wonderful as I had my arms tight around you, and I could lean over and kiss you now and then. Do you miss me Sunday morning, Darling? I wake and just think of you and the lovely times to come. We're going to be so happy. I'll just go on loving you more and more all the time.

Con and Mair were over this evening. I was washing my hair. The rest of the family were out, so they had to entertain themselves for a while. It's no wonder they made us sit looking at one another when we were all at their place. That's how they are. One sits reading the paper, while the other stares into space. We'll never be like that, will we, Honey? We'll read the paper together. I'll treasure every minute we're together. You'll always be my beau.

Right now my back is cold. Can't you do something about it, Darling? I'd give anything if I could just put the light out and snuggle into your arms and just forget the rest of the world. Every time I think about those things, I feel as though I can't wait, but I will. It's just that I love you and want you more and more all the time. You're so very wonderful, and I want you to know how I love you.

I feel awfully sleepy tonight. Anyone would think I'd done a hard day's work. So do you mind if I make this a very short letter? I'll dream extralong dreams of you instead. I love you twice as much as I did last night. You have loads of love saved for you, Darling. I can't wait until you make a withdrawal. I hope it will be very, very soon too. Love me all you can, and miss me all the time.

All my love always and always,
Mary

February 25, 1946

My Darling,

A wonderful letter from you today, written on the thirteenth. I can't understand why you aren't getting my letters, Darling. I know you must be worrying just a little. You know I'm yours for always, though, don't you? I am your wife, you know, your sweetheart for always too. Can I have a big kiss for that please? What I would consider an adequate reward for that, you know better than I do. I'm prepared for more than thirty days and nights with you, Darling. I'm prepared for the rest of my life. We'll just go on loving one another until we have to sleep. Wish you were here now so we could start. I love you so very much, Darling, and I'm awfully lonely this evening. If only I could reach out and have you in my arms. You fit so nicely. But they were made for you, just as I was. There'll never be anyone but you for me as long as I live. You have my heart with you, wherever you are. I can't wait until I'm all with you so I can hear you say you love me. Those words and all the other wonderful things you say make up for all the times I'm lonely, and I miss you so very much. Do you realize how wonderful you are, Darling? I hope you don't. Otherwise you may forget about me, and that's the last thing I ever want to happen. I want you for always.

You're awfully good to me, Darling, buying that silk, I mean. You don't know how welcome it will be. There are so many things I can use it for, but I don't know how you can send it. I suppose it is illegal to send materials here, but I'd like to have it soon. They're only giving us fourteen coupons to last six months, and it's eighteen just for a coat or suit, so I don't know. Even if I had to pay a lot of duty on it, as long as it would come through all right, it would be well worth it. But if they'd allow it is the trouble. What a peace! It's almost as bad as war except my darling isn't being chased by Germans, and that's what worried me most.

You only bought a Swiss watch because you were afraid my watch would keep better time than yours, I know. The magazines haven't arrived yet, but they usually take a couple of days longer than letters. I'm looking for them though. You're a genius, my darling husband.

I'm glad your father sends his regards to me. I'm going to make his boy the happiest person in the world, and I hope he'll like me too. I wrote to Virginia again, in case that letter didn't get to her. The letter she sent me was so nice.

Van Johnson certainly isn't anything as wonderful as you are. I just like the way he acts. Anyway, Alan Ladd is my favorite now. That's only because he's the same size as you are, and I love everything that reminds me of you. You're my only pin-up, Darling, and you're perfect. I love you and miss you every minute, so love me a little, Honey.

All my love always and always,
Mary

February 26, 1946

My Darling,

Didn't have a day off again. I had to take the telephonist's place. Hazel is busy getting things ready for her wedding, so she had my day off instead. I only stay in bed anyway, so I might as well be at work. When I saw five o'clock coming around, I was thinking how wonderful it would be if you were taking me home. Oh, Darling, I miss you so very much, and everything's so empty without you with me. Walter insisted on listening to a fight on the radio this evening, and that's something I really don't like. I was just waiting for the hours to go until I could come to bed and be alone with my thoughts of my Irwin. I love you so much. Today I got the lovely letter you wrote on the fifteenth. When I read how you love me, the time when you'll be with me for always can't come quick enough. I'm the luckiest person in the world to have your love, and you don't know how I treasure it. I'm yours, all of me, Darling.

I know how impatient you are, Irwin, as I'm the same way. You have lots more chances of going out and having fun than I do, but I couldn't stand the thought of you being with someone else. I'm selfish, Darling, and I know I am, but I love you so, and I want you to be just mine. I'll never betray your trust. I never want to. I like to think of you wanting me to be this way, so I'll never go out, even when things make me very miserable. Your love is the most important thing in the world to me, and I have so much to look forward to. Cheating now would, I'm sure, reflect on our future happiness, and I want nothing to spoil that.

I'm awfully glad that you had my two letters. I don't know what happened to the rest of them, though. I am writing regularly to you, Darling. You'll get them all in time. Then you'll love me lots. As you know, I'm getting all your letters, so if you want to send money, it should be quite safe. You asked me if I'd deposit the money for you and said, "You will, won't you?" What do you think I'd do with it, Darling? Maybe I've told you before, other people's money doesn't tempt me a bit. Naturally, I look after it, but that's all. So you can depend on me banking all the money you send.

I'll give that solitaire game to Con. I've tried to figure it out, but it seems crazy to me. If you start playing that after we're married, I'll, well, I guess I'll have to watch you, but, my darling husband, you won't be able to concentrate very hard. Your little wife is going to pester you to death. Can I start now, please?

Your flowers were beautiful, Irwin. They still are. Mother won't part with them until only the stems are left. So every time I look at them, I want to be with you, to give you a great big kiss for being so wonderful to me.

Good night, Darling. I'll be on your side in a couple of minutes. I'm going to be a nuisance tonight. Last night we had a wonderful time. You know I'm loving you and missing you more all the time. Bless you. Love me lots.

All my love always and always,
Mary

PS: Reading over the letter, I discovered what I said about money sounds nasty. I didn't mean it to sound that way. I just wanted to assure you, I'll take care of it.

I love you.
Mary

February 27, 1946

My Darling,

Wish you could have been here tonight. You would have laughed as much as I did. John kept me company, and he started talking about his job. He's at a wholesale chemist's place, and the sooner he leaves, the better it will be. Dorothy came in later on, so be became bolder and told us all the interesting things they have in stock. Dorothy started giggling, and he told her not to be so silly. It's only the facts of life. You should have seen the expression on his face, though I didn't know how to tell him to keep quiet. I was afraid of the answer I may get, and he just rattled on all the time, until my mother came in.

Darling, I had four wonderful letters today, written on the fifteenth, sixteenth, seventeenth, and eighteenth. It was lovely going downstairs this morning and finding them there. Thank you, Irwin, for writing me as often as you do. I don't know what I'd do without your letters.

What you wrote about the party at your camp made me want to be with you more than ever because when I'm anywhere and see couples together, I miss you extra much, and when I think of you eating in the same room as all those people having a good time, I imagine you wanted me a little too. Did you, Darling?

You know, when I started reading the letter you wrote on the eighteenth, I was wondering what was wrong, but I was tickled pink when I reached the end of the page. You know, the supposed letter from the colonel. Oh, Darling, I love you so much. You're crazy, though, and that's the way I like you. Wish I could get a plane and then jump out right into your arms, even if we only had a couple of hours together. I could use a few hundred kisses right now. Could you?

It's late, Darling, eleven thirty. I'll be late for our date if I don't hurry. Wait just a little while for me, will you, Irwin? Keep waiting for me until I'm really with you and love me more all the time 'cause I'm your wife, remember? You're wonderful, and I love my darling more than I can say.

All my love always and always,
Mary

March 1, 1946

My Darling,

Do you love me lots? You do. I think I love you more, though. Everyone's in bed, Irwin. We can sit on the floor now, or would you rather be where I am now? Yes, I'm in bed. It's awfully cold too. Oh, Darling. I miss you more and more every minute. Hurry and come to me. I want to see you so much, my wonderful husband.

This morning I went to work rather late. The colonel was already there. He was looking through the mail, and he handed me an envelope. I was wondering what it could be. It was your cheque, Darling. I thought you sent it home this time. It's in the bank now, anyway. The colonel asked me how I was connected with the US government as though he didn't already know. He told me I'd be a lucky girl if I got to the States. I'm wondering what he meant. Though I have heard him say what he thinks about Americans, and it's all been good. My little American is the best person in the world, so I don't worry about the rest of them.

You wouldn't have liked me this afternoon, Irwin. I lost my temper and told Mr. Clements exactly what I thought of Glamtax. Remember me telling you that when I did this extra work, I'd have a lot more money? These last few weeks I have been working hard, honestly, and Mr. Clements told me I'd be having my increase today. So you can imagine how I felt when it didn't come, and when I asked him about it, he said he's forgotten. When I think of what I told him, I feel a little ashamed of myself. I said he wasn't capable of being in charge of people, and I told him I wouldn't do any more of the other firm's work until I had the money for it. I was expecting to be thrown out any minute, but he knows what I could tell Captain Evans if I wished, so he has to be careful. I'll have the money next week too. He told me not to mention it to the colonel.

I'm glad you didn't accept the PW as our servant. I wouldn't like him around our place all day. I can cook for you, Darling. Don't worry about that. You'll love me more if I do. Won't you, Darling? You have to have lots of energy to work all day, don't you?

You know when you end your letters you say things that make me imagine I'm right there with you, and when I come to bed, I move over on to your side, and my arms are just as though you were in there. If only you were, Darling. Just think of how much love I have waiting for you and all the time that's wasting. Well, I'm going to dream that we're not losing any time now. I love you with all my heart. Miss me lots.

All my love always and always,
Mary

March 4, 1946

My Darling,

Love me more today? I do you. I'm not even going to say anything about you coming home late tonight. I've even cooked an extraspecial supper for you. Do I get a big kiss for that?

Went to see *A Thousand and One Nights* this evening. It was the fairy story type and not bad at all. The princess asked her father if he thought she was very beautiful, and Elaine yelled out "No!" before he could answer. That was the biggest laugh I had out of the show.

The colonel asked me today if I minded him smoking his pipe. I told him I was quite used to it, but his tobacco didn't smell half as nice as yours, Darling.

Good news on the radio tonight. Less coupons for clothes and we'll have nice shoes, and no austerity clothing by autumn. When I heard that, I danced around the room. John asked if I'd gone crazy. He wasn't at all interested. That voice of his makes me shudder.

Mrs. Jones was telling my mother about her daughter going to Sweden for her holidays this year. Then she asked where I was going. That was just another way of fishing for information. I told her I was going to Langland. She seemed very surprised. Then she said not everyone was as fortunate as her daughter. She can boast about her marriage. I thought of telling her to wait until she was married. I'm sure she thinks I envy her. I have the most wonderful person in the world. He's the only person for me, and I love him with all my heart. I'm so awfully lucky to have his love too.

I'm tired, Darling. Put your arms around me and let me kiss you good night. Wish I could, Darling. I miss you so very much. For always in my mind, you're with me, telling me you love me. Miss me lots.

All my love always and always,
Mary

March 5, 1946

My Darling,

This morning I stayed in bed until twelve thirty. I was thinking hard about you. I woke around nine o'clock, and after that, I just went over all our wonderful memories. Then I thought of all the wonderful times to come. You are in them all. It was nice planning our home and wondering how you'll be in the mornings. You'll always be wonderful to me, though. Even if you should be a little grumpy at breakfast, I won't mind a bit, honest.

When I finally went downstairs, there was a lovely letter waiting for me written on the twenty-fourth. I asked Mother why it wasn't brought to me. She said she thought I was sleeping.

Went to see *Perfect Stranger* with Mother this afternoon. It was very good. Then this evening, we sat by a nice big fire and listened to the radio, until the Voice, John, came home from school and pestered me with his algebra. He's trying an examination this week, and we have to know all about it too. I came to bed again at ten o'clock. There's a lot of time being wasted, isn't there, Darling?

You're terrible, Irwin Deems, reading those awful books. I suppose you won't tell me about those until after we're married. I'm making a list of all these things you know. What could you possibly learn out of those books? Will you tell me, Darling? I should know, shouldn't I? I can't wait until I'm in your power again, anyway. I'm yours for always.

What does that PW mean by calling me Maria? I told you those pictures of me weren't very nice, didn't I? I'll have to speak to that German. It's all right for you to laugh about it. You should defend me, Darling.

I know stockings are scarce in the States. I read about the GI brides wrecking the stores and buying all they could, so Virginia will have a rough time getting them. So I won't be disappointed if they don't come, Darling.

It's funny you should say about a husband is what's left of a sweetheart after the nerve is killed. I meant to write and tell you that after hearing the same programme. I thought of you at the time. Your nerve will take some killing, won't it, Darling? You'll always be my sweetheart, though. Yesterday afternoon, when Elaine and I were having tea at the Albert Hall, an American sergeant came in. He was a nice-looking boy too. And with him was a girl—she must have been his wife—and a baby. Well, the girl was the untidiest and the most repulsive-looking thing you could ever wish to see. She had the baby wrapped in a dirty shawl, and the poor little thing was yelling. Seeing them was enough, but when she started to eat, it was the end. Everybody was looking at her. Elaine turned around to me and said that sight was enough to put anyone off marriage. If she thought she'd ever get like that, she'd have a divorce now. That's the way it made you feel, though. I felt sorry for that boy.

I'm awfully anxious to see that house you liked so much in *The Post*. The other magazines haven't arrived yet though. Can you have houses built in the States now, Darling? I think I saw an article in *Yank* about people sleeping in parks. The living accommodation was so bad. Or is that just in one particular state? I'd like whatever you want, Irwin. I want an upstairs, though. You do as well, don't you? We'd miss our exercise without that. I couldn't race you up the stairs.

Good night, Darling. Love me for all your worth and miss me too. I love you so very, very much. You're wonderful.

All my love always and always,
Mary

March 6, 1946

My Darling,

It's cold in bed tonight. I know where my feet would be if you were here. Yes, Darling, on your back. Would you mind?

This morning I had two lovely letters from you and also a letter from the magazine people. I'll send it on to you. They want money, my dear husband. That's your department. I had a big laugh when

I read it this morning. I said to Mother, "We have bills already, and we're not even married yet." She laughed about that.

One magazine came too. *Collier's*. That came direct from America. Do you want me to save them for you, Darling? You know, after we're married, will you bring me magazines home? I love to think of things like that.

What did they give you three days holiday for? I wouldn't have minded you going to Paris or Brussels, Darling. I say that now because I know you didn't go, but if you had, well, I would have worried a bit. I don't like to think of you being lonely, though, Darling. On the other hand, it makes me feel wonderful to know that you're that way because of me. I love you so much, Irwin, and knowing that you're being as good as I am makes our love perfect. I'd hate to spoil it by taking a chance of a night out.

Darling, my little black thing, as you call it, is still waiting to be displayed for you, my husband, though that weekend I spent in London with that man, I can't remember his name, didn't leave it brand-new, as it was. He was rather rough, you know. Imagine that. I didn't tell you about it before, did I? You know, Darling, you're the only man for me. You'll never have to suspect those things. I'm all yours for always. My arms were only made to wrap around you. I couldn't imagine anyone ever taking your place, not even for a second. So love me for always, Darling.

That Passion perfume you gave me made the drivers have a good laugh today. I walked into the office, and someone remarked about the lovely smell, as he put it, and I said it was my passion. Well, you should have heard them. They said it was the first time they knew of passion in that form. So all day, they've been asking if my passion still smells.

Harry and Kit were over this evening. We played cards and talked until eleven thirty, so I'll be late for our dreams tonight. But wait for me, Darling. Harry doesn't like his work now. Not enough money to have an expensive time. They suggested having a party on my birthday. Kit said she had a bottle of sherry and could get the food. Then I remembered about the whiskey you gave me. But when I went to the cupboard for it, it was half empty. What do you think? My mother and Mrs. Jones have had bad colds since you left. They've been drinking it in tea every morning. We teased her about it. I told her I'd tell you about my drunken mother. She said you wouldn't mind as long as it cured her cold. I said I'd put her name on the list at the wine stores so she could always get it. She didn't think she'd have any more colds, though. Well, Harry couldn't stop laughing. She used to create such a fuss about people drinking. Anyway, we called the party off. I didn't want it. There's nobody I'd want to invite. My Irwin is the only person I'd want, and he's over in France.

I hope you're not tired of waiting for me tonight. Sorry I'm so late, but you know how it is. I love you with all my heart, Darling, and miss you so very much. Love me.

> All my love always and always,
> Mary

March 7, 1946

My Darling,

I love you, remember? You wouldn't get any sleep tonight if you were here. I have oceans of loving in store for you. I can just hear you say, "Oh, for Pete's sake, go to sleep." Would you, Honey? I can imagine that, but am I going to love you, Honey? Just wait and see. (What's wrong with me saying "honey" all the time? That's what comes of trying to remember how you talk. I only have to think for a moment, though, then there you are, as wonderful as ever, telling me you love me. Memories are wonderful too.) Wish my darling would hurry and collect some of this love.

Went to see *Body Snatchers* with Elaine this evening. It wasn't as gruesome as we expected, so we were a little disappointed, and what's more, we stood for two hours until I felt too stiff to sit down. Now I feel really tired. Wish I'd stayed home.

There was a Welsh play on the radio at nine thirty. I was wondering if you were listening to it. It was funny. Even though it makes the Welsh people seem like half-wits.

Well, Darling, my eyes are almost closed, so do you mind if this is a very short letter? You know I love you twice as much as I did yesterday, and I'm wishing so hard that I could see you soon. I miss you so terribly, my darling husband. Love me all you can, and be good for me.

All my love always and always,
Mary

March 8, 1946

My Darling,

Wish you were here so I could give you a great big hug and a kiss for the beautiful flowers. I'd like you to see them, Irwin. They're super. And what do you think? I had anemones as well. Thank you, Darling. You're wonderful to me.

I worked until six forty-five this evening. If I could be independent of Glamtax and jobs were easy to get, I'd have told Mr. Clement something this afternoon. He's a two-faced old so-and-so, and he's giving me work as well as the colonel. I'm tired of hearing their voices. When I came home this evening, I was too tired to speak. Con and Mair were here. Con asked when you were coming home. I wish I could have given him an answer. Oh, Irwin, I miss you so terribly, and it seems ages since I saw you.

Saw a picture of the state highway in Pennsylvania today. It looks something like the road that goes up to the top of Mumbles. I was thinking hard of you when I saw it, wondering how many times you'd driven along there and lots of other things.

Well, Darling, I feel sleepy again tonight. I won't make a habit of these short letters, but I'm liable to fall asleep writing if I don't stop now. I love you more than I can ever tell you, Darling. I'm all yours forever. Love me all you can, and miss me every minute. Thank you again, Irwin, for the lovely flowers.

All my love always and always,
Mary

March 9, 1946

My Darling,

Why can't you be here or me there? I miss you so much, Irwin, and it's Saturday night again. Time seems endless without you with me.

We're having lovely weather lately. The sun shines all day. We must be having our summer before time or something. Elaine and I went shopping this afternoon. At least we looked at things. At least it was fun. After we walked through every shop, we had tea and discussed the things we'd like, if we only had more coupons. This evening we went to visit Elaine's friend. She lives about ten miles from here. We had more tea there and played cards for the rest of the time. Her husband was at the pub. She didn't mind that though. Now I'm in bed again, and it's only ten thirty. Can't we do something about that narrow strip of water that's between us, Darling? Wish you were making use of that ladder tonight.

Tomorrow I'm going to Penclawdd. Elaine's people are going away for the weekend, so I'm staying with her tomorrow night. I'll be thinking hard of you when I'm there as every time I hear the word Penclawdd, I think of you the same time.

Hazel's been crying all day thinking of her sister going to America. She's sailing Friday. I've never seen anyone cry so much as Hazel does. She knows her sister wants to go more than anything, so she shouldn't feel miserable.

Haven't had a letter from you since Thursday. I know that's nothing to complain about after the weeks you've waited for my letters, but I miss yours so much that the day seems empty without one,

Darling. I want to read how much you want and miss me. I know you do, but it's a lot nicer hearing it or reading it. Will you tell me you love me every morning after we're married, Darling?

I'm going to dream about you now, Darling. Don't bother to shave tonight. It's such a waste of time, and I love you just as much when you don't. You know I love you for always no matter what. Keep loving and missing me, Darling.

All my love always and always,
Mary

March 12, 1946

My Darling,

Had a morning in bed again today, so I did some more dreaming and thinking of my Irwin. We had a wonderful time, Darling. I was considering whether or not I should get up around twelve o'clock when Mother came rushing into the bedroom with a parcel. We opened it in record time. It was the silk, Darling. It's lovely. Much better than we could buy. I don't know how I can tell you how grateful I am. You're so good to me. When people give beautiful things like that, they usually get a great big kiss for it. You know there are thousands of those kisses waiting for you, Darling, and how I wish I could put my arms around you right now and just go on kissing you until we had to pause for breath. I love you with all my heart forever, Irwin. You're mine too, aren't you?

Mother hasn't recovered from seeing that lovely silk yet. When it came, she thought there'd be duty to pay, but there wasn't any, Irwin. I can have some nice things made out of it, and I hope that the next time you see it, I'll be underneath it and I'll be your wife. You don't know how hard I'm wishing and praying that things will be as we want them. I can't imagine life without you, Darling, but it isn't going to be that way, is it? I want you so much, Irwin. Didn't get a letter again today. It's funny, not hearing from you since last

Thursday. I know that's not so long, but it's the longest time without a letter since you were here, and your letters are so important to me. There's always tomorrow, though. I don't have to worry about whether or not you still love me, do I? I want to think of you missing and loving me, almost as much as I do you.

Mother and I went to see *Our Vines Have Tender Grapes* this evening. It was quite good. Margaret O'Brien is sweet, isn't she? Before we went to the show, we called at the garage. I left a coat there yesterday. Hazel was sitting there alone, looking awfully miserable, and she's getting married in five weeks. She showed me pictures of the hotel and its surroundings where she's spending her honeymoon. It looks a lovely place, and reading about it made it sound like a little heaven. It's in Cornwall. Have you ever heard of it? They call it the English Riviera. Hazel doesn't want to go there, though. She's scared in case people will dress for dinner, and she hates masses of people around her. Mother said it would be a nice place for Elaine and I to spend our holidays this year. I said it would be and dropped the subject. Then on the way to the show, she said how sorry she felt for Hazel and asked if I'd take my holidays when you came on leave. I said I would, then she said we should go away for a week, and Cornwall would be a nice place to go. We have other plans, don't we, Darling?

Headlines of our local paper this evening were "Swansea Girl Gets Proposal of Marriage by Telephone from America." Do you know what she said when he asked her? "I don't know." She met him two years ago, hasn't seen him since, but he must love her lots.

Good night, Darling. I'm always thinking of you. I love you so much, and you're so wonderful. Keep loving and missing me, Irwin. Couldn't you come here for a few minutes right now? I want a good night kiss, and you're the only person I want to kiss me. When you dream about me tonight, make sure you get a super hug and kiss for the silk. Be good for me.

All my love always and always,
Mary

March 13, 1946

My Darling,

Gosh, I had an exciting day. At eight twenty, a telegram arrived for me. Before I opened it, I was all excited. I thought you were coming home. Then I soon found out it was from you, giving your new address. That was nice, though, 'cause it was from my darling. Where are you now? I'm curious. Hope you're missing me. The postman brought a lovely letter from you and also one from Ken. He said he'd be home soon and not to write anymore. When I came home from work this evening, another telegram arrived. Ken was arriving at eight thirty this evening. Then there was one mad rush. I had to take all my belongings from my bedroom to make way for him. Isn't it a shame? Since he arrived, we've had neighbors and the rest of the family all talking at the same time in the house. Now I'm in bed before Mother comes. It's about twelve o'clock, and this bed is terrible. You wouldn't like it either.

I'll answer your letter tomorrow, but you know, Darling, you're the most important person in my life, and my heart is right there with you. I love you more and more every minute, Irwin, and miss you so much. Love me lots, Darling. I'm your wife, remember?

All my love always and always,
Mary

March 14, 1946

My Darling,

If I could only tell you how much more I love you today, you'd like me a little too. I realize more and more, all the time, how very fortunate I am to have your love; you're so wonderful. Oh, Irwin, I'd give anything to be in your arms right now. I'd even be content just to hear you talk. As you can see, I'm missing you extra much. I love you so, Darling.

My brother is quite a house full. He just sits around like some-one lost then suddenly speaks in a very loud voice. I'll be a nervous wreck before his leave is over. Mother is happy to have him home, yet he's wearing her down a little too. She's doing her best with the rations to give him good food, and then he always asks for some-thing different and keeps moaning about everything. Mother even sent him to the pub with Walter tonight so she could have a break, and she said to me that it was nice to have him safely home, but she'd rather have Irwin here. She keeps telling Ken about you, all nice things too, until Dot says, "What about my Sid?"

I'm glad you've started to get our home together. We don't need the alarm clock, though, do we? I have some china, cutlery, and tablecloths, but you have to take me as well. I was tickled pink when I read about you getting those things. You can be Mother all the time if you want to. Are you sure you went to see *Kitty* the night you didn't write me? That's something I don't have to worry about, do I, Darling? Was *Kitty* a good show? It's coming here shortly. It seems quite good, what I've read about it.

Imagine you getting Chanel perfume for me. Thanks loads, Darling. I'll keep it for our wedding night, then maybe you won't read a book. I'll allure you into my arms. You'll be sorry.

If you like the picture of the French street, I know I will. It sounds lovely. I can hardly wait until it's hanging in our house so I can say to the neighbors, "It's just a little thing my husband picked up in France, you know." Oh, Darling, I love you so much.

I understand about the hose all right. I can't expect Virginia to give up her share, after the way they have to fight for them. She was more than kind to write me anyway. I hope she gets my letter too.

Another night in this awful bed. I didn't sleep at all last night, so I couldn't dream, Darling. Maybe tonight I'll have extra wonder-ful dreams to make up for it. I certainly hope so. Bless you, Darling. Remember I love you with all my heart forever. Keep loving me and miss me all you can.

All my love always and always,
Mary

March 17, 1946

My Darling,

Did you think I was lost? I'm sorry I haven't written these last two nights, but you remember that awful cold I had when you were here in September? Well, I had another one just like it, only this time I stayed in bed. So you will forgive me, Darling? I felt too rotten to do anything. I was thinking of you the whole time though.

Yesterday morning I had six wonderful letters from you and also one that I wrote on February 12 with "Addressee Returned to US" marked on the envelope. What do you know about that? I've burned all the letters I've had returned. Only kept the envelopes as evidence. I'm sorry, Irwin, but I didn't think of sending them again. I'm crazy, aren't I? I love you tons and tons, though, and that's not crazy, that's lovely.

I'd love to be with you when you take those trips, you doing the driving. How do I fit in with your one-arm efforts? Don't make me dream so much, Irwin. It makes me so terribly impatient. Won't everything be perfect when we are together for always? You're so wonderful. Don't take any risks when you're driving along icy roads, will you, Darling? You know you're my whole world.

I'm glad you have faith in my love for you, Darling. You need never doubt it, and however much Kaplan kids you, you know I'm all yours for always. I have no doubts about you at all. You're my Irwin, I know, and how I love you, Darling. So I never want to think of losing you. I never thought anyone could ever mean so much to anybody as you mean to me. Love me for always, won't you, Darling.

Ken seems to fill the house. I'm glad you're your size, my little husband. Big men don't look right in houses. You're big, of course, but not too big. (You were just getting mad too, weren't you?) How I wish I could be wherever you are. I need some love, Irwin. That means I should be in your arms. Oh, Darling, it seems such a long time since you asked me if I loved you each day and how much. I don't know what I'd do without all our wonderful memories.

I'm starting work again tomorrow, so I'd better get some sleep. Wish you were here so I could put my cold feet on your back and hear you complain about it. We'd soon get warm, though, I know. I've had some super dreams lately. You've been as bad as I've wanted you to be. It's a lovely life, you just wait. Love me all you can and miss me lots. I love you with all my heart and miss you so very much.

All my love always and always,
Mary

March 18, 1946

My Darling,

Do you want to know how much I love you tonight? You do. Well, let me think how best I can explain. I love you, Irwin, twenty times as much as I did when I last saw you, and all these lonely evenings convince me more how necessary you are to me and how fortunate I am to know I'm waiting for you. I love you so much, Darling.

Went to work today. They'd all missed me, I think; anyway, they said they had. Elaine came around at four o'clock, so we had tea and then went to see *Love Letters*. I liked it a lot. Maybe some people would think it was too sentimental, but it just made me want you near. I'd like to have seen it with you. I miss you every minute, Irwin. When are you coming to see me again? I want to be with my wonderful Irwin. I love him so very much, you know.

You certainly did a lot of work when you left your last camp. You're not working too hard, are you, Darling? I really think I should be there to take care of you. Don't you think so too? I've never seen any ten-pound notes with "Issued by the Military Authority" written across them, so I don't know if they have any value now. The ordinary orange notes are all right. They're the old ones, just as the green one-pound notes are.

Listen, my darling husband, you've made me very curious about the surprise you have in store for me. I just can't let it wait until I see you. Can't you tell me now? You wouldn't hold out on me if things were all right for us, would you? You know, if we could make a date to get married, I mean. I've thought of everything, but you make it sound such a secret. I'm all confused. My intuition is slipping, I guess. You haven't grown a moustache, have you? You said I'd be pleased though, so that wouldn't be it, 'cause that used to spoil the Irwin-Mary routine. You wouldn't want me to go crazy trying to guess, would you? Or do I have to wait, Darling? If you say I do, I will.

Mother is just coming up the stairs now. I wish it was you, Darling. Dream about me and miss me more than ever. You know you have all my love with you. I'm all yours, Irwin.

All my love always and always,
Mary

March 19, 1946

My Darling,

I was thinking about you working hard while I was dreaming in bed this morning. Wish time would go much faster so we wouldn't waste these mornings. It's been a terrible day. I don't know where all the rain came from. Ken wanted me to go to a show with him, but I still have a cold, and I didn't want to sit around in wet clothes for a couple of hours, so he persuaded Walter to go with him instead. Then Mother went to the Manor, John went to school, and Dorothy went to her friend's, so I'm all alone. If you are where I like to think you are, then you are lonely too. What can we do about it, Darling?

This afternoon, I had a *Collier's*. They came in good time. It's strange about those other magazines, though. They must be lost. It's such a long time since you sent them. I think that's the first lot that haven't arrived since you've been sending them.

Of course I'm interested in your work. Darling, you keep on telling me all you have to do. I'm your wife, remember? So I should know. I forgive you for not writing when you worked until eleven thirty. You must have been awfully tired, so I wouldn't expect you to write. I'm glad the army thinks you're good too, though. If you don't want to go to Le Havre, I don't want you to go either. I think you were wonderful to write the night you had to stay in Paris, I do, not that I expected you to be running around, but you must have been tired after all the work you did that day. I love you, my Irwin.

Didn't get a letter today. Maybe tomorrow, though. I hope so. The crowd is starting to drift in now, so I'd better leave you. I'll see you in my dreams, though. Don't be late, sweet. Love me, Darling, and remember how very much I love you and miss you.

All my love always and always,
Mary

March 20, 1946

My Darling,

Here I am again, loving you twice as much as I did yesterday. I deserve a big kiss, don't I, Darling? When can I collect it? Wish you were within reach now. I'd just love you and love you and love you more. Are you scared, Honey?

Gwenda phoned me today. She's only been married seven weeks, and already she's home with her people for a couple of days. You wouldn't get rid of me like that, Darling. I'll be around all the time. She's coming to see me tomorrow and tell me all about her wedding, etc. She was married at the Civic Center and went to her husband's farm for the honeymoon. Do you know what she said? I didn't think it was a bit nice. "Haven't you ended the affair with Irwin yet?" She can't get over the fact that she met a dope that wanted to marry her, even though he isn't up to her expectations. Had a lovely letter from you today, Darling, written on February 27. You were missing me and loving me lots, so I've been feeling extra good today.

It seems I wrote you a very depressing letter one Saturday night. I didn't mean to complain. Honest, Darling, 'cause I'm not losing anything by staying home Saturday nights. You see, Irwin, when I'm not with you, nothing seems worthwhile. You know, Irwin darling,

285

that if I ever wanted to go out, I would, but I never want to without you. It's just that I miss you so much sometimes that it gets me feeling lonely, then I suppose I write to you, and the words don't mean the things I mean. You know, though, that you're my whole world, and there's no one else for me. You too have to spend lonely nights. I realize that, but you never seem to complain the way I do, and I'm glad of that. We'll have lots of fun together, though, won't we, Darling? I have tons and tons of love saved for you. We won't want to take walks on Sunday mornings for a long time after we're married. I can just imagine us waking and jumping out of bed right away. It will take at least an hour before we even consider it. Then you'll have to drag me out. I can be very strong when I want to, so you'd better conserve all your strength for those tasks, Darling.

I don't write in bed anymore. It's only eight thirty now. I have to make supper for Walter. He's going to work. Mother has gone to a concert at the church and taken Ken with her, thank heaven. I'll have to leave you now, Darling. But I'll have wonderful dreams of my Irwin later on. Love me lots and miss me a little too. I love you with all my heart, Darling, and miss you so much.

All my love always and always,
Mary

March 21, 1946

My Darling,

I've had a busy day, not working, of course. Elaine met me at four o'clock. We went to see *Stork Club*. It was good too. Then I went to Con's. Stayed until nine thirty. Now I'm home, and Harry and Kit are here. I feel ready to get nice and close to you and sink down in a lovely bed while my darling tells me he loves me. Would you like to do that too? Oh, don't be a meanie. Come on, I promise not to bother you too much.

Haven't had a letter from you since you've been at your new place. You still love me though, don't you, Darling? Only one letter I've had this week so far, and I miss you so very much, Darling.

I'm writing this while all the family are talking for the most. Irwin, I wish I could see you soon. Even if we can't be married, I want to use some of that love, Darling.

It's been raining all day again. My hair is still wet. Why aren't you around to help me dry it? You're neglecting me, Darling. That's what you're doing. I'm only kidding. I know you want to be with me, almost as much as I want to be with you. Wish time would go faster.

Have to leave you now, Darling. Dream lovely dreams about me and love me loads. I love you, and I'm yours forever and ever.

All my love for always,
Mary

March 22, 1946

My Darling,

This morning I was very lucky. I had seven wonderful letters from you, written from the eighth to the fourteenth. As you can imagine, I was later than usual getting to work after reading them. But I didn't care. You're the most important thing in my life.

That was a very special letter you wrote on my birthday. I certainly hope we are together next year, and I don't care if there's another person there, either, as long as she'll be as good as you say she'll be. How do you know, anyway? I wish you could come here, even if it will only be a couple of days. I want to see you so very much, Darling, and I'm bored to tears with everything right now. So come and see me as soon as you can.

I can't understand why brides-to-be are kicking up such a fuss about nighties. Maybe they think they look nice folded at the bottom of the bed, though I showed the article to Hazel, and she just blushed.

Irwin, would you expect me not to be discouraged after all this time we've been waiting? I honestly think sometimes that it will never come. Your divorce, I mean. I know you're as impatient as I am, and I know everything will be worth waiting for when it does come. At times, though, I wonder how much longer it will be, and maybe I should tell you I wouldn't wait any longer. Then I remember how much I love you and how empty life would be if you weren't the center of it. I get myself mixed up on times. When I'm very miserable, I wonder about lots of things, then end up by loving you more than ever. You know though, I'll wait for you, whatever happens.

I'm glad you reached Le Havre safely. It seems a very nice place you're living in. Any room for me, Darling? I could have lots of fun chasing you up those stairs. You seem to have an important job, my clever husband. Don't work too hard though, will you? Remember I'm here waiting for all your love, and how I could use some now. Oh, Irwin, I'm missing you so very much.

You won't want to listen to the radio in bed after we're married, will you? Well, who's going to turn it off then? I'll sing to you instead, Darling. It will be just as good. Both of us can sing, then we'll wake up all the neighbours. Wish I could hear you sing "Honey" now, though every time I think of it, I start to laugh. Oh, you're wonderful, Darling.

You know something? I'm jealous. Yes, I am. When I saw the letter from Paris on the fourteenth, I thought, some lovely French girl will take my Irwin from me. I don't like you being there. That hotel sounds wonderful. Wish I could have been there with you, then I wouldn't let you out of my sight. I'd even go to the tailor's with you. What are you buying all those army clothes for? What sort of jacket is it, Darling? I'll have to wait and see. You won't tell me anything, you meanie.

Who did you take to the show in Paris, Darling? You know the part of the letter you wrote after returning from the show. Well, I keep it so you can see for yourself. It looks as though someone was holding your hand when you were writing. I'm only kidding. You must have been tired. I'm sorry you didn't enjoy the show, though, and I know you were missing me.

Good night, Darling. I have to go to bed now. I love you more than anything in the world. Keep loving me and miss me all you can.

All my love always and always,
Mary

March 22, 1946

My Darling,

I've written you once this evening, but my conscience is bothering me. I'm in bed now, and I've just been thinking over what I wrote you. I said something about being discouraged about waiting so long. Well, you know I didn't mean it that way. It's just that I'm so anxious to be with you for always. Waiting isn't hard at all. I love you so much, Darling, that the thought that you love me too makes up for all the lonely hours I spend. You understand, don't you, Darling? You're the dearest person in the world to me. I wouldn't want to write anything that would make you miserable. Sometimes I wish that I could speak to you when I wanted to tell you exactly how I feel. Words never seem to sound right. I always want to be with you, though.

Forgot to tell you too what I've been doing with myself today. I worked until five o'clock then came home to find Ken filling the house up. Every evening I wish that I could wait for you to come, and then I'd forget everything else. Or better still, I'd like to be home every day, doing things for my Darling, so when he'd come home to me after a day's work, he'd find everything nice. Then he couldn't help loving me all the more.

The colonel came into this office, this wonderful office of ours, this afternoon and started talking of his great American friend. He'd had a letter from him today, and in it, he told him of a crazy number just out. The colonel started reciting it. I was weak trying to control my laughter. I forgot the exact words, but it was something like, "Onesy, twosy, I love yousy. Threesy, foursy, you love me moresy." He thought it was terrible and said that if this is the postwar world, to h——with it. Mr. Clement had to leave the office he was so tickled. The colonel's friend works in the Chrysler factory, and he said that British cars over there coast $1,600. That's a lot of money for them, isn't it? Cars like our taxis, I mean.

Wish you had been there to brush my hair tonight and unfasten me. Tell the time to hurry, Irwin, so that I can help you shave. Time for dreams now. Don't me late. I want to love you loads tonight. I won't be a sissy, either. Love me all you can and keep missing me, Darling.

All my love always and always,
Mary

PS: Warm my place in bed tonight, unless you want me over on your side. All right, forget about my side then. That's what I wanted you to say.

March 23, 1946

My Darling,

Had another lovely letter today, written on the thirteenth. That's eight letters in two days. I'm awfully lucky to love you, Darling, and I don't know what I'd do without your wonderful letters.

It's been a real spring day today. You don't know how I was wishing that you were with me. I've been in the mood to pitch lots of woo. You forgot to tell me what Paris is like in spring, Darling. It's supposed to be lovely. Tell me that it couldn't be nice without me. That's what I want you to say, because without you, nothing could ever be complete for me.

I just worked all through the sunshine, though we can see it now. I forgot to remind you that it's Saturday again. I hope you're missing me loads just now, as it's only eight thirty. I've been washing my hair, and I'm ready for bed. Would you like to join me? I miss you more than you'll ever know, Darling.

My five brothers escorted me to work this afternoon. They were going to the football. Our house is the meeting place. You should have seen us. I was stuck in the middle of them, and we couldn't get on a bus. I had to run to keep up with them. Swansea lost again today. John hasn't made any comment on the game yet. He gets mad when they don't win.

You asked me if I was tired of hearing you tell me you love me. That's something, Darling, that I want to hear every second of my life. Remember that you have my heart with you, and I love you so very, very much.

I'm afraid to look forward to seeing you for those few days when you might come to England on business. You know something, Darling? I love you a hundred times more since I last saw you, and I'd give anything to see you soon, if it's only for a few minutes. I hope more than anything that you'll make that trip. I have tons of assorted hugs, kisses, and loads of love waiting for my husband, and I'm longing to be in his arms again as his arms are the only ones I ever want to be in. They were made for me, just as you were. Dorothy is here writing too. She wants to know what she can tell him. She's funny.

Elaine works until nine o'clock some days, and today is one of them. I didn't feel like going to a show this evening, anyway. Do you have a theatre at your new place? You really aren't so very far from me now. Wish I was a super swimmer.

I'm going to have something to eat. Then I'm with my darling again. You were wonderful last night. Mother told me I was talking in my sleep. I wonder what I was saying. It must have been about you as you are the last person I think of at night, and then I dream of you, wake, and then I think of you right away. And so it goes on every day, and I'm loving you more every minute.

You know Mrs. Hill, who works at the office, her brother has just returned from Greece, and this morning he had a cable from a girl he went around with out there to say she's on her way over to see him. He doesn't want her here, but they don't know what to do about it now. She had some nerve, though. I was asking Ken if we could expect a girl from Greece or Italy to arrive. He told me he's seen enough of women and is never going to marry. After he went out, Mother said she hopes he won't be on her hands all her life. Honestly, Irwin, he takes up all the air in the house, and he speaks so loudly. I don't know if he thinks he's still in the desert.

There's a variety programme on the radio now. Our Music Hall. Do you hear it? It's wicked, isn't it? Who said Saturday night is the loneliest night of the week. Someone's impersonating Charles Boyer now. He hasn't anything on you, Darling.

I really am going to bed now. I love you and love you so much, Darling. Love me all you can and miss me lots.

All my love always and always,
Mary

PS: Did I tell you I had a *Collier's* one day this week? It's addressed to Irwin Deems c/o Mary Thomas. That sounds lovely to me. I love you, Darling.

Mary

March 24, 1946

My Darling,

Did you have a nice sleep this morning? You wouldn't have had a moment's peace if I had been there. I was at work at nine o'clock, and I thought of you snoring away when I could be loving you almost to death. But there are lots of Sunday mornings to come when I'll have you all to myself. Wish they'd hurry and come.

Ken has been helping me with the cooking this afternoon, making himself a general nuisance. He's gone to church now, though, with the rest of the family, except Walter, of course. He's gone to his club. So here I am, Darling, waiting for you to come and play house with me. You can be Daddy all the time. I don't mind a bit.

I've just been listening to a programme on the radio, crazy people imitating the Americans. Her name was Myrtle, and his name was Irwin. I had to laugh the way she said "Oiwin," though. Would you like me to call you that.

Had to leave for a couple of hours then. Con and Mair and Nancy's mother all walked in together. It's now eleven o'clock, and here I am in bed again, another day over. There's always my dreams of you before work again tomorrow morning though.

Ken asked when we were getting married this afternoon. I told him I didn't know. He said that it's better to get married at the Civic Center than in church, as not so many relations gather there. He thinks of everything.

Think I'd better go to sleep now. I was up early this morning. Do you mind if I leave you for a few minutes, Darling? I love you with all my heart, Darling. Love me too, and miss me lots.

All my love always and always,
Mary

March 25, 1946

My Darling,

Miss me tonight? I miss you lots, Irwin. Wish I could see you and tell you how much I love you. I do. You're wonderful.

The cheque for $275 arrived today. We're getting awfully rich, Darling. We're millionaires with all the love we have saved though, Darling. Just wish we could use our interest now.

Gwenda came to see me this morning. Everyone at work asked her what she thought of married life, and she said it wasn't too bad. That didn't sound right after only a few weeks. She didn't have much time then, so she arranged to meet me at five o'clock so we could go to a show. Everyone thought she looked terrible, not that she ever was very beautiful, but she looked as though she had lost interest in herself. Of course I heard it all this afternoon. A week after she was married, she was rushed to hospital. You can guess what for, and she had a serious operation. When she went back to the farm, she naturally wanted her husband to make a fuss of her, but he didn't even bother to ask her how she was. So she came home. Now she's waiting for him to come and take her back. You wouldn't be like that to me, would you, Darling? When she was telling me about it, I was thinking to myself, *Imagine Irwin treating me that way.* I'm so lucky to have you. You're perfect, and I have no doubts at all about our happiness. Our love is for keeps.

Would you like me to work in France, Darling? Gwenda had to go to that shop where you went one day, to buy makeup, remember? The people who run it had a very big beauty salon in Swansea, London, and Paris, before the war. Mr. Langley, the owner himself, was there when we went there this afternoon, and after talking for a few minutes, he turned to his wife and said I'd be the girl for beauty work, so I asked him if he'd like to take me on. I thought he was just kidding, but then he said he's sending girls over to France for the new treatments and new ideas on everything, and he'd willingly fit me in. He was quite serious too. So I told him I'd let him know. After that, of course, Gwenda was telling me how wonderful it would be, and I was full of ideas. Then I told my mother. She just shatters all my dreams and makes them seem ridiculous. It would be super if I could be over there with you and doing different work to what I'm doing now. I'll wait for you here instead, though. I love you, Darling.

Went to see *This Love of Ours.* It made me cry, but I enjoyed it. Ken is going to London tomorrow. He won't tell us how long he's going to stay there. He must have a girl to see or something.

Good night, Darling. You're wonderful, and I love you so very much. Love me lots.

All my love always and always,
Mary

March 27, 1946

My Darling,

You know something? I missed writing last night. Will my darling forgive me? I love you tonight so much. The more I think of you, the more wonderful you are. I'd give anything for just a quickie right now. I held my breath for a minute then. I'm in the front bedroom, and a car stopped right outside the door, and I thought it was you paying an unexpected visit. I was ready to jump out of bed. That would have been wonderful. But it was the man next door. I want to see you so badly that I'm sure my prayers will be answered, and you'll come to me. I miss you terribly, Darling.

Ken went to London yesterday morning so I moved all my things back to my bedroom again. You wouldn't believe how happy I felt about it. Yesterday afternoon, Mother and I went shopping. She insisted on buying me a dress. It's only something to wear on a real summer's day. I promised to go and visit Nancy. So I went there to tea, played with the baby all evening. He has a tooth now, and he's a cute little thing. I take back all I said about him. It was eleven thirty when I reached home. It was nice sleeping in my own bed. You might think I'm crazy, but it's the next best thing to being with you. I think all the wonderful things I want to do without worrying about talking in my sleep or something afterwards. We had lots of fun last night.

This morning I received a bundle of magazines, not the one with the bracelets, though. I wonder what happened to those? They were lovely magazines anyway. Thanks loads, Darling. Haven't had a letter since last Saturday. Do you still love me? Of course you do! Guess what? I love you much more, Irwin.

Went to a show with Elaine this evening. *Indiscretion*. It was silly. I don't think you'd like it either. I was coming home on the bus. I saw an RAF boy getting on too. I thought he looked like Ken, but he was in London. The next minute, Ken was sitting next to me. I had the shock of my life. He went to stay with a boy who was overseas with him, and he insisted he spend half his leave at his home as he's the only child. He knew Ken was coming. Met him at London and said casually to him, it would be all right to spend the night with him. That surprised Ken. When they got to his home, his mother started talking about extra work and no time for visitors, so Ken left. He didn't want to stay in London alone, so he's home again. Mother was shocked to see him walking in. That was awful for him though. He expected a great welcome there. Some people are funny. You'd think his mother would have been glad to see his friend, and it wasn't that he hadn't been invited. So now I've had to move all my things back to this room again, and I have to control my imagination a little. Why can't you be here, Darling? I wouldn't pester you too much, honest.

Well, Darling, it's time for dreams again. I love you and love you and love you all I can. Love me lots and miss me too.

All my love always and always,
Mary

March 28, 1946

My Darling,

I've spent a lovely evening sitting by a nice big fire and reading your magazines. Wish you could be with me all the time. I miss you so very much. You know, don't you?

More magazines arrived this morning. The watch bracelet was in one package, the gold one for Mair. It's very pretty, Darling. I meant to take it to her this evening, but the fire looked so nice, and they'll be here tomorrow evening, and I know she'll be awfully pleased with it.

I've been looking through the magazines trying to find the house you mentioned, but I can't. Maybe it's in the other package, the one with my bracelet in.

When I arrived home this evening, there was a lovely letter from you there, written on the sixteenth. I was beginning to worry about your trip back from Paris as I hadn't heard since last Saturday. I think all sorts of things. You're on my day all day and night. I love you so very much, Darling. Now I'm happy again. You're still missing and loving me, and that's what I want to hear all my life, though. I want to be there with you so you won't miss me at all, and I'll make sure you won't forget my presence either. You have tons of love to use. Darling, it's going to take every spare second you have.

Irwin, please don't ever think that I'm not waiting for you, even though you don't get my letters. I'm waiting for you more now than ever before. And remember how I love you, Darling. You shouldn't have any doubts in your mind at all. I'll send a cable tomorrow. I know how you feel not hearing from me. I'm writing all the time though. If only I could see you to tell you just how much you mean to me, then I expect I wouldn't say a word, but you'd know by just looking at me. You're my all too, remember? Won't it be wonderful when we don't have to bother with letters. All we have to do is touch one another, and you know the rest.

What a pin-up in the January *Esquire*. Walter is fascinated with it. I didn't have much to do at work this afternoon, so I took that *Esquire* to pass the time away. I called at the bank on my way, and the cashier asked if he could look at it. You should have heard him when he saw that girl. He wants to know what the Americans want our beauty over there for, when they have things like that to look at as well. You couldn't give her a sucker bite, could you, Darling?

Good night, Honey, and thanks for the magazines and bracelet. Remember that I love you for always and always and miss you every second. Love me and miss me all you can.

All my love always and always,
Mary

March 3, 1946

My Darling,

How's my little Yank tonight? I love you lots, but how impatient I am waiting to see you again. It's been a long time, and I want your kisses and your arms around me again. Then it will seem as though you hadn't been away from me. I miss you so much, Irwin.

Had a lovely letter today, written on the twentieth. Keep remembering, Irwin, that I miss you just as much, if not more, than you miss me. I look at your pictures too and remember what you were saying and how wonderful you looked at the time, though I remember everything that happened whenever we were together. So you can imagine how much I want to be with you for always. Wish you could send me some love by mail. I need loads of it.

You still remember the black-out girl, then. I didn't know she even had one of your kisses. You never told me before. I see her quite often. She smiles at me too. But in future, I'll ignore her. You don't know the awful feeling I get when I think of you kissing someone else. I must be jealous, but I love you so terribly much, Darling, and I'm saving all my love and kisses for you. I'd hate to harm our love in any way by kissing anyone else, just once. I'm yours for always. I'll keep wishing that you have to accompany English money to London very soon. I'm longing to see you, Irwin. What makes you think I'd say "If you want to"? If you only knew how much I miss you, you'd fly here. I was wishing you were near me this morning, when I read that. You'd be sorry. Mother asks me every day when you're coming again, so I told her about you going to London, and she asked if you'd be able to travel to Swansea. I said I wasn't sure. Anyway, she said I could go to London to see you. So, Darling, just let me know when you'll be there, and I'll be there waiting for you. Wouldn't it be nice?

So you had your new camera. We can do all kinds of things with it if it's yours. I'll take you in the mornings and tease you when you look so good afterwards. Of course, you'll have to teach me how to operate it first. That's if you know yourself.

What are you doing in a show until twelve o'clock? Don't you get tired sitting down all that time. I'd be sleeping. Did I tell you that the other night when Elaine and I went to a show, a sailor sitting near us snored the whole time. It sounded awful, but I couldn't help laughing. Elaine was getting mad though, so we moved away from him.

Ken has been teasing me all the evening, chasing me with a scissors to cut my hair. We had a real fight. I have a few bruises as a result of it. Raymond, the boy who used to spend so much time at our house, is getting married shortly, so we bought him a wedding present today. I bought one for Gwenda the same time. She was my friend, so I couldn't forget her wedding. I have to buy one for Hazel too. It's getting monotonous, all these people getting married like this.

Just as I was leaving this afternoon, Mr. Clement told me some exciting news, as he thought. On April 30, the whole Glamtax staff, all the branches, have to attend a victory dinner at Cardiff. We'll have the cars at our disposal, and they have the biggest hall in Cardiff for the occasion. I can just imagine what it's going to be like. There'll be more beer in that one place than in any other place for miles around. I'm not going unless I have to.

Con and Mair didn't come over today, so I gave the bracelet to Walter. He sees Con at work. Con was very pleased with it. That is all Walter will say. Ken reads the *Popular Science* from beginning to end. He thinks it an excellent magazine, and believe me, it takes a lot to please him.

It's Saturday again tomorrow. That's the loneliest night of the week for me, all right, but you know I don't mind being lonely. It's just that tomorrow afternoon, I'll be thinking all the time, about those wonderful days when I could see you then. I miss you the worst way. I want to be in my darling's arms, dancing or otherwise, then I have my whole world with me. Sometimes people I haven't seen in a while phone me, and it's usually on a Saturday, wanting me to go out somewhere. That's when I prove to myself how very, very much I love you. I refuse without the slightest regret at all, even though I know I'll spend the evening alone at home. I just couldn't go out with someone else. That's how I know I'll love you forever, Darling. Then I look around me at people like Elaine and others, who, ever since they were married, have just carried on making dates and, in their opinion, having a good time. Our love is different from that, isn't it, Darling? It must be. I know how miserable and horrible I'd feel if I should prejudice our love, even for a minute. You're everything to me, Darling.

You said something in your letter about receiving my letter, so I didn't cable you. You do know I'm all yours, don't you, Irwin? I am.

Nobody could ever love you more than I do. You're so wonderful, Darling.

Have to leave you now. Mother's coming to bed. I'll be with you in a few minutes, though, and am I going to be terrible in our dreams tonight, just you wait. Love me all you can, more than that even, and miss me every minute.

All my love always and always,
Mary

March 30, 1946

My Darling,

We're having lovely weather here, and it makes me miss you more than ever. It's a lovely and starry evening. You don't know how I long to be with you, Darling. I love you so very much.

The other bracelet arrived this morning. I don't know how to thank you for all these lovely things. You're wonderful to me, Irwin. I also had two super letters from you written on the eighteenth and twenty-second with the five pounds in one of them. I put it with the rest of the money right away.

Don't think that I'm patting myself on the back when I agree with you that if you had gone to the States last September, we'd be together now. I know one or two girls who were waiting for just the same thing as I'm waiting for and their intended husbands returned to the States to settle things, and now they have joined them. Do you think you'd save any time if you returned now? I don't want you to go in one way, and yet I'm longing to be with you always, as soon as I can. You know I'll wait for you though for just as long as you want me to. I'm all yours for always.

You say it's harder waiting for your next leave this time. It's funny you should say that. I feel the same way too. You're more important to me now than ever. You're on my mind every second. I wonder what you're doing and if you're missing me too. And all the time, I just love you more and more. I'm so glad I love you. There's nobody else in the world like you. You're perfect, and you know I have all my faith in you.

I certainly do remember using your pen. It was very good. Thank you, Darling, for getting me one like it. We managed to buy one for John for Christmas. That's the one I use now, and it's murder. It doesn't even fill.

Don't say anything about what I said about the money. I didn't mean it the way I wrote it, and I don't want to hear you say something may happen to you. That would be the end of the world for me, so we won't talk about what happens to the money then. I'll take care of it, Darling, until you'll be asking me for a few shillings to buy tobacco. Then you'll be sorry you let me keep it. We're going to have lots of fun, Darling. I'm glad you didn't want to go to the dance with the other two officers. I don't want you to dance with anyone else. You're too wonderful to do that. I trust you but I don't trust the girls. I remember so well how nice I thought you were when I first danced with you. I loved you right away. That's why I don't want you to go to dances, Darling.

Did I tell you we have a new girl telephonist? She was a WAAF and keeps telling me what she did to win the war. She was on radar. It makes me feel awful. She's engaged. Her boyfriend is in Burma, and she's met someone else that she likes better since he's been there. She doesn't know what to do now. She asked me if I'd go to Langland with her tonight as she has no friends here. I told her I was going to a show with a friend. She's a girl I could never like. I don't want to start going around with her. She thinks I'm crazy because I don't go to dances when you're away, but she wouldn't want to if she really loved someone. There's no pleasure in dancing with anyone else. I can wait until we have lots of evenings together, and then I'll forget about all this time we've been apart.

You didn't know we were married, did you? Some girl told Nancy we were, and today Mother met someone who told her the same thing. It's wonderful how these stories circulate. I wonder who invents them in the first place.

Well, Darling, it's getting late, and I have to get up at eight o'clock tomorrow morning, Sunday, and just think. My husband will be sleeping peacefully for a few more hours. Wish I could be with you, Darling. I'd pester you until you get mad. I don't mind how much you pester me, Darling. Good night, and remember I love you with all my heart and miss you so very much. Love me all you can, and dream nice dreams. I'm always over on your side.

All my love always and always,
Mary

April 2, 1946

My Darling,

It's no wonder you're not having my letters. I had three returned this morning. I'll enclose them in this letter tonight. I also had a lovely short letter from you too. I did wrinkle my nose as I saw it, as you said I would, though I understand how difficult it is for you, Darling, when you don't hear from me. I'm loving you more and more all the time, Irwin. You know that, 'cause you're my husband.

It's been a beautiful day again, and how I miss you. I worked for a few hours this morning then, this afternoon, went shopping with Mother. Met Elaine at five o'clock. We had tea, and the show at the Albert Hall was *Divorce*. I know it was silly of me, but I didn't want to see it, but Elaine did, and there wasn't anything else in town to see. All it was, Irwin, was a parable on how divorces don't work out. It only lasted fifty minutes, but it made me think, all right. I felt uncomfortable, and if you ever see it, you'll understand why.

People were swimming here today. If it's as warm as this this weekend, Elaine and I are going to see how it is. Wish you were with me, Darling. I need you with me all the time though. I love you so very much.

You're going to wrinkle your nose too when you see this short letter, but this spring weather makes me feel tired. This would be a good excuse for us to get up the stairs, Darling. I'm making believe right now that I only have to turn around, and I'm in your arms. Lovely dreams tonight. Love me and miss me lots.

All my love always and always,
Mary

April 3, 1946

My Darling,

Do you mind me writing to you on your stationery? I'm sorry, but Dorothy used mine to write to her Syd this evening. You love me, anyway, don't you? I love you lots. Today I had three wonderful letters from you, with 5 pounds in each. That's 212 pounds, 1 shilling, and 10 pence we have in the bank. What are you going to do with the money, Darling?

It's been warm today. I was thinking how nice it would be if you could be here. Then you wouldn't grumble about our weather. Whatever the weather is like, though, I always want you with me. I miss you so very much, Darling. You can never realize just how much I do. What I wouldn't give for a super kiss from my darling right now. You're so wonderful. When can you take money to London? Tell them to make it very soon. I have tons of love waiting for you.

Elaine and the rest of the girls at her office were having a sort of picnic this evening. She asked me to go along, and I was, until I learned that it was an affair where they were going to stop at every pub. That's when I refused the invitation. I went for a walk instead, all alone. It was nice though. I imagined you were with me. Wish you could have been. I want to tell you how I've been missing and loving you.

The Glamtax Party on April 30 is the chief topic at the office these days. We can all take a friend with us. Brookman is our representative. He was at Cardiff yesterday making all the arrangements. I'm quite sure I'm not going. I see enough of them every day. Mr.

Clement must think I'm a genius. He asked me today if I could write a short play for some of our staff to entertain the other people with. They'll have me singing next. Then they'll be sorry.

I saw *Lost Weekend*. It was a dismal affair. What a drunk he was. I told Walter to see that. Maybe it could change him. I'd love to see you fooling around with your camera. You wouldn't have any peace. When you get the camera, be sure you get me some views of Le Havre. I want to see where my husband is. Of course, I want lots of you too. I'll never see enough of you.

That was very nice of Rankin, inviting you to his place. He's awfully proud of everything, isn't he? He has good reason to be, though. Maybe we'll be a lot more satisfied with ourselves, though. I know we're going to be so very, very happy, especially me. I'll have you all to myself, every evening and every night. Wish time would hurry. I want you near so I can love you all I want.

Gosh, Irwin. I don't know what to say or how to thank you for getting me those handkerchiefs and the Shocking perfume. You know how grateful I am, though. You're just wonderful to me. That Shocking sounds awfully nice. I've almost used all my Passion. That tickled everyone. The name, I mean.

Yours letters, Darling, are more wonderful to me than those in *Love Letters*, but I don't just love you for them. I love you and everything about you. Every letter you write me, though, makes me miss you more and more.

Good night, my own Irwin. I'll dream about you tonight. I can see you every time I close my eyes. You're my everything. Love me all the time and be good for me, 'cause I love you with all my heart.

All my love always,
Mary

PS: I forgot to tell you, I had another letter returned today, which I'm enclosing.

I love you,
Mary

April 4, 1946

My Darling,

I love you, guess how much? You'd never guess, so I'll tell you. I love you more than anyone could love anyone else. You're my whole life, and I'll never stop loving you. Even that doesn't sound enough for the way I really feel about you. But you know, don't you, Darling?

Had a lovely letter again today with five pounds enclosed. You seem to be having my letters, now. I'm glad of that in case you start thinking again. You know, though, that I'm yours for always.

Ken was in a bad mood tonight, and I was wondering what had upset him. He waited until we were all having supper and then turned to me and said was I crazy. I was about to ask him why, when he said something about divorce. We hadn't told him about that. We thought he'd never know, but some nice person took the trouble to inform him, and that annoyed him more than anything. Of course, Walter said his piece as well, and that was the topic for the next hour. I'm used to it, though. It doesn't bother me a bit. We have a new driver. He's been in the army. He's a sarcastic and conceited thing. This afternoon he annoyed me more than usual, and his head was through these spaces we have in front of the office, so I just tugged at his hair. It must have hurt him, but I thought he just walked away, but the next thing, he pulled the chair, and I was sitting on the floor, and I went with it. I gave a scream, and Mr. Clement came out. I had a hard time explaining that one. He told me to be more careful about the way I sat on chairs in future. I've got some super bruises, and I can't show them to anyone, only you, of course. Would you be interested? I thought you wouldn't be.

Why can't you tell me what the surprise is? You shouldn't have said anything about it, then I wouldn't be so curious. I hope I can see you soon. It seems such a long time since I was in your arms, and I'm longing to be there again. Can't you do something about making the weight for two planes? Two days would be heaven. I miss you so much, Darling.

I did write to thank you for the lovely silk. It's so lovely. I just can't tell you what I think of it. I had the watch bands too. Mair has hers. She told me to thank you for it. Suits her watch perfectly. Thanks loads for everything, Darling. You have tons of super kisses waiting for you.

Dorothy has gone to visit Sid's people this evening. They live about ten miles from here, so she's staying the night with them. My grandmother wanted me to spend the night with her, but I wasn't having any.

Good night, Darling. I have to go now. Dream about me, and love me lots. You know how much I love you and miss you.

All my love always and always,
Mary

April 5, 1946

My Darling,

Bet you didn't stay in bed this morning if it's so nice at Le Havre as it's been here. You don't know how I was wishing we were together when I saw the sun this morning. I closed my eyes and imagines that we were deciding what we'd do. I love you more and more each time. I think of you, and I'm thinking of you all day long. I don't think there are many more people in this world who are loved as much as I love you.

It was such a lovely day that I just couldn't settle down to work. I played cricket with the men instead. Mr. Clement came along, and he played too. We have a good stretch of open ground at the side of the garage, and that's our cricket pitch now. They wouldn't let me bat or bowl, because cricket is a man's game, and the ball is very hard, so I did the fielding for them. They bought me ice cream afterwards too. That was a good day's work done.

This afternoon I went for a walk with John. We went to the top of the hill, and then he was tired. We saw a fire burning a little distance away and went to take a look. The gorse bushes had caught fire by the sun shining on them. It was spreading too, but we came away and left it. I think John was embarrassed walking with me. He kept saying that he hoped the boys wouldn't see him as they'd think he was a sissy going out with his sister.

This evening, I read more magazines. I have to laugh every time I read the article "Do You Know How to Make Love?" I know one person who could show them a few things, my Irwin. He's wonderful, you know. Wish he was demonstrating on me right now.

Hope I get a letter from you tomorrow, Darling. I want to know how much you love me. Love me with every bit of love you have. You have all mine. I miss you so awfully much, Irwin. Be good for me and dream nice dreams about me.

All my love always and always,
Mary

April 6, 1946

My Darling,

Sorry I missed writing last night. We had another family gathering, and I didn't get to bed until twelve thirty. Am I forgiven, Irwin? Say yes. I love you lots and lots, remember?

I was all ready to go dancing tonight, but you didn't show up, Darling. So I just sat around reading magazines all evening. They're playing "I Can't Begin to Tell You" on the radio right now. I like that. I'm all alone at home. Wish I could expect you to come in. I'm lonesome, Darling. I want to hear you say you love me. If only I could see you for a few minutes. I know as well as you do that I wouldn't be satisfied with that. I'd want to keep you with me. But right now, a few minutes with you would be wonderful.

When you talk in your letters as though we were already married, I feel envious of myself in the future. Don't you watch me washing my neck. You look after your pipe instead. I have to laugh every time I think of that night at the Brangwyn, when those women left that corner and looked at your pipe when I could smell something burning, remember? You're wonderful. Oh, if you were only near now, I'd just about love you to death. Just before I go to sleep, I can feel your arms around me again, and I just lose myself in a wonderful dream. You're all my dreams. Sometimes I wake up in the morning and feel terribly disappointed when you're not at my side. It's not fair. I want you so much, Irwin.

Ken was supposed to receive his orders today, but they didn't arrive. I think he's a little disappointed about it. He wanted Walter and me to go to Langland this evening, but you know what I did.

Elaine wanted me to go swimming this afternoon, and I arranged to meet her at two thirty, then at one o'clock I was leaving the office when the colonel told me he was expecting an important phone call at four o'clock, and as Mr. Clement and himself wouldn't be there, I'd have to take it. I couldn't say a thing, as officially I'm supposed to work Saturday afternoons, so I cancelled my date with Elaine and sat around that dismal place until the call came through. I was mad. It was such a lovely day.

Time to dream of my wonderful husband again. I don't know what I'd do without dreams and memories of us. I love you with all my heart, and I'm longing to see you, Darling. Miss you so terribly. Love me lots and miss me all you can.

All my love always and always,
Mary

April 8, 1946

My Darling,

I think I've got chicken pox or something. Quite a number of people have it here, and I'm feeling sick. What are you going to do about it? I'm only kidding. I never felt better in my life. Just ready for lots and lots of love. Hurry and come to me, Darling.

Went with Mr. Clement to buy a wedding present for Hazel this afternoon. She's getting married next week. We bought a clock. Nice too. It was funny shopping with Mr. Clement, though. Don't know why he took me along. He knew what he was going to buy.

This morning, I had a lovely letter from you, written on April 1, and also two of mine returned. I'll enclose them in this letter. It's no wonder you don't get much mail from me. Wish letters weren't the only means of me letting you know how very, very much I love you.

I started this letter at seven thirty, but Harry and Kit came in, and I had to listen to her baby talk again. Ken told her not to talk that way when John was around. She didn't like that either. It's now eleven thirty, and here I am in bed again. Guess what I wish would happen? You're right, first time. I want you so much, Darling. I want you to wolf me all my life.

I'm tickled pink about you listening to the Welsh Home Service. I can't understand all they say myself, so I can imagine how difficult it must be for you. Wish I could be there. We don't need a radio or anything. Just us. Wish I could see you. You don't know how I'm missing you, Darling.

I feel sleepy now. You too? All right, you can come over on my side tonight, and I'll make you comfortable. Dream about me and love me all you can. I'm always loving and missing you, my Irwin.

> All my love always and always,
> Mary

Part Seven

APRIL 18, 1946–MAY 5, 1946

*I've been thinking about you and
your leave in the States.*

April 18, 1946

My Darling,

I miss you so much. It doesn't seem only this morning I was with you. I want to see you, Irwin. Seeing you leave this time was much harder than any time before. I love you, Darling. Wish I could tell you how much I do. You're my whole life though, and I'll just go on loving you more and more all the time.

It was a wonderful surprise when you called this afternoon. You seemed so close to me that I dared to hope for a second. The office was full of people at the time. Hazel and Eddie were being presented with the clock, so if I sounded a little odd, you can understand why. You know how I love you though.

When I walked out of the station this morning, one of our cars was just moving out. I couldn't resist the temptation of running, so I had a ride back to the office. I couldn't work properly, though. I felt as though most of me was with you. Well, my heart was. But I just couldn't settle down to do anything. I started to miss you right away.

Going home to lunch alone was awful too. Mother seemed awfully disappointed when she knew that you did get your train. She went over to Harry's place this morning. Kit said something about people talking about me. Mother told her that people should mind their own business, and that upset her a little, and to make matters worse, she said if she wasn't going to have a baby, she wouldn't live with Harry. So all day long, Mother's been worrying about that.

Miss Baldwin told me today that Elaine phoned Monday. She hasn't been to work for two weeks, so now I know why I haven't heard from her.

You would have laughed if you'd heard the speech Mr. Clement made when he made the presentation this afternoon. He said that marriage was the most wonderful thing in the world, and you know the little gangster, with the remains of a battle on his forehead, well, he stood up and said, "I second that." I gave a yell. He made Mr. Clement's words sound so funny.

I came home at six this evening. Mother was reading *Amber*, and I felt so lonely. I had a hot bath and came to bed right away. It's only eight thirty now. This time last night we were on our way home from the Manor. I want you with me always, Darling. Life is so empty without you. You're so wonderful, and knowing that you are all mine makes me feel so good. You know I'm yours for always. I'll never stop loving you.

I feel tired. Do you, Darling? I'm ready for lots of love, though. Why can't you be with me? My little bed seems so nice tonight, and really there's lots of room for both of us. I want to be so close to you, my wonderful husband. I can just feel myself in your arms right now. Life's wonderful.

I forgot to thank you for the lovely time I had with you. You're so good to me. I know our life together will be just as wonderful as the few precious days just gone. We'll always be happy.

Love me more and more all the time, Darling, and miss me all you can. Remember that all my love is there with you. I'm yours forever. I'm going to have super dreams tonight. I love you so much.

All my love always and always,
Mary

April 20, 1946

My Darling,

Have you missed me? Wish you were here to answer my question. I realize more than ever how much I need you. I do, Darling, for every second of my life.

Yesterday morning I was shaken out of my dreams at seven thirty. Ken had arrived home again for indefinite leave, so I started to move my things back again. What a life! I worked hard all day without even lunch until six thirty. Went home. Nobody there at all. You can imagine how I was missing you. I love you so much, Irwin. I did lots of odds and ends, then read the *Cosmopolitan* that arrived yesterday. Then I thought I'd make supper for everyone and wait until I got to bed before writing you. Well, it was twelve thirty before they were home. Mother went to my aunt's, and Walter worked late. I'm sorry I didn't write, Darling. I was mad at myself. But you understand, don't you?

Mother misses you lots. She says how strange it is to see me coming home without you. It's much worse for me though. The first thing Ken asked when he arrived yesterday was if you were here. Wish I could have said yes. You do seem to be the biggest half of me now. You're mine, aren't you, Darling?

Went to see Hazel's wedding this morning with Miss Baldwin and Mrs. Hill. We waited outside to see her walking up the steps. There were quite a number of people there, and when she arrived, instead of the people exclaiming with joy, they all made pitying sounds. She looked so small and pale. I felt like crying. You know something? You don't have to promise to obey your husband in the wedding ceremony now. You'd better be careful, Darling. I'd never go through a fuss like I saw this morning. I'm sure you wouldn't like it either. I didn't go to the reception. We went and had coffee, then back to the office. One of our drivers came back and said that hazel was asking where I was, so Mrs. Hill and I went to wish them luck. We had wedding cake and a tiny glass of wine. It was like a madhouse. They wanted us to stay, but I had lots of work to do. As Hazel was leaving for her honeymoon, she fainted and fell down the stairs. It must have been all the excitement. Her mother made me read a letter from the daughter that's just gone to the States. She doesn't seem very happy. It's a very quiet place where she lives, and all her husband's friends and relatives only speak Serbian, so you can imagine how she feels.

I came home around six o'clock this evening, and the flowers were there. Wish you could have seen them, Darling. They're wonderful. Lots of them and roses too. Thank you, Irwin. I'll never be able to repay you for all the wonderful things you do for me. I do love you with all my heart, though, and maybe I'll really be able to tell you one day how I appreciate all you give me. You know how dumb I am with words, though. I just want to make you the happiest person in the world. You deserve so much.

Do you know what I did tonight? I took all your letters out of the envelopes, filed them nicely, and burned the envelopes. Guess how long it took me? Three hours. There were mountains of letters. I read almost every one as I went along. The one you wrote in December 1944 after your terrible experience, even though it's only a few lines, tells me more than any of them how much you love me, and it's my very special letter. They're all wonderful though. I'd hate to ever part with them. You should see all your writing, Darling. It made me very proud to see it all for me. I'm awfully conceited about having your love, though, and to know you want me too. I want you for my own for always.

Saw Nancy, her husband, and the baby today too. She asked when you were coming. I told her you had been, and then I had to make excuses for not visiting her. She hasn't had a place to live at London yet. It doesn't seem to bother her, though.

Mr. Clement told me I was to present a bouquet to the managing director's wife at the party. He wouldn't accept my refusal of the invitation. I'm not going, though.

Well, Darling, I feel sleepy again. It's only four o'clock. This time last week we were on our way home from Langland and then, remember? I was terrible, wasn't I? I wish I could be that way tonight. Well, I just want you with me, then my life's complete. Love me and miss me all you can. I'm all yours, and I love you with all my heart. Dream wonderful dreams, and be good for me.

All my love always and always,
Mary

April 21, 1946

My Darling,

Remember last Sunday? We were on top of the hill around this time. When I think of all those wonderful days we had together, I can't realize it isn't a dream. You're so wonderful, Irwin, and I miss you so terribly.

I worked this afternoon. Well, I wrote more invitations for the party, and when I came home, I felt tired. So after tea, I had a nice bath and sat in the front room surrounded with your lovely flowers. I was wishing so hard that you'd come and at the same time wondering if you'd reached Le Havre and if anything was said about you staying the time you did. Well, you're on my mind every minute of the day. Wish I could be with you. I want to know how much you love and miss me. I need all the love you can spare. Please save it all for me, Darling.

Con and Mair came over this evening too. I explained to Con about our problem. He's fixing it for me. Everything will be fine, Darling. That will be a load off my mind and yours too, I know. We'll benefit a great deal from it, and no questions will be asked. Are you satisfied now? I am.

Do you mind if I leave you for a few minutes now, Darling? I feel sleepy but still ready for lots of love. Don't keep me waiting. I'll see you in my dreams. Love me all you can, Irwin, and remember how I love and miss you.

All my love always and always,
Mary

April 23, 1946

My Darling,

I'm cold again tonight. Why aren't you with me? Are you missing me, Irwin? I want to see you again. It doesn't seem just a week ago tonight we spent the evening sitting by the fire, remember? I love you and miss you so much. You're my whole world, and you're so wonderful.

Worked again today. Elaine phoned this morning and asked me to go out tonight. I thought she meant going to a show so I said I would. Then she said she had a date, and he wanted to make it a foursome. Just go for a few drinks somewhere. You know what I told her then? She didn't say anymore. Then about an hour later, she phoned again. She said she'd broken her date and would I go to a show. Well, I couldn't say no, but knowing Elaine, if I turned up, there'd be two men with her. So, Darling, I stayed home. It's bothering me a little now, just in case she was on the level, but I wasn't taking any chances. You know something, Darling? A few months ago I didn't think any less of her as a girl for going around, but today when she said she had a date, I felt sick, and I could have slapped her if she'd been near. I don't want to see her again. Isn't that strange? I just can't imagine myself with anyone but you. I'd hate to be in anyone else's arms. You have all me, for always, Darling. Please want me, Darling.

This morning, I had a lovely letter from Virginia. She's missing you too and wonders why you are away so long. Am I selfish for wanting you to stay, Darling? She sent a picture of herself and the children receiving her husband's medal. They all look lovely. I was thrilled with it.

The *Collier's* arrived this morning too. I was reading it this evening when Harry and Kit arrived. They've taken a certain dislike to me. I don't know why, unless it's because I don't fuss over them. I'm not worried, anyway.

Hope I get a letter tomorrow. I'm getting impatient again. I just can't realize that you love me as you say you do. I want you to myself for always. I love you with all my heart, and I'm missing you every second. Love me and miss me loads.

All my love always and always,
Mary

April 25, 1946

My Darling,

Came to bed tonight and turned the radio on as loud as possible so I could write to you and listen to Jean Sablon, the French crooner, at the same time. He's singing "Stardust" right now. I like his voice very much.

It seems a long time since you were here. Time goes so slowly, and I don't even have a trace of a sucker bite left now. I love you more and more every minute, and I want to be so near to you. You're in my thoughts and dreams all day and night through, but I miss you so much. I want to make fudge, Charles. Didn't get a letter today again. You do love me though, don't you?

Went to see Nancy last night, and what do you think? I gave the baby its bath. It's easy. He liked it. I almost had a bath too, but it was fun. I didn't get home until eleven thirty. I had to walk the whole way. So you see, Darling, I didn't write last night, but I had some wonderful dreams. You're my ideal, all right.

Haven't heard from Elaine since I didn't turn up the other night. I'm awfully glad I'm finished with her. I'm not easily led, but she could have involved me in a few escapades that would start out quite innocently and end up the other way. I think I'll fix her up with Eva. They'd be a good pair.

It's been raining all day today. Ken was home all the evening. He kept throwing things at me, banana skins, orange peel, and everything he could lay his hands on until I could have screamed. Mother was trying to read *Amber*, and she was getting annoyed with him. It was like a madhouse. I think I'll stay in work until bedtime tomorrow. There's more peace there.

Are you in your tent yet? I think I'd better come over and take care of you. You don't know what you may pick up. Don't let anyone take you away from me. That's my big worry. I want you for all my life, Darling. You're my whole world. You're just wonderful.

Good night, Darling. Love me loads and miss me all you can. I love you with all my heart, and I'm all yours. Everybody wants to be remembered to you. Dream about me, and be good for me.

All my love always and always,
Mary

April 26, 1946

My Darling,

Didn't get a letter today. I feel miserable now. Wish we were together for always now, Irwin. I love you too much to keep it to myself for the time we have to wait. I want to be loved too, and you're the only person in the world that can do that. So hurry back to me, Darling. I want to be your wife as soon as I can. You want me, don't you? I want you so very much.

Waiting this time is so very much harder than other times, but I'll wait for just as long as you want me to. There's no substitute for you anywhere. I love you with all my heart, Darling.

This evening, Ken and I were alone in the house, so I showed him my collection of foreign coins. I have a big collection now. Ken gave me more too. Egyptian, North African, Italian, and Greek. I'm worth some money. I'd like to tell you what I've done about the other sort too, but I'll guess I'll have to wait until I see you.

I bought a new dress today too. I don't know what to think of it now I've got it, and Walter and Ken thought it was terrible, so that made me think a little. It will be all right for the office, though.

Nothing special to tell you tonight. I hope you think that the fact I love you more and more each minute and you know how I loved you when I last saw you is special though. 'Cause I do, Darling, and I miss you for all I'm worth. Love me all you can, Darling, and miss me too.

All my love always and always,
Mary

April 27, 1946

My Darling,

Saturday night again and I'm lonesome for you. Wish I was wherever you are. I look at that picture of your room and think of you sitting around and then wonder if you're in your tent. I want to see you, Darling. I haven't had a letter yet. I hope you still love me. You do, don't you, Darling? I love you more than anything. I don't want to go dancing tonight. Let's spend the evening at home. I want you all to myself.

Spent the evening alone. I listened to the radio, wrote a letter to Virginia, then came to bed. It's only ten o'clock now. We're wasting lots of time, Darling. Just think of what we'd be doing if we were together. We'll make up for it soon, though. I'm going to love you so much.

Mr. Clement asked if I was looking forward to the party Monday night. I told him again that I wasn't going, but he said I have to, so I don't know. If I go, I know I won't have a good time, and it isn't worth staying out until two o'clock for. I certainly hope he doesn't insist. He said he'd ask my mother if I could go, and then I'll have no excuse. Imagine going to a party with our drivers. But they'll have their wives with them, so it won't be too bad.

Wish I had a letter to answer. I'm worrying about your trip back now. I'll be completely happy when I'm with you all the time. Then I won't have to wonder how you are, where you are, and if you still love me. I was mad today. I looked at my Shocking, and what do you think? It's evaporating. At least it must have been the way I had it in my drawer. The perfume had run out of the bottle. So now I have it standing up. I hope it will be all right. I like it a lot.

Good night, dearest. I'd give anything for a super kiss and hug right now. You're so wonderful, and I love you so very much. Love me with all your heart and miss me lots. Dream nice dreams.

All my love always and always,
Mary

April 30, 1946

My Darling,

I had two wonderful letters from you today written on the twenty-first and twenty-second. I was awfully glad to get them too after not hearing where you were and if you had returned safely. I love you so very, very much, Darling.

Went to the party last night. You didn't mind me going, did you, Irwin? I had to go out of decency. The men kept saying that I didn't want to mix with them, and Mr. Clement was annoyed too. We left town at five o'clock in a bus. They were singing all the way. We reached Cardiff at seven o'clock and had a lovely reception. Every lady was given a little present and introduced to everybody. They had a nice band too, but after looking around, I started to feel bored, and I was missing you so very much. Darling, I sat in the lounge with one of our telephonists most of the time. She's young and wasn't at all interested in dancing with old men, and neither of us went for the drinks we were supposed to have. We just sat looking miserable, and a man asked me to dance. He looked different to the drivers. I told him I didn't want to dance, but he insisted. We'd only gone two yards when the band stopped, and Captain Evans started walking me up to the stage with the man behind me, and we won a prize each for something. I had a shopping bag, and he had a shaving mirror. I discovered afterwards that the man I danced with was our head director's son. That shook me a little. They played a few party games. I danced with a few of the men, but you know, Darling, that I didn't touch your account in any way. I'm all yours, every part of me, and I'm so very lucky to belong to you. You're more than wonderful, Darling. I didn't get home until two o'clock. I was awfully tired and hungry, so I didn't get to bed until three o'clock. Then this morning I got up around ten o'clock to see if there were any letters for me, and I was lucky. Went to see *Because of Him* this afternoon with Mother and read magazines this evening until coming to bed at eight o'clock. I want to see you, Darling. Oh, how I love you.

As I was leaving the house yesterday afternoon, Mother said, "No fooling around with any men tonight." She knew better, but I liked to hear her say that as if I'd fool around with anyone when I have you and your love. I wouldn't want to spoil our love for anything. Nobody could take your place, not even for a second, and you know that too.

I'm feeling pretty tired right now, Darling. I'll see you in my dreams for sure tonight. You're so wonderful. Love me and want me all you can, Darling. You have all my love and all my heart too. Wish I could say good night with a super kiss and hold you close even for a few minutes, our minutes. Darling, I wouldn't let you go tonight. Miss me lots and dream about me, Darling.

All my love always and always,
Mary

May 1, 1946

My Darling,

It's a lovely evening. Would you like to go for a walk? I feel extra miserable tonight, and all day I've been thinking of you and your leave in the States. I know you're going to help our future along, but I have some awful doubts in my mind, and to tell you the truth, I'm scared. I am, Irwin. When you get there and see your people, you mightn't realize how much you'd be giving up for me, and you know I don't hold you to anything. I want to be your wife, more than you'll ever know. But I guess I'm selfish. I want you all to myself. You are all I ever think about, and I'd love to know that you felt the same way, too. And yet you couldn't be blamed if you changed your mind. I'm all mixed up, Darling, now that it comes to your going. I want you so very much, Irwin. I just couldn't let you go now. Promise me too that even though things may not work out as we planned, you'll come and see me. Wish you were here tonight so I could talk to you. I think I could say more than I can write about this.

You can see what kind of a mood I'm in tonight, so will you excuse the short letter, Darling? One thing that doesn't change with all my moods, and that's the way I love you. I just go on loving you more and more all the time, and I miss you so terribly much, Irwin. Please keep loving and missing me always. I'm all yours forever. You're my whole life.

All my love always and always,
Mary

May 4, 1946

My Darling,

It's Saturday night again, and I feel extra lonely, wondering how much further away from me you are right now. I haven't had a letter since Tuesday when you were seeing about going to the States. Maybe you're on your way right now. I will see you again, won't I, Darling? I love you so very, very much and want so much to be with you for always.

Went to the Manor this evening with Mother and saw *The Way to the Stars*. It was very good. It was a British film but showed American airmen on duty here. Mother was tickled pink with them. They were so lovable. We managed to meet Mrs. Jones inside, so after seeing the whole show, I left the other two there. They saw it over twice. It's only nine fifteen, and here I am in bed. I just made a wish. There's a new moon tonight. I only hope that it comes true soon.

Should I keep writing when you're in the States, Darling? You might not even get this one when I come to think of it. Now I don't have any way to keep reminding you how much more I'm loving you every minute. You won't forget me, will you, Darling?

I want to finish my book before I sleep tonight, so I'll leave you now, Darling. Are you going to read too, or are you going to pester me for a while? Darling, anything you say. I wanted to come over to your side anyway. It's so nice, and tomorrow's Sunday. We have lots of time. You won't say you have to work tomorrow and want to go to sleep right anyway. I love you, Darling. I'll see you in my dreams tonight. I don't want to be good wither. Please love me all you can and miss me wherever you are. I'm loving and missing you wherever you are. I'm loving and missing you every minute. Good night, Darling. Be good for me.

All my love always and always,
Mary

May 5, 1946

My Darling,

Right now I'm remembering the last Sunday evening I was with you. Remember? We did a lot of walking. Life was wonderful. That's how it always is when I'm with you though. I love you, Darling, so very much.

It's only seven thirty now. I thought of going for a walk alone, but it's awfully cold and looks like rain. So instead, I'm curled up in front of the fire. I'm missing you, Irwin, more than you'll ever know. Wish I could hear you say you love me right now. I've only had two letters since you returned. I wish they'd do something about the mail. I want to know how much you're missing me. I want you most of all, though. You're my everything.

Ken and Walter are here now. You can guess how they're performing. Walter has his new suit on, and I won't look at him, to say how it looks. Men are worse than women.

Are you pleased about going to Marseilles, Darling? You didn't say anything about it. It's a long way from me, though. Isn't it? Will you be able to come to England on leave from there? I don't even know what I'd do if they stopped that I want to see you so much, Darling. I'll never see enough of you. The south of France should be nice for you, though, especially this time of year. Wish I could be with you. Imagine sun for weeks at a time and you to share it with. It would be wonderful.

Mother and Dorothy are patiently waiting for the snaps. I'm not so anxious myself. I hope the ones I took of you will turn out all right. Those are the most important to me. Mother has finished reading *Amber*, but she wants to know what happens to her afterwards.

I'm not getting much peace to write this letter, so I'd better leave you now, before it's torn out of my hands. I love you and love you and love you all there is and miss you so terribly. Love me and miss me every minute and hurry back to me.

All my love always and always,
Mary

Part Eight

MAY 26, 1946

*Remember me telling you of my biggest
fear for our happiness I had?*

May 26, 1946

My Darling,

It's wonderful to be able to write to you. I've missed telling I love you every night before I dream about you. I love you more than ever now, Darling. I've had all your letters now. Eight arrived yesterday, including the one with your brother's address. I hope this letter gets there in time.

Thank you, Darling, for thinking of Mother and sending flowers. She had them all right, and you should have seen her face. She wanted to write and thank you, but of course, like me, she couldn't do that because of your trip, but she thought it was wonderful of you, Darling.

We had the snaps this week too. Everyone was thrilled with them, Darling. You look just as you are, super. Mother hasn't stopped looking at them yet. Con and Mair are having theirs enlarged, and Dorothy has sent hers to Sid.

Are you missing me way over there, Darling? I miss you more and more every second. Just wish I could see you and talk to you instead of writing right now. There are lots of things I could explain much better to you if you were here.

Since about the first minute I saw you, I loved you. But from about the same time, I never thought you'd do all this for me. Naturally, this makes me terribly happy. If you weren't so wonderful, and if I didn't love you so very, very much, it wouldn't be hard at all to tell you what I'm going to tell you. You know how much I want to be with you, Darling. And I want to make you just the happiest person in the world. But when those papers arrived for me to sign this time, and I had to send a cable with my answer to you, something happened to me. Remember me telling you of my biggest fear for our happiness that I had? Well, Darling, I didn't want to think about your children, but I just couldn't help it, and then I wanted to see you more than ever before. You see, Darling, I wouldn't want anything to spoil our happiness, but for a few days, I was scared of risking these things, and that's why I didn't send that cable. You must think I need a lot of reassuring and that I'm a dummy. But you understand, don't you, Darling? I'm yours, forever and ever, and I want you to be all mine forever too.

Irwin, you're going to get mad now, so hold your breath and count ten. I want to be your wife as soon as I can, but, Darling, after all this time, things have developed all of a sudden. What I'm trying to say is, will you wait another month longer? Ken will be out of the RAF by that time, and things will be settled at home, and I'll have new clothing coupons too. I know it's a lot to ask after you going to all this trouble for me, but can you do that? I'm all excited right now, just thinking about us together for always, and I don't want to wait any longer than is necessary for that time. But Mother has been pretty good about everything, and I have to consider her a little too. I hope you won't love me any less for it, Darling, 'cause I want all the love you have. Please save it for me.

That house you picked out in the magazine is a dream. Ever since I saw it, I've been fixing it up in my imagination, and in my dreams last night, we were living in it. It was wonderful. Could we really have a home like that, Darling? I don't care about having a fireplace. It looks just perfect as it is. The stairs are just where I want them, and there are big windows. It looks like something I've always wanted but never thought I'd really have. We'd be so happy living in a house like that. We'd be happy anywhere, I know, but we'd have so much fun making fudge in that kitchen.

I have a girl from Manselton working with me now. She's married. Her husband's an officer in the Navy. That's his career, but she loves him almost as much as I love you. So we go to shows together, play tennis in the evenings, and spend our spare time at one another's homes. I've known her all my life. We went to the same schools, but I never knew before what a lovely girl she is. She lives with her people and just works to take her mind off her husband being away. She won't see him again for another two years. I know how she must feel about it. Her Jack and my Irwin are our only interests. It's wonderful to meet someone like her after knowing Elaine. By the way, this girl's name is Peggy. You'd like her too.

Almost forgot to tell you, I had a letter from Virginia this week and a snap of herself. She looks awfully nice. I'm going to answer her letter this evening. She told me about the hosiery difficulty, and she'll explain the rest to you. I understand about the way things are there. I'm awfully grateful for her just writing to me anyway.

How do you like being home, Darling? You know that I want you to say that you're missing me, but I hope you're having a good time and being good too. I bet everybody was surprised to see you. They're awfully lucky people. Wish I could see you as well. I mustn't be selfish, though. They're still lucky, all the same.

This is Sunday afternoon. It's raining hard right now. Just think. I have disgusting thoughts. Do you, Darling? Lovely, though.

It's time for tea now, so I'd better leave you. I hope everybody asks about me. I love you and love you more every second, my wonderful husband, and miss you so terribly much. Have a lovely time, and be Good for me, Darling. Miss me lots and love me all you can. I'm all yours, Irwin.

All my love always and always,
Mary

Part Nine

JUNE 28, 1946

Are you pleased about being in Paris, Darling?

June 28, 1946

My Darling,

What's happened? I haven't heard from you since last Monday, and I'm awfully worried, Darling. You do love me, don't you? Remember me asking you to write and tell me if you should change your mind? I don't want that letter, but I'd rather know. I've been thinking all kinds of things. I'd never know if anything happened to you, and that's making me more worried. I love you so very, very much, and this suspense is terrible. I know it's only a week since I heard from you, but it isn't like you to miss writing for as long as that. I hope that you've just been too busy to write and there's nothing else wrong. I'm lost without you, Darling.

I went to church tonight. I prayed hard there, that everything was all right for us. You don't know how very important you are to me. You're my whole life, Irwin. How I wish you'd walk in this minute, then I'd know how you felt and that you're all right. I've kept thinking about the things you told me about what happens to jeeps. I guess I've just worried about everything there is to worry about.

I just can't write a letter tonight. My mind is on you all day and night. Now I know how you felt when you didn't hear from me, and I hate myself for making you worry so much.

I hope I get a letter in the morning telling me that you still want me. I'll always love you, Irwin, whatever happens. There'll never be anyone else for me.

Al my love always and always,
Mary

Part Ten

JULY 20, 1946–AUGUST 8, 1946

Wedding arranged for August 26.
Try and make it. Love, Mary

July 20, 1946

My Darling,

Here I am again. Have you missed me? I can't tell you how wonderful it is for me to write you after all this time. I love you so very much, more than when you last heard from me.

I have so much to tell you that I don't know where to start. Isn't it wonderful that everything is over? I just can't realize it.

I want to thank you, Darling, for writing so often when you were home. You're so nice.

I had your wire telling me you were on the boat and had your lovely letter too. Then this morning I saw the boy coming to our house with a wire and thought at once that you were coming to see me. I was a little disappointed, well, you know how disappointed I was, when I found it was just your address. Are you pleased about being in Paris, Darling? I am, because you're nearer to me. I've missed you so terribly, Irwin, and I want to see you so badly, but take care of my heart with the Paris girls.

Ken came home tonight for sixteen days leave. He thought you'd be here too. Mother was expecting you too, and she mentioned you saying to Ken that you'd be home before him. You don't know how I want you here. It seems years since I saw you. I've missed you more than ever this time.

Ken and Walter have gone to Langland tonight. I'm in the house alone. Peggy's husband is home on leave too. I feel so lonely. Why can't you be here, Darling.

You know the sergeant who was in the 108th? He came to see me about a month ago. He expected you to be here. He was awfully nice. I believe he spent most of his leave in London. He phoned me when he returned to see if you were here, but I hated to tell him you weren't. He seemed disappointed too.

I'm glad you saw Doc again. Glad for you but not for him. I met Eva not very long ago, and she said she'd had one of her letters returned from Doc in April, with just a line, "How could you?" So she wrote for an explanation, and he wrote back telling her that he'd had a detective trailing her and so found out that she was going around with different people. I told Eva that Doc was married, but she wouldn't believe me, so I don't know. I don't have any room for her, though, after what she said she'd done. Did you know she lost a baby last year? She told me she'd like to go out with me one evening, but I told her I didn't go out. I don't think she liked that, but I don't worry. I've been awfully good for us, Darling. You know that, though. I love you so much, Irwin, and I wish we could be together for always. I'll never be satisfied until that time comes. I know we'll be so happy wherever we are, and I'll be so proud of my wonderful husband.

Nancy is going to London to live on Monday. She's awfully thrilled about it. I've spent a lot of time at her place lately. The baby is a darling. I wish he was mine. I've slept with Nancy a few nights, and when he wakes at six o'clock in the morning, Nancy brings him into bed to keep him quiet. Because I was there she went to sleep then, so I had him pulling my hair and crawling all over me until it was time to get up. It's fun, though.

I've had wonderful dreams about you, Darling. They just convince me more, that's if I need convincing, how empty everything would be without you. You're my whole life, and there'll never be anyone but you for me. I never thought there was anyone as wonderful as you are in the whole world. I'm so awfully lucky to have your love.

Wish I could talk to you. I want to hear you tell me you love me. I want lots and lots of love, and I've saved tons and tons of love for you. I could love you just about to death, but I want you with me all my life, every minute that's possible. Gosh, I want to hear all about your trip to the States too. Hurry to me, Darling. I want you so much, so very, very much. How many kisses can you spare?

Have to leave you now, Darling. Time for dreams again. It's time some of these dreams came true now too. It's so nice to tell you again that I love you with all my heart and miss you every minute. Love me all you can and miss me please.

All my love always and always,
Mary

July 22, 1946

My Darling,

You must think I'm slipping, not writing yesterday, but I went to sleep with Nancy for the last time. I'm sorry, Darling, but you know you are the most important thing in my life. I love you and miss you more than you'll ever know. You're so dear to me. I wish I could see you. I did expect you this weekend, and you know how disappointed I was.

I had two wonderful letters from you today, Darling, one written on the fifteenth from Germany and the other one on the eighteenth from Paris.

Mrs. Jones is talking here now. Her daughter is married now. Went to Switzerland for her honeymoon, and we haven't heard the end of it yet.

I know you'll keep your job in Paris, and I'm awfully glad you like it. It was nice of the colonel to remember that you wanted to come here. I hope that Major comes back early in August. I want to see you, Darling. I've been breaking the news to my mother very gently this evening, that I want to get married in August, but she just says there's plenty of time. But I'll get her used to the idea before then. It would be so wonderful if I could return with you. I want to be with you all the time, every possible moment. It's going to be heavenly. I can't wait, but you know I will until we are together in our little home, wherever it is.

I wrote to Virginia. Will she think I have a nerve for asking for a swimming suit? I do need one, and I'll be awfully grateful if she sends it. I hope we have nice weather when you come here, then we can swim, amongst doing all the other things we'll want to do. Are we going to have fun? You'd better reserve all your energy. I'm taking vitamins. I'm going to love you and love you and love you. Wish you were here now. You're so wonderful.

Time for bed now, Darling. Don't be late in my dreams because I feel wonderful tonight. I'll be on your side all night. You don't feel tired, do you, Darling? Good night, Irwin. I'm loving and missing you more every minute. Love me all you can and miss me too.

All my love always and always,
Mary

July 23, 1946

My Darling,

It's awfully late, twelve o'clock. I hope that right now you are dreaming about me. I love you, Darling, and I want you to think about me all the time. But please don't take so much room up in bed tonight. I'll be falling out.

I worked this morning. Gwenda phoned me and asked if she could meet me. So I took her home for lunch and spent the afternoon shopping. We went out for tea and then saw *The Harvey Girls*. Do you know what she told me? I don't know if she's trying to disillusion me or not, but she said that married life has too many responsibilities, and you're always wishing you were single again. I don't think she's very happy, do you? I've thought over all those things and know that whatever happens, I'll only be happy when I'm with you forever. I'm even prepared to obey you. Darling, see how much I love you. I got home around eight thirty, then Harry and Kit came over with some bad news. Kit went to see the doctor this afternoon, and he told her she'd have to go to hospital tomorrow. She should have had the baby on the sixteenth, and he just told her everything was wrong. Harry's too worried to speak, and you can imagine how Mother is. We've been talking until now, and I'm so tired I could fall asleep right here. Please excuse this short letter. I'll be with you in a few minutes though, ready to pitch lots of woo. You're so wonderful. You can be Daddy tonight too.

Love me every minute, Darling. I'm missing you and loving you more than you'll ever know. Be good for me.

All my love always and always,
Mary

July 24, 1946

My Darling,

I love you, remember? I hope you're loving and missing me loads too. I'm in the mood for lots of loving, Irwin. How I wish you were here. I'm awfully impatient. I want to be so close to you.

Mr. Clement is on holidays this week, so I have to work just a little bit harder. I didn't get home until six thirty this evening. Mother has gone over to Kit's place, and I've been talking to myself all evening. I've had a fine time. I'm awfully lonely, Darling. Can't you do something about it?

Dorothy's boyfriend, Sid, wrote and told her he had met a girl in Australia, and she writes to him quite often, so Dorothy's heart-broken now. She says she's lost faith in men. You should hear Walter teasing her.

I wish we were married right now, Darling, so we could be some place together. You don't know how I'm looking forward to the day when I can do all the things that a wife should do for her husband. The GI Bride Club in Swansea doesn't exist now, so I couldn't have my cookery lessons. But I've been doing all I can at home, in spite of the nasty remarks I have from the family. I'm not scaring you, am I, Darling? I'm improving all the time.

Dorothy just came in with her friend now. I won't get any peace at all. I'll finish this letter after supper, Darling. Do you mind if I leave you for an hour? I'll be back.

Here I am again. Since writing to you, Con, Mair, Ken, Walter, Mother, Kit, and Harry have arrived. Quite a gathering. Kit had an x-ray at the hospital. She'll have the result on Friday. I hope everything will be all right for her. It's late for me again tonight, and I have to save all the sleep I can in readiness for sleepless nights to come, lovely nights.

Good night, Darling. Dream about me and remember how I'm loving and missing you. Love me and miss me a little too.

All my love always and always,
Mary

July 29, 1946

My Darling,

I had two wonderful letters from you today written on the twenty-fourth and twenty-fifth. So please don't take any notice of that worrying letter I wrote yesterday. I was awfully relieved this morning, though, when I read that you were still loving me. I love you loads too, Darling. You know that.

I want to be your wife as soon as I can, Irwin, and I'm talking Mother into it as fast as I can. She's too worried about Kit at the moment to think about anything else, but I'm certain everything will be fine for us. We can't get married in a church, so you don't have to panic about it being a big affair. I'd like to get married about 9:00 a.m. Then we wouldn't have many people around. I just want you there. You're the only person that interests me. I love you with all my heart for always.

Mother is still keeping on about me staying home every night. It hurts me more than anything. I don't want to go out. If the weather was nice, I'd go to the beach, and I do go to shows. But there's nothing else that interests me. I've tried to explain that to her, but she can't see it. I'm quite happy, well, not happy, but contented to be this way, until I'm with you. It's so well worth waiting for.

Are you sure you didn't make a mistake when you said we'd have $411 a month to live on? That sounds like an awful lot of money to me. Wish I could talk to you. There's a lot I want you to tell me about.

I'd like to eat part of our meals where you eat now, for a while. Then I'd have a good idea what you like and how different the food is to ours. After that we could eat at our own place all the time. But you mustn't fool around while I'm cooking, otherwise, you know what's going to happen. We'll starve, and we'll need lots of food for lots of strength.

Gosh, you're clever, sewing buttons on your shirts. What do you want me for, Darling, when you can do all these things? It will be wonderful taking care of you, though I wish time would go faster. I want to be with you so much.

The girl, you know, Mrs. Jones's daughter, she went to Switzerland for her honeymoon and waited three months for her passport to go there. I wonder if it would be the same process for me to obtain one. It would be terrible if we had to wait that long.

Ken should have been out of the RAF in July, but there's some delay, and it's September now. I'll have to give my room up altogether then, but I'm hoping I won't be here to use it anyway. Guess where I want to be? I want to be in your arms wherever you are. Darling, how I love you.

I have a day off tomorrow, so I'll have extralong dreams tonight. Hurry to me. I love you and miss you every minute. Love me lots.

I'll my love always and always,
Mary

July 31, 1946

My Darling,

The days go awfully slowly, especially when the mail is so bad. Last week I had one letter, then two on Monday, and since then I haven't had any at all. I thought it would be better now you're in Paris. I miss you loads, Darling, and I want to know how much you love me as often as I can.

Yesterday morning I had your wire saying you hadn't received any mail. I can't understand that either, because I've written you regularly since having your address. I guess you must have been worrying as you haven't heard from me for months, so I went to town and wired you. I don't want you to think I've forgotten you because I just love you more and more and want you more every day. I hope you've had my letters by now, Darling. I know how I'd worry if I were in your place.

Yesterday afternoon, I did some shopping then went to see *The Years Between* with Mother in the evening. It wasn't very good, though. A British show. Mother took Walter's points, and we bought a box of chocolates. I ate a lot of them, and when I got home, I felt sick. Ken has to open his big mouth and tell Walter why I was sick. Walter was mad, so I went to bed early. I felt terrible. That's why I didn't write, Darling. You'll excuse me, won't you? Walter hasn't spoken to me all day today. He's like a big baby. He didn't want the points, but nobody else should have them.

Wish you were here, Darling. I feel like dancing tonight. If you were here, though, I wouldn't mind where we went as long as I was with you. I just want to be in your arms, dancing or otherwise. I haven't had any loving since April. That's a long time, isn't it? I'd do anything for a super kiss from my Irwin right now. But it's all well worth waiting for, and it's so wonderful to know that I have your love, and when this waiting is over, I'll have you for always. Life's certainly wonderful.

Hazel's sister in America wants to come home. Her husband's people are awful to her. Hazel came to the office this afternoon especially to tell me this. I don't know what I was supposed to say, but I asked her what her husband was doing about it. I saw snaps of Doreen, Hazel's sister, taken outside her home. It's a real little shack with a tin funnel sticking out of the roof, but she wouldn't mind that if she loved her husband. And there are lots of people without homes at all. But she expected so much

I sent my last letter to you by airmail. I didn't know there was a service to Europe. Will you tell me if it gets there any quicker that way?

It's getting late. I'm writing in bed tonight. It's nicer this way. Monday night I had super dreams. You're wonderful, Darling. Last night I didn't dream at all. So I was at work early this morning. I hope you're in my dreams again tonight, terrible as I want you to be. I'm ready for all the love you can spare. I love you and love you all there is. I want to be so close to you, though. Love me all you can and miss me lots. Be good for me. I'm afraid of all those girls in Paris, but you're mine for keeps, aren't you, Darling? I love you so much.

All my love always and always,
Mary

August 1, 1946

My Darling,

No letters yet. I feel so miserable when I look around for them in the morning and find there aren't any for me. I wonder what's wrong, Darling?

This morning I had a *Collier's* and a *Good Housekeeping*. That's a very good magazine, but how did I get that this time? There must have been a mix-up, and it was sent instead of *Cosmopolitan*. I've spent all evening looking at the lovely houses and wonderful recipes for cooking.

Yesterday we were told not to sing in the office, and today we were laughing and were told to stop. It's getting just like the army there. We have a new general manager. He's a silly-looking thing but likes making new rules. I even have to be in work at 8:00 a.m. now. I don't like him a bit.

It's just like writing a letter to myself as I don't know when or if you'll get this, the way they're messing our mail around. I want you to know how very, very much I love you. I do, Darling. It's raining here now. A good excuse for us to go to bed early. You can read, and I'll turn over for you (the pages, I mean). It would be heavenly if I was wherever you are. I've saved so much love for you I just can't keep it to myself for much longer. So hurry to me, Darling.

I don't feel in a very good letter-writing mood tonight. I'm missing you so terribly, Darling. So excuse the short letter. I'm going to dream early tonight so I can be with you. I love you more than ever. You have no idea how I'm missing you, Darling. I wish I could see you. Love me and miss me all you can.

All my love always and always,
Mary

August 8, 1946

My Darling,

I missed writing last night. I'm sorry, Darling. Ken and I went to visit Con and Mair. We left there around ten o'clock, and when we got home, Nancy's mother was here. She wanted me to stay with her over the weekend as my uncle has gone to London, and she's alone in the house. So that's where I went last night, and that's where I'll be tonight and tomorrow night.

I had a lovely letter yesterday written on July thirtieth that came in good time. I read something in the paper about postal workers in Paris being on strike. Would that affect our mail?

It's one of those holiday weekends again here. Everybody's going places. I feel so lonesome, Darling. Why can't you be here too? I love you and miss you so very much. I'm jealous of those British civilians working in your office. Take care of our account, won't you, Darling. I'm taking no chances with my account at all. It's in perfect shape.

I'm awfully glad you had letters from me at last. I've sent all your letters by airmail since your wire. I'm not going to let you forget that I love you for always and always.

Sergeant Christy told me he was going to Marseilles when he returned. He thought he'd meet you there. I liked him too. I hope I see him again.

Have to go to my other home now, Darling. I don't want to sleep there, but I can't refuse. Love me more than ever, and dream nice dreams, all about me. Be good for me. You have all my love over there with you. I'm yours for always. Miss me, Darling.

All my love always and always,
Mary

WIRES

Have written every day. Everything is all right. Mary

Have written. Wedding arranged for August 26. Try and make it. Love, Mary

Their wedding took place on August 27, and they left for Paris, where Irwin was stationed, and the Hotel Miami, where they lived for the next six months. According to legend, the seats and the floor of their train compartment were strewn with rose petals.

Mair, Irwin, Mary, and Dot

This story of love amid the backdrop of war is the story of my parents. Their honeymoon in Paris lasted about six months as Irwin was stationed there as part of the occupation forces. They lived in the

Hotel Miami, went to the Opera and the Folies Bergere, climbed the Spanish steps, played tennis, and grew to love Paris.

Irwin's next posting took him to Fort Jackson, South Carolina. In order to travel to South Carolina, Mary traveled on a troop ship, the USS *Goethals*, with other war brides. She met Irwin's family after arriving on the United States. They welcomed her, but everyone knew and still saw his first wife and his children, so there must have been some tension. But she was a charmer.

South Carolina presented Mary with a world about which she was ignorant. She saw chain gangs working outside her home, men dressed in prison clothes guarded by men with guns. One morning she found that overnight a spider had made a nest in her hair. With no family around, she made friends with other young Army wives and went to work in a department store, work that she loved. She left that job when she became pregnant. Mary gave birth to me, her only child, at Fort Jackson in an Army hospital in July of 1949. The experience was horrific and lonely and rarely mentioned.

From Fort Jackson, Irwin was sent to Korea and was stationed at the prisoner of war camp in Koje-do. Mary took me to Pennsylvania, where we lived with Irwin's brother and his wife. That arrangement didn't last long. The story is that I was not a good guest. Soon Mary decided to return to Swansea, where we lived in her mother's home for about a year. The house was crowded—austerity Britain—but it was a happy year.

Mary and Irwin then completed the paperwork necessary to move Mary and me to Japan, where Irwin was stationed after his tour in Korea. Mary delighted in exploring Tokyo. At first we lived "on the economy." Mary became great friends with a Japanese woman her age who had also endured war and bombings. With her new friend, Mary explored tea ceremonies, bath houses, and Kabuki. There were journeys into the mountains to go trout fishing. Mary's world was opened up, and she embraced the different culture. Sundays were often spent in downtown Tokyo with the Imperial Hotel as the focal point. She no longer dealt in stereotypes; she dealt with people she came to know, people with shared experiences.

After Japan, the family returned to the States to live on an Army post in Maryland in a house on the water, a few miles from my home today.

After three years, Irwin was posted to Germany. Here, Mary began work at the Officers Club, work that she loved. She also befriended the woman who came in to clean for us three days a week, a woman who had met her husband when he hid from British bombs in her garden. Both women had experienced war; both their marriages resulted from wartime encounters. They spoke of the war often, sharing experiences, fears, hopes, and horrors that brought them closer to one another, bound by their wartime experiences. Living in Germany brought my family closer to Mary's family in Swansea. We would drive to Swansea from Giessen several times a year, first in a bright-pink Buick, and then in a Jag. Mary's mother loved the big cars, the Buick more than the Jag.

After four years, Irwin retired from the Army, and for six and a half months, the family moved back to Swansea to consider the next move. The decision was made to return to the States, to Maryland, a difficult transition. Eventually Mary went to work at the Officers Club on Post and loved her job. She dreamed of owning a dress shop in the city of Havre de Grace, Maryland, where I now live. Mary visited Swansea in the fall of 1966. In the summer of 1967, her mother and her mother's neighbors, with whom I had lived when we were in Swansea in 1960–1961, came to visit. Mary didn't feel well that summer. In October she entered the hospital and died on December 30, 1967, from cancer, a word that was never mentioned. She smoked, but she had also worked at Glamtax, unprotected from the fumes.

Through her letters Mary lives on as young woman in love with her future before her, full of adventure and travel and the unknown.

ABOUT THE AUTHOR

Deborah Stathes taught high school English for forty years and is now retired. The daughter of an American career soldier and a Welsh war bride, she has been in possession of her mother's war-time letters to her father for many years and used time during the COVID lockdown to prepare them for publication. She lives with her husband in Havre de Grace, Maryland, and Mumbles, Wales.